TRADING THE INTERNATIONAL FUTURES MARKETS

THE MARKETS, THE SYSTEMS, AND THE STRATEGIES FOR ACHIEVING THE TRADER'S "EDGE"

TRADING THE INTERNATIONAL FUTURES MARKETS

THE MARKETS, THE SYSTEMS, AND THE STRATEGIES FOR ACHIEVING THE TRADER'S "EDGE"

JAKE BERNSTEIN

NEW YORK INSTITUTE OF FINANCE
NEW YORK • TORONTO • SYDNEY • TOKYO • SINGAPORE

Library of Congress Cataloging-in-Publication Data

Bernstein, Jacob
Trading the international futures markets: the markets, the systems, and the strategies for achieving the trader's "edge" / Jake Bernstein.—2nd ed.
p. cm.
ISBN 0–7352–0136–6
1. Futures. 2. Futures—United States. I. Title.

HG6024.A3 B53 2000
332.64'5—dc21

00–041836

Chapters 5, 7, 8, 9 and 12 have been adapted from *How the Futures Markets Work* (second edition)

Acquisitions Editor: *Ellen Coleman*
Production Editor: *Eve Mossman*
Interior Design/Layout: *Dee Coroneos*

Printed in the United States of America

10 9 8 7 6 5 4 3 2 1

ISBN 0-7352-0136-6

NEW YORK INSTITUTE OF FINANCE
Paramus, NJ 07652

On the World Wide Web at http://www.phdirect.com

FOREWORD

The French expression *plus ça change, plus ça meme chose* means "the more things change, the more they stay the same." While this may very well be true in many areas of life, it is anything but true in the futures markets. Changes in the futures industry and in the futures markets themselves since the 1960s have been significant and vast, accelerating rapidly since the mid-1980s.

I began my career in the commodity markets of the 1970s. The markets then were much less complicated than they are today. The premier markets were grains, livestock, tropical commodities, metals and lumber. Price moves were less volatile (more often than not), there were fewer markets, and the factors directly affecting prices trends were relatively simple to discern. Currency futures trading was still in the very early development stage, and stock index futures had not yet been initiated (but was being actively discussed).

The world of the commodity trader was circumscribed and centered primarily in the United States. Futures exchanges existed in various other countries, but their trading volume was minor in comparison to what was generated at the leading exchanges located in Chicago and New York. It was during these relatively "calm" days of futures trading that I first met Jake Bernstein, the author of this book. Although we both went in our separate directions within the futures industry, we were destined to meet again years later. While I developed the presence and scope of my brokerage business, Jake grew his career as a trading adviser, author, trader and educator. His research and seminars took him all over the world. He taught traders in Europe and Asia how to trade in the U.S. markets. My business became international in scope as well, attracting overseas traders to the U.S. markets and, more recently, U.S. traders to the overseas markets.

With the growth and expansion of free trade and third-world economies came increased demand for grain, livestock and metal commodities. The inflationary era of the 1970s kindled significant interest in gold and silver futures. Severe weather, strong demand for food commodities and the inflationary economic trend prompted large rallies in many commodity prices which, in turn, attracted many new traders to the futures markets, increasing trading volume dramatically. Over the next decade, futures trading in a new breed of futures contracts forever altered the landscape and complexion of futures trading.

The addition of interest rate futures, currency futures, stock index futures and petroleum futures opened the commodity markets not only to vast new areas for speculators and hedgers, but also fostered the birth of international markets. The corn and wheat traders of yesteryear could no longer function in a market that remained relatively immune to currency fluctuations in Europe and Asia. By the early 1980s such important fundamental developments as the effect of currency exchange rates on grain prices, U.S. interest rates on the Japanese yen (and other currencies), the cost of crude oil on Treasury Bond futures, and the foreign trade policies of the Asian nations on the price of livestock futures were major considerations for the futures trader.

Many traders adapted slowly to the new fundamental relationships, seeking to understand their role in determining price trends. But the task was a vast one indeed. The amount of information was vast. Among the factors needing study and evaluation were weather, supply and demand, government policies, political events, domestic and foreign interest rate trends, economic trends, military policies and/or confrontations, currency exchange rates, the role of cartels, crop conditions, and more. While some traders developed methods of collecting and integrating all of the above (and more) into a viable decision-making procedure, others were not so capable. Rather than spend their time attempting to understand the multiplicity of fundamental factors, they took refuge in technical analysis. Rather then attempting to understand the effect of "mad cow disease" (Kreutzfeld-Jacob syndrome) in England on the price of beef in the United States, or the role of Chinese human rights policies on U.S. grain sales, they studied chart patterns, formations, technical indicators and timing signals. The use of technical analysis offered a relatively simple entrée to futures trading to the new trader.

Futures trading continued to expand in response to several other factors as well. The availability of sophisticated computer technology at affordable prices, increased cooperation in foreign trade, the breakup of the Soviet Union, the European Union, relative peace in the Middle East (subsequent to the Gulf War), strong economic growth in many economies, and, more recently, the Internet have all contributed to the expansion of futures trading.

Producers, financial institutions, governments, and corporations in virtually every phase of business and in virtually every country can now use the futures markets as a means of hedging risk. Speculators and investors are able to participate in the markets more actively than ever before. While not all countries have futures exchanges as yet, it is likely that within the next few years they will. While not all countries currently allow their citizens to trade futures, within a few years they will. For the first time ever, the futures markets are truly international in scope.

While the futures markets offer vast profit potential to all participants, they are not without their new challenges and obstacles. Today, more than ever, traders must, at the very minimum, have a working knowledge and awareness of the international markets. Even the pure market technician must emerge from the protected cocoon of technical indicators into the light of market awareness. Lack of knowledge can be costly not only in the form of losses in actual trades, but also in the sense of lost opportunities. The U.S. commodity markets, once world leaders in commodity trading volume, have fallen into second place, giving up their lead to the new EUREX and LIFFE (London International Financial Futures Exchange) exchanges. The German Bund contract (at the EUREX) is now the largest market in terms of trading volume.

In *Trading the International Futures Markets,* Jake Bernstein guides you carefully through the international waters of commodity trading. He provides you with an overview of the markets as well as specific advice on which exchanges offer futures contracts that are viable and worthy of consideration as trading vehicles for the speculator. He also discusses emerging markets, the unique characteristics of the markets, and specific trading methods that can be applied to virtually all futures markets. Learn about the challenges and opportunities that await you. Whether you attempt to make your profits in the EuroBund, Japanese Bond, dried cocoon futures, or the CAC-40 stock index futures, take your time and become educated. Read this book carefully. Welcome to the world of international futures trading.

—Jeffrey H. Fox
Fox Investments

PREFACE: INTERNATIONAL TRADING HORIZONS

In January 1998, I traveled to London and Milan to conduct a futures trading seminar. The seminar theme was "Real-Time Futures Trading." Specifically my goals were to teach a variety of trading systems and methods, and to implement them in real-time trading using the London International Financial Futures Exchange (LIFFE). Prior to presenting these seminars, my experience in trading the overseas futures markets was limited to research and analysis.

Although I had been trading the U.S. markets since 1968, the European markets were still relatively new to me and my understanding of their mechanical operation was minimal. I expected the task of trading these markets in real time—as my students watched—to be a true "trial by fire." Therefore, I wanted to be certain that I was fully prepared. While it was not imperative that I make money on my LIFFE trades (no system works on every single trade), making money while demonstrating my methods would make a far stronger statement in support of their efficacy.

In preparing for the seminar, I did a substantial amount of research to determine which technical trading systems, indicators or analytical methods (if any) I might use successfully to trade the European futures markets. After all, the fundamentals and underlying structure of the markets were different from those of the U.S. markets, and this might well make traditional systems and methods useless.

To my pleasant surprise, I discovered that many of the technical trading methods I had developed and used for the U.S. markets worked exceptionally well on the European futures markets. In fact, in many cases the historical back test results were far better than those on the U.S. markets.

Assured now that the methods I planned to teach in London and Milan would give traders the tools they needed to trade profitably, I was also confident that my own trading in real time at the seminars would be successful. I taught my methods for the first two days of the seminar, and on the third day, I traded them in real time as the attendees watched, asked questions and learned. I made two trades in London. I bought the FTSE-100 Stock Index at the LIFFE at 5231 for a day trade, and sold it the same day at 5259 for a profit. I also bought the London Italian Bond (BTP) at 116.91, also for a day trade, and exited profitably at 117.17.

I was greatly encouraged by what I had seen. Not only was the trading enjoyable, but dealing with the floor brokers at the LIFFE was a pleasant experience. They were prompt, efficient, and, above all, polite. London was a positive experience in all respects, and I continue to be impressed with the caliber of service at the LIFFE as well as with their commitment to developing a viable and liquid futures market.

I repeated my performance in Italy several days later. This time I day traded AC Italiana Bonds, closing them out by the end of the day at a profit.

My audience in Milan was considerably larger than the one in London. Indeed, I felt somewhat intimidated by this group. Futures trading had been growing substantially in Italy and the level of interest was extremely high. The Milan attendees were not only inquisitive, but also highly motivated and exceptionally well educated in futures trading.

Many of these attendees were new to futures trading, and were making the transition from equities to futures. Although their questions were often basic, they were excellent students. In spite of my one-hundred percent profitable trading of the BTP at the LIFFE, the Italians maintained a healthy level of skepticism about its validity over time. Therefore, I was pleased that several months after the seminar I was asked to return. Now, over one year later, I still receive e-mails with questions from attendees.

Clearly such a small sample of trades, whether successful or not, cannot be taken as a guarantee of the future, or as confirmation of my prowess as a trader, or as proof that my trading methods are valid. However, the results were consistent with what my research had revealed about the European markets.

Perhaps the most rewarding aspect of the entire experience was the recognition that traders in Europe are similar to traders in the United States, with the same conflicts, the same struggles and the same concerns. In fact, from talking to traders from Japan, Korea, China, Taiwan and Australia, I have concluded that traders all over the world confront essentially similar issues, conflicts, concerns and psychological struggles.

A NEW WORLD MARKET

My experiences in trading the LIFFE markets revealed a whole new world of futures trading. I chided myself for clinging to the ethnocentric idea that the U.S. futures markets were the best markets to trade. Since the ability to trade in virtually any world market is now open to all traders, clearly the new futures markets are here to stay. The important question was whether these new exchanges could create sufficient interest among traders to provide the liquidity and volatility essential to the success of a futures market.

Upon my return to the United States, I embarked on a detailed analysis of futures markets around the world in order to understand what was available out there in the world of futures trading. Although the United States was, for many years, and still is, the center of world futures trading, new exchanges have been popping up all over the world. In fact, the third largest futures exchange in the world (in terms of trading volume) is the LIFFE exchange in London.

One factor that has helped accelerate the growth of foreign exchanges, such as the LIFFE, is the encroachment of restrictive government regulations on futures exchanges in the United States. Traders who wish to make large transactions without limit or scrutiny have been forced to participate in foreign markets, thus increasing trading activity and adding to liquidity in those markets.

On the other hand, in some countries, futures trading is so very new that the markets are essentially untradeable due to poor liquidity. But in time they will grow—as long as economic viability continues. In addition, as the international financial community has become more closely connected both monetarily and electronically, events affecting the markets of one country can have significant consequences on the markets of other countries. Such relationships are not new, they date back hundreds of years. What is new, however, is the speed with which information travels. Hence, the impact of a market reaction in London will likely be felt in Paris, Chicago, New York, Singapore, Moscow, Milan, etc., immediately.

For example, recently the Asian economic and financial crisis has had a serious impact on stock markets all over the world. Again, in early 1999, devaluation of the Brazilian *real* resulted in a sharp knee-jerk market decline in the United States. These are only two examples of what can be expected to occur as international financial markets grow increasingly interdependent. Therefore, it behooves futures traders, market analysts, investors, economists and governments to be familiar with foreign markets and with the futures contracts that are traded in those markets.

As economies worldwtide grow and mature, the transfer of risk becomes an increasingly important issue. In order to effectively transfer risk in the form of a hedge either against production or costs, the cultivation and growth of a viable futures market is necessary. Without an organized exchange, whether in the form of the traditional "open outcry" system or the more modern electronic trading, effective trading is impossible.

In writing this book I hope to:

- Increase your awareness of futures trading around the world.
- Familiarize you with the futures vehicles traded in different world markets.
- Provide a synopsis of futures contracts and their general specifications.
- Analyze market liquidity and viability for trading purposes.
- Illustrate the efficacy of various technical trading systems and methods in different world markets.
- Provide details on how you may participate in these markets.

In offering a summary of technical trading systems, I understand that there are limits to what I can present. Clearly this book is not a definitive study of systems trading in various international futures markets. Instead, I have provided you with an overview of these methods so that you can decide for yourself which you prefer and which you would like to investigate further.

Jake Bernstein

ACKNOWLEDGMENTS

Gathering the facts for this book has truly been an international effort. Exchanges throughout the world were contacted via e-mail and telephone. Hundreds of web sites were located and catalogued. Promotional materials were studied. I thank Nan Martin Barnum for her valuable assistance in this monumental undertaking. I also thank Ellen Schneid Coleman, executive editor at Prentice Hall, for her expert reading and corrections to my manuscript; Barry Richardson at Prentice Hall deserves a special thank-you for pulling this project together. I am grateful to my family for their usual patience, support and input during my many hours of writing. And lastly, I thank my office manager, Marilyn Kinney, and my office staff for their valuable assistance in this project from its inception as an idea to its completion as a finished product.

Jake Bernstein

INTRODUCTION

Would you like to trade gur or hessian futures? Perhaps you'd feel more comfortable with a position in pepper or turmeric futures. Should these not suit your taste, you might take a plunge into peanut kernel or dried cocoon futures. Whatever you do, you'll need to be educated, first in futures trading, and second in the characteristics of each market you intend to trade.

The nature and scope of futures trading has changed dramatically since the early 1980s. The "good old days" of futures trading are gone forever. The Chicago Mercantile Exchange (CME) and the Chicago Board of Trade (CBOT), once the preeminent futures exchanges in the world, have slowly, but surely lost their edge as new exchanges in Europe and Asia have emerged to challenge their lofty positions. The London International Financial Futures Exchange (LIFFE) has, in a relatively brief period of time, become the third largest exchange in the world and threatens to overtake the CBOT as number two.

Several reasons account for the rapid growth of world futures exchanges. Foremost among these is the growing interdependency of world economies and currencies. Whether this is a potentially positive or negative development remains to be seen. As always there are several schools of thought. Some economists and market observers feel that this is a positive development, whereas others are concerned that close global market interdependence could very well result in a domino effect of financial collapses in the event of a financial panic. (One example is the 1994 global crash in the bond market, which resulted in huge losses for major investors and large corporations around the world.)

As the financial centers of the world become closely interdependent, extreme fluctuations in prices have become commonplace. In the course of only a few days or even hours, currencies can change their relationships dramatically, gyrating from low to high and back to low again, as speculators who are unprepared or unable to withstand large intraday moves topple like bowling pins under the weight of a heavy ball.

The three major currencies of the world, the U.S. dollar, the Euro (ECU) and the Japanese yen, have all fluctuated so widely in the last few years that it is increasingly difficult for international businesses to depend on exchange rates without being hedged in the futures markets. Participation in the international futures markets has become a matter of survival to many firms.

Futures trading, no matter where it takes place, is the quintessential form of financial speculation. Until the 1980s most futures trading found its home in the United States. However, many events—economic, monetary, political and technological—have all combined to facilitate the growth and development of futures trading in virtually every country of the world. Yet the growth of futures exchanges, in and of itself, does not guarantee that the road to riches has become readily accessible to the average trader. In fact, most traders will, for lack of discipline, knowledge and effective trading methodologies, continue to be overall losers in this high-stakes game.

The winners will be those who have developed the prerequisite skills and trading systems that make futures trading a profitable venture. Whether these traders base their decisions upon technical systems and/or fundamental analysis, it is the very idea of having and following an operational methodology that differentiates the relatively few winners from the many losers.

Access to winning tools is not the exclusive domain of professional traders. Today, the tools of the professional trader are also generally available to the aspiring trader. Numerous software programs and computerized data analysis are available at reasonable prices, putting them within the reach of virtually any trader who is willing to make the financial commitment.

Those who have traded the U.S. markets have the benefit of experience over those in other countries who are new to trading futures. The lessons to be learned are many and painful. The tuition for learning the game is high, and tuition alone will not guarantee success. Experience, self-discipline, organization and persistence are the behavioral keys to success; while they can be taught, it takes work to become a successful trader and some may not make the grade.

One of the major factors contributing to the international growth of futures trading and futures markets is the need for organized markets that will help producers and end users plan for their needs. This is true for the producer of agricultural commodities as well as for those who deal in currencies, stocks and interest-rate vehicles. The ability to lay off or hedge the risk of currency, interest rate and/or stock fluctuations is crucial to the efficient and profitable operations of financial institutions and governments.

Finally, the formation of the European Economic Union has created a new and powerful economic force that will make extensive use of the futures markets. This, in turn, has resulted in a new group of professional traders and speculators, and has made the need for viable and active futures markets in Europe greater than ever.

Trading volume on the Asian and Australian futures exchanges also has been increasing steadily. As Asian economies resume their strong growth cycles, their futures markets have expanded. Trading activity in a variety of futures vehicles promises to increase dramatically by the year 2010. As activity increases, more traders and speculators have been attracted to the markets and their growth has accelerated.

Yet, as I noted above, the mere expansion of markets and trading volume is in no way a measure of profitable trading by the individual speculator. The rules and principles of effective trading still hold true. Although the size of the available monetary pool may increase, thereby increasing liquidity, the value and importance of knowledge and experience will not be diminished. Rather, the reverse will be true. In order to trade profitably in any domestic or foreign market, the speculator and/or professional trader will need:

- A thorough understanding of the markets to be traded: their general contract specifications, trading hours, tick values, basic fundamental characteristics and unique aspects of operations
- A knowledge of systems, methods and/or timing indicators that have been proven effective in the markets to be traded
- Knowledge of the liquidity, average trading volume and volatility of the market(s) to be traded
- A clear understanding of currency exchange rates between one's domestic currency and the currency of the market(s) to be traded
- Familiarity with rules and regulations of local governments regarding futures trading by foreign traders and entities
- An understanding of the technical considerations that may be unique to the specific markets being traded

In chapters that follow, you will find information about each of these rules and principles. Where specific information is available, I will supply it. However, in cases of markets that are currently in the development or growth stage, I urge you to contact the exchanges themselves, or brokers who deal on those exchanges, for up-to-date information. Remember that world futures markets and exchanges are changing rapidly. (India is a good example of this.)

In many cases, new contracts are being added and new exchanges are being opened. In other cases, contracts that have not attracted sufficient trader interest or participation are being abandoned and replaced with others. Finally, some exchanges have merged, for example, the European Futures Exchange (EUREX), as markets in Europe consolidate due to the new European Economic Union.

In addition, you'll find an overview of the international markets as well as some of their history. I will also familiarize you with the markets that are traded, their location and general characteristics. I will illustrate for you how some of the more traditional trading systems and methods perform in these markets. Finally, I will show you some specific systems and methods that I have developed especially for those markets, given their often unique characteristics.

CONTENTS

Chapter 3

FUTURES TRADING IN EUROPE AND THE AMERICAS / 31

Chapter 4

FUTURES TRADING IN ASIA, THE PACIFIC RIM, AFRICA AND THE MIDDLE EAST / 53

Chapter 5

FUNDAMENTAL ANALYSIS OF THE INTERNATIONAL FUTURES MARKET / 69

Chapter 9

DEVELOPING A TRADING STRATEGY / 159

Chapter 10

TRADING SYSTEMS IN THE INTERNATIONAL MARKETS / 175

Chapter 11

DAY TRADING THE INTERNATIONAL MARKETS / 199

Chapter 12

MAKING THE INTERNATIONAL FUTURES MARKETS WORK FOR YOU / 209

Chapter 13

SUMMARIZING THE INTERNATIONAL TRADING EXPERIENCE / 219

Appendix I

WORLD FUTURES MARKETS / 223

Appendix II
CONTRACT SPECIFICATION LISTINGS / 251

Appendix III
SYSTEM DETAILS AND COMPUTER CODE / 297

Chapter 1

THE FUTURES GAME

Dictionary definitions of "futures trading" are woefully inadequate because they fail to convey the essence of what trading is all about. Most state that futures trading is "the speculative purchase and sale of commodities for future receipt or delivery." While this may have been true when the markets were first developed for grain transactions, things have changed dramatically. Modern futures trading not only includes grain and livestock markets, but also "intangible" commodities such as stock indices, interest rates, currencies, electricity, insurance and freight costs. In many cases there is **no** delivery of the commodity itself; settlement of the contract is achieved in a cash transaction, and even then the cash does not physically change hands, but is transferred electronically.

In its most basic form, futures trading is a high-stakes speculative game, in which competitors buy and sell things that don't exist—with money they don't have. Futures trading is the ultimate capitalist tool. While traders in the United States have known this for many years, the rest of the world has only recently recognized its potential benefits (and risks).

AN UNORTHODOX HISTORY OF FUTURES TRADING

Futures trading has existed in various forms since the 1400s. While the original purpose of the futures markets was to provide a marketplace for producers and end users of agricultural commodities, speculators realized that the marketplace was an ideal location for them as well. As markets grew more active with increased foreign trade and domestic consumption in China and Japan, speculative activity increased and eventually culminated in Europe with the Dutch Tulip Mania of the 1600s. The futures markets continued to serve their original economic purpose of buffering violent price swings by matching buyers and sellers, but they also grew steadily as vehicles of speculative trade.

Although speculators were often held in disdain as opportunists, they nonetheless served a functional economic purpose. When the supply of a given commodity was limited and prices rose to high levels, speculators were willing to sell in the hope that prices would decline. When markets fell due to oversupply, speculators were often willing to mitigate the decline in prices by buying in the hope of reaping a profit as prices rose. While governments and bona fide traders officially frowned on speculation, they realized that the role of the speculator was a vital one if markets were to remain liquid and viable.

Texts on economics and futures trading still tout the economic purpose of the futures markets, but I believe that over time this purpose has been obscured by the growth in speculation. Well over ninety percent of all activity in today's futures markets is speculative.

In practice, only a very small percentage of all futures contracts traded eventually terminate as completed delivery and receipt of commodities. The primary function of the futures markets, as a vehicle for hedging the risk of production and the risk of costs in the manufacture of foods and goods, has been overshadowed by massive speculation. The futures markets of today are more like international lotteries than markets whose purpose is to buffer risk. In fact, it appears that speculative activity, which continues to grow daily on exchanges throughout the world, is so substantial that risk is paradoxically increased as opposed to being diminished.

The Role of Speculation

Speculation in matters of finance can be traced back to the dawn of humankind. As civilizations developed and man evolved into a more social being, speculative activities in financial matters increased accordingly. As empires flourished and vanished, speculative activities rose and declined. Eventually, speculation reached a frenzied peak with the Dutch Tulip Mania of the 1600s. The climactic rise and fall of the tulip bulb market was a sobering lesson to speculators in Europe, subduing speculative activity for many years.[1]

Except for relatively brief periods of sharp price increases and declines, world commodity prices were stable for literally hundreds of years as prices fluctuated within a small range. The stock market crash of 1929, prompted in part, but not entirely, by excessive speculation, ushered in a new era of fiscal restraint as the Great Depression brought the American economy to its knees. Speculative activity remained at relatively reasonable levels until the early 1970s, when inflationary pressures began to take their toll.

As the financial markets grew, speculative trading increased dramatically. Periods of economic boom and bust led to a number of speculative phases, primarily in the U.S. stock market in the 1960s. Although commodity prices were affected periodically, they did not occupy center stage. Occasionally a drought or crop disease resulted in wild commodity price moves, but there was no consistent up or down trend in prices as a function of price inflation until the early 1970s.

Since the 1970s, virtually all world markets have fallen prey to a host of economic influences that include everything from the weather to political machinations and war to inflation. World markets have entered an era of unprecedented volatility.

[1]For more information, I strongly recommend Charles Mackay's *Extraordinary Popular Delusions and the Madness of Crowds*. New York: Harmony Books, 1980.

Speculative activity is at its highest level ever in virtually all futures and stock markets all over the world. Record high prices in many stock markets, as well as significant fluctuations in currency exchange rates, have created the backdrop for speculative activities that frequently set new records in terms of volume and magnitude.

The frenzied buying of precious metals and the inflationary "blow-off" of the early 1980s was yet another period of rampant speculation. At the time, attention was focused not on stocks but rather on gold, silver, so-called strategic metals, coins and even jojoba beans. Speculators rushed to invest in these supposedly safe havens in an effort to protect themselves from what was predicted to be a complete economic collapse. This, of course, did not happen, and the U.S. economy made a safe transition into the greatest period of stock-market growth ever.

Yet panic ruled the trading pits in 1987 as a market crash followed a period of excessive stock speculation. The crash, however, ended quickly. Slowly, but surely, speculative stock-market activity increased as the twentieth century came to a close. It has been said that fear, greed and uncertainty are the key ingredients of speculation. Indeed, the international sociopolitical and economic climate at the end of the century is awash in these factors. It is no surprise, then, that traders the world over jockey for financial position and use the futures markets as their weapon. In their desire to get the "edge" over other traders, speculators are often willing to assume massive risk, but the risks taken are not always commensurate with the anticipated rewards. The expectation of large gains often leads to speculative bubbles, which culminate in a climactic top.

As of this writing, there is massive speculation in the stocks of Internet-related companies, many of which show large deficits, but which have been bid up to unprecedented highs. This speculative activity will no doubt end, as have all others. Whether it ends with a whimper or with a bang is the issue. It is not my goal here to prognosticate; instead, I urge you to consider all speculative activity in stocks, commodities, real estate or tulips within the context of history. The history of speculation is one of boom and bust. The cyclical nature of "free" economies results in speculative bubbles and crashes.

The wise trader and speculator will be aware of signs and symptoms that precede and accompany such periods of high risk.

For example, the Great Depression of the 1920s and 30s was preceded by a highly speculative stock market. The economic peak of the early 1980s in the United States and Europe occurred after sharply inflated commodity prices reached their peak. The Japanese economic decline of the late 1990s followed a period of accelerated growth.

Finally, traders should be aware of the fact that some markets are inherently more speculative than others. New traders would do well to avoid markets that are either too volatile or too risky, leaving them instead to journeymen traders who are willing and able to take large risks. While speculation will always be a major factor and force in the futures markets, the knowledgeable trader will choose his or her battles carefully, engaging in those where the probability of success is high.

FUTURES TRADING IN THE TWENTY-FIRST CENTURY

The long-accepted justification for futures trading is that it serves an economic purpose. We are told that the futures markets exist in order to provide an organized medium by which producers and end users can either buy-hedge or sell-hedge their products. In so doing, the producer can lock in a profit or minimize a loss. The end user can buy products in advance and lock in costs. Sandwiched between the producer and the end user we find the speculator.

In theory, the role of the speculator is to buffer price movements, therefore providing liquidity to the markets. As a potential reward for assuming risk, the speculator stands, at least in theory, to profit from market fluctuations.

This traditional view of the markets is essentially correct and has served its purpose well. However, as speculators have increasingly dominated the markets, the characteristics, purpose and efficacy of the marketplace have changed. Speculator reaction to and anticipation of news and fundamental events have prompted wide market swings. Such swings often undermine the stability of bona fide market hedges and transactions by forcing producers and end users to take positions in order to protect themselves from the inherent volatility. These actions, in turn, create more volatility to which few markets have proven immune in the 1990s. In a global economic environment, futures markets tend to fluctuate in a chain reaction of volatility as news sweeps across international boundaries within seconds.

Increased market volatility is both good news and bad news. It creates opportunities as well as risks. At times, the risks clearly outweigh the potential opportunities. There is growing concern among professional traders that international market volatility has become so immense that it may potentially cause a collapse of the system.

THE "REAL" PURPOSE OF FUTURES TRADING

In my view, whether the true hedger trades for the purpose of locking in a profit or costs or not, the fact remains that the overwhelming majority of futures trading is speculative to varying degrees. While the commercial trader may have a crop or product against which to balance a futures transaction, the speculator does not.

In any event, the trader should not confuse the goals of the game with the purported economic purpose of the game.

Although the vehicle may be soybeans, Italian bonds, crude oil or the CAC-40 Index, the end result is the same: a profit or a loss. The true purpose of futures trading from the perspective of the speculator is to make money. There is not and cannot be any other reason or purpose.

George Soros, master player of the international markets, lamenting the global trend toward increased volatility, said: "*I cannot see the global economy surviving. . . we have entered a period of global disintegration only we are not aware of it.*"[2]

As a result of the growing volatility in all markets, their original purpose of futures trading has been masked by the amount of speculative activity taking place. Although the markets will continue to have an important economic function, they will, in reality, function as a legitimized arena for high-stakes financial gambling. (I have replaced the euphemism "speculation" with the word "gambling" for a variety of reasons that will become clear although it may ruffle some feathers.) It is clear that, today, traders or speculators worldwide compete with one another for the same prize—money. While systems, methods, techniques and strategies are some of the tools that are used in attaining the goal, the fact is that, in order to succeed, traders must be intently focused on the goal.

For this reason, profitable traders must not be idealists or moralists. They must have a clear direction that leads to profits. There is no room for fantasy, wishful thinking or hopes. Successful traders in any world futures market must cut losses when they have reached their prescribed limit (as determined by a system or method), and must ride profits to their prescribed end. Traders who spend too much time thinking about the whys or wherefores of market moves will be tempted to disregard the system they are using, and the end result will be losses. Idealism has no place in the futures markets.

---

[2] Soros on Soros: *Staying Ahead of the Curve*. New York: Wiley, 1995.

RULES OF THE GAME: U.S. FUTURES TRADING REGULATIONS

In order to maintain orderly markets, governments throughout the world have adopted a formalized set of rules, laws and regulations that govern futures trading. Their purpose is to curb excessive speculation, and they are central to the effective functioning of these markets. However, they are not always effective. As in all cases of bureaucratic oversight, government agencies must walk a fine line between excessive regulation on one extreme and *laissez-faire* on the other.

Most of the largest futures exchanges in the world are located in the United States. In addition to exchange-traded financial derivative instruments, the U.S. futures regulatory authorities allow a limited number of off-exchange commodity options. All sectors of the U.S. futures markets fall under the jurisdiction and authority of the Commodity Futures Trading Commission (CFTC), but they are essentially self-regulated.

The regulatory role of the CFTC and the National Futures Association (NFA) has long been a subject of controversy. There are concerns that the strict enforcement and interpretation of NFA rules may be forcing traders and money managers to shift their business to markets outside the United States. In part, the restrictive regulatory climate in the United States has helped the growth of exchanges such as the London International Financial Futures Exchange (LIFFE), where the regulations are not nearly so limiting.

The CFTC regulates and oversees the operations, procedures and contracts traded at the various exchanges as well as the legislative provisions governing derivative instruments. It also has regulatory authority over all traders and trading in the futures markets. In spite of its broad jurisdiction, the CFTC does not conduct day-to-day supervision on the retail trading level. Rather it monitors regulatory compliance through the authority of the exchanges and the clearinghouses. The CFTC also monitors and regulates trading advisers, newsletter writers and others who hold themselves out to the public as experts on futures trading. Brokers and money managers in futures are required by law to pass various proficiency, ethics and background checks in order to be licensed.

Commodity exchanges must also be licensed by the CFTC. Exchanges must meet a variety of minimum standards in order to acquire and maintain their licensure. They must develop their own rules of conduct in order to ensure the implementation of mandated standards as well as the facilitation of trade in their various trading vehicles (i.e., futures contracts). Before a new futures contract may be introduced, exchanges must obtain CFTC approval. In evaluating the appropriateness of new futures contracts, the CFTC determines if the proposed contracts meet a variety of economic criteria and preconditions. Exchanges are required to demonstrate that their proposed contracts will serve an economic function beyond their potential use as speculative vehicles.

Manipulation of futures prices either by conspiracy to corner a market or by a variety of other means constitutes a violation of the futures laws in the United States. The Commodity Exchange Act (CEA), enforced by the CFTC, prohibits fraudulent and noncompetitive trading practices in the futures markets in order to assure that customer orders are executed fairly in competitive market conditions. Constant monitoring of trader position limits and trading practices by these agencies assures fair and free trading.

Rules, Restrictions and Realities

The rules of futures trading offer participants the opportunity to conduct their businesses in a regulated environment that guarantees the fulfillment of obligations by both buyer and seller. As in all business undertakings, there is an optimum level of regulation.

While some speculators may prefer insufficient regulation and minimal rules of operation, such a situation erodes confidence in a market. On the other hand, excessive regulation inhibits the growth of markets and dissuades traders from participating.

Developers of the new international futures markets are well aware of this; hence, they have designed their markets to reflect the best qualities and characteristics of existing markets.

The success of any modern futures exchange will depend on its ability to balance regulations and restrictions with opportunities for trading; trading restrictions regarding position size and limits are necessary for the effective functioning of a market. Harsher restrictions, however, can seriously impair liquidity, which can result in the quick demise of a market. The job of the futures exchange is to implement and enforce regulations that will facilitate rather than inhibit trade. The realities of trading require this functional balance.

As every market has its unique set of rules and regulations, traders in the international futures markets should become familiar not only with such basic information as trading hours and tick values, but also with unique characteristics of each market. Some close for the lunch hour and then reopen, while others trade straight through the day. Some markets only have open outcry trading, while others stop open outcry trading at a given hour and become electronic markets.

It is imperative that anyone trading these markets keep up with changes and new developments. One of the best ways to do this is to ask your broker(s) to keep you informed. You also may consult the exchanges' web sites on a regular basis.

The regulatory scope and role of the CFTC is changing considerably as this book is being written. It appears that such changes are being implemented in order to allow the U.S. futures markets to compete more effectively with the new, less restrictive and rapidly growing overseas markets.

WHAT'S TO BE GAINED?

While some traders may claim that there is enough activity in their own domestic markets, other traders throughout the world are not able to enjoy the benefits of hedging and the profit potentials of speculation that viable futures exchanges can offer. Consequently, they must look to the international futures markets to conduct their business. Whether your goal is to sell-hedge production; to buy-hedge raw commodities for manufacturing; to lay off risk of currency, stock or interest-rate fluctuations; or to speculate, the international markets offer many outstanding opportunities. The ability to trade in markets other than those in your own country has opened a new arena of potential profit.

But with this come new risks. In order for the gain to exceed the risk, it is necessary, as always, to correctly evaluate the risk-to-reward possibilities in the international markets. Although there is much to be gained in the form of opportunity, there is also much to be lost if trading decisions do not adequately reflect conditions in the international markets. Among the factors that must be considered in this determination are the following:

- Trading volume
- Type of trading approach (i.e., fully electronic, partially electronic, open outcry or otherwise)
- Accessibility of your broker or brokerage firm during the trading hours in foreign markets
- Viability of the market for short-term and/or day trading
- Currency exchange considerations
- Rules regarding futures trading by foreigners
- Tax considerations

- Limitations on withdrawal of profits from trading accounts in the given country
- Ability of brokerage firm in your own country to execute orders in the foreign markets with speed, accuracy and efficiency
- Trading hours as they relate to your own schedule
- Availability of price, volume, open interest and other trading information that may be necessary to maintain your specific trading system(s) or method(s)

Provided all these factors are conducive to your goals, you have much to gain by trading the foreign markets. The potential may be especially significant to those whose businesses require bona fide hedges as opposed to those who seek merely to broaden the scope of their speculative activities. The ability to hedge foreign interest rates and currencies by trading in their countries of origin may prove highly profitable to manufacturing firms, banks, governments, importers, exporters and food processors.

Your broker will be able to provide you with valuable information on the markets that are most active. In addition, your broker will be able to answer specific questions regarding the order-entry procedures and arrangements they maintain with floor traders on the various international exchanges who fill their orders. Ask your broker to assist you in selecting the markets that are most suitable for trading. Market conditions will change in time, often dramatically. Such dramatic change can provide many potentially profitable trading opportunities for the investor and should be considered as a positive aspect for traders.

SUMMARY AND CONCLUSIONS

The game of futures trading can now be played on futures exchanges throughout the world. Although opportunities abound, risk is always a fact of market life. Traders who focus only on the potential for profit while ignoring the probability of loss are asking for trouble.

If you plan to trade the international futures markets, be sure to know the details of each. Traders who are new to futures should take small steps at first, trading their domestic markets or the U.S. markets, where liquidity is high.

As international markets expand their operations and, concomitantly, their trading volume, opportunities for trading will grow. At the present time, the best thing traders can do is trade only in markets where liquidity is high, while closely watching developments in other markets.

Chapter 2

INTERNATIONAL MARKETS: WHAT IS TRADED; WHERE IT'S TRADED; HOW IT'S TRADED

Given the proliferation of futures markets throughout the world, it would be best to consider the general categories of futures markets before discussing where these markets are traded. These categories include:

AGRICULTURE/FARM PRODUCTS
Grains & Oilseeds
Meat & Dairy Products
Foods (other food products)

INDUSTRIAL PRODUCTS
Energy
Metals
Other Industrials
Textiles

FINANCIAL PRODUCTS
Currencies
Equity Options
Financial Futures & Options
Indexes
Interest Rates
Stock-Index Futures
And, **Other Products** (which fit into none of the other categories)

MAJOR EXCHANGES OF THE WORLD

The rapid growth of futures exchanges throughout the world has given us literally hundreds of new exchanges. The vast majority are still in their infancy. Competition for trader business is high. I have included only the more active exchanges in this book. The most active exchanges are marked with an asterisk. You will find a comprehensive list in Appendix I (page 223), along with specific contact information in Appendix II (page 251).

FIGURE 2.1

COUNTRIES WITH FUTURES EXCHANGES

Argentina *
Armenia
Australia *
Austria *
Bahrain
Bangladesh
Barbados
Belgium *
Bermuda
Bolivia
Botswana
Brazil *
Bulgaria
Canada *
Cayman Islands
Chile *
China *
Costa Rica
Côte d'Ivoire (Ivory Coast)
Croatia (Hrvatska)
Cyprus
Czech Republic
Denmark *
Ecuador
Egypt
El Salvador
Estonia
Finland *
France *
Germany *
Ghana
Greece
Honduras
Hong Kong *
Hungary *
Iceland
India *
Indonesia *
Iran
Ireland *
Israel *
Italy *
Jamaica
Japan *
Jordan
Kenya
Korea (South) *
Kuwait
Latvia
Lithuania
Luxembourg
Macedonia
Malaysia *
Malta
Mauritius
Mexico
Morocco
Namibia
Netherlands *
New Zealand
Nicaragua
Nigeria

Norway *
Oman
Pakistan
Panama
Paraguay
Peru
Philippines *
Poland
Portugal*
Romania *
Russian Federation *
Saudi Arabia
Singapore *
Slovak Republic
Slovenia *
South Africa *
Spain *
Sri Lanka
Swaziland
Sweden *
Switzerland
Taiwan
Thailand
Trinidad and Tobago
Tunisia
Turkey *
United Kingdom *
United States *
Venezuela *
Yugoslavia
Zimbabwe

African and Middle Eastern Exchanges

Futures trading in Africa and the Middle East is still relatively new and trading volume is limited. Exchanges are located in South Africa, Turkey and Israel. The markets are thinly traded (limited activity) at this time; however, this may well change.

The South African Futures Exchange (SAFEX) trades a wide variety of contracts in many types of markets. Established in 1988, SAFEX was officially licensed as a derivatives exchange in 1990.

The organized securities market in Turkey began after the Crimean War, when the first market in the Ottoman Empire was established in 1866 under the name of "Dersaadet Securities Exchange." The Istanbul Stock Exchange (ISE), founded in 1985, trades a variety of financial futures and stock-index products.

Israel's Tel Aviv Stock Exchange Ltd. (TASE) began trading futures in 1953 and derivatives in 1993. In August 1997, TASE launched a computerized trading system for continuous trading. Orders that are taken by the Tel Aviv Stock Exchange include LMT (Limit), MKT (Market) and ATO (At the Opening Price). It is interesting to note that Israeli income-tax regulations define options and futures on the Exchange Index as "shares," so that the profits from options trading are exempt from capital-gains taxation (which is, of course, subject to restrictions set in the law).

Asian Exchanges

Although there is considerable futures trading activity in China, information on the exchanges is not so accessible as it is in other parts of the world. There are numerous exchanges in the various Chinese provinces. Among these are the Beijing Commodity Exchange (BCE), the China-Commodity Futures Exchange, Inc. of Hainan (CCFE), the Guangdong United Futures Exchange (GUFE), the Shanghai Cereal and Oils Exchange (SCOE), the Shenzhen Mercantile Exchange (SZME) and the China Zhengzhou Commodity Exchange (CZCE). Futures and securities in China are regulated by the China Securities Regulatory Commission (CSRC). Foreign investors may not enter the Chinese futures market. Additionally, some futures exchanges limit certain trading practices to prevent excessive speculation. State-owned companies may only trade futures to hedge their own production.

Although Hong Kong has a long tradition as the center of commodities trading, the Commodity Trading Ordinance, the first regulatory body for the colony, was only established in 1975. This was closely followed by the establishment of the Hong Kong Futures Exchange Limited (HKFE).

At the Indian Commodity Exchanges, about half the futures trading is estimated to be speculative. Day traders conduct half of what is termed "scalping" (the term *scalper* usually refers to a pit broker or speculator who trades frequently during the day for very small moves). Farmers in India rarely use futures markets directly for hedging; however, they benefit indirectly by using cooperatives or other intermediaries to help them obtain better prices for their own goods by using futures markets.

Futures trading in India is regulated by the Securities and Exchange Board of India (SEBI), the Reserve Bank of India and the Forward Markets Commission. Foreign investors are required to register with SEBI in order to participate in Indian securities markets. As of this writing, regulations governing foreign institutional investors allow investment only in listed securities. Buying, selling or otherwise dealing in securities as a foreign institutional investor is not permitted unless the investor holds a certificate granted by SEBI. The Over-the-Counter Exchange of India (OTCEI) is the most well-known exchange.

European Exchanges

Trading in Europe (which will be elaborated upon in Chapter 3) has enjoyed a colorful history that dates back hundreds of years. The newest European exchange is the European Futures Exchange (EUREX), which was established in 1998 in Germany through the merger of the Deutsche Terminborse (DTB) and the Swiss Options and Financial Exchange (SOFFEX).

Some of the more well-known European commodity exchanges include the Belgium Futures and Options Exchange (BELFOX), the Mercato Italian Futures (MIF), the Amsterdam Exchanges (AEX—Optiebeurs) and the Spanish Financial Futures Market (MEFF Renta Fija). With the onset of the new millennium, a new market structure in Paris was created in 1999 as four French market operations (SBF, MATIF SA, MONEP SA and Societé du Nouveau Marché) merged to form a single entity, the ParisBourse SA, "home to interest rate, equity and commodities derivatives markets." Although MATIF SA no longer exists as a market operator, the MATIF is still performing as a market for interest-rate and commodities derivatives along with the MONEP, another of the derivatives markets that is now a part of the ParisBourse SA.

London offers a wide variety of trading vehicles and exchanges, among them, the International Petroleum Exchange of London (IPE), the London Commodities Exchange (LCE), the London International Financial Futures Exchange (LIFFE), the London Metal Exchange (LME) and The London Securities and Derivatives Exchange (OMLX).

Futures trading in the states of the former Soviet Union is conducted through the Moscow Commodity Exchange (ME), the Russian Exchange (RE), the St. Petersburg Futures Exchange (SPBFE) and the Siberian Stock Exchange (SibEx), among others. Any person or legal entity may trade at the RE as a trader but if trading as a clearing firm, specific requirements must be met. At this writing, trading in Russia was, for the most part, virtually inactive.

LATIN AMERICAN EXCHANGES

The development of organized capital markets in Venezuela began in 1805, when Don Bruno Abasolo and Don Fernando Key Muñoz founded a trading house in the Santiageo de Leio de Caracas. In 1807, the government issued a *reglamento* (regulation) designed to regulate traders and trading activity. They also founded an organization of traders, who authorized six traders in Caracas, as well as developed certain sanctions for those who did not fulfill their requirements for approval. After several attempts to create a formal marketplace, *La Bolsa de Portillo* was established in 1840, offering two trading sessions per day. In 1917, the National Congress approved a Commercial Exchange Law and, in 1947, the first formal exchange was registered.

In 1917, Brazilian exporters, businessmen and commodity producers founded the São Paulo Commodities Exchange, Bolsa de Mercadorias de São Paulo (BMSP). This was the first Brazilian institution to offer forward transactions. Eventually, the BMSP established trading in agricultural commodities, especially coffee, live cattle and cotton. In 1986, the Bolsa Mercantil & de Futurus Exchange (BM&F) was established. Trading activities began the next year. In 1991, the BMSP and BM&F merged to create the Bolsa de Mercadorias y Futuros, retaining BM&F as its official title.

In 1997, the Brazilian Futures Exchanges (BBF) of Rio de Janeiro, which was founded in 1983, joined BM&F. This strengthened the domestic commodities market and consolidated BM&F as the major derivatives trading center in Mercosur. Mercosur is a common market comprised of Brazil, Argentina, Paraguay and Uruguay, and represents the third largest trading bloc in the world after the European Economic Union and the United States, Canada and Mexico, a bloc that was formed by NAFTA, the North American Free Trade Agreement.

Several other South American countries have futures exchanges that have been active for many years. Chapter 3 (page 48) discusses futures trading in Argentina from its inception in 1854 at the Buenos Aires Grain Exchange (BAGE) to the Buenos Aires Futures Market (MATBA), which began in 1907, to the Rosario Futures Exchange (ROFEX), which was established in 1909. In Chile, the Santiago Stock Exchange (SSE) pioneered the implementation of futures markets since it began trading in 1993. In Venezuela, futures are traded at the Caracas Stock Exchange (BVC).

North American Exchanges

Futures exchanges in North America are among the most active in the world. Recent mergers in New York have resulted in two major exchanges—the New York Board of Trade (NYBOT) and the New York Mercantile Exchange (NYMEX/COMEX). The NYBOT absorbed the former Coffee, Sugar & Cocoa Exchange, Inc. (CSCE), the New York Cotton Exchange (NYCE), the New York Futures Exchange (NYFE), the FINEX and Citrus

Associates of the NYCE Inc. NYMEX/COMEX merged the New York Mercantile Exchange (originated in 1872 as the Butter and Cheese Exchange of New York) and New York's Commodity Exchange, which was formed in 1933.

Chicago's Board of Trade (CBOT) and Mercantile Exchange (CME) are also major world centers of futures trading. Other exchanges that have also shown reasonably good trading activity are the Kansas City Board of Trade (KCBOT), the Minneapolis Grain Exchange (MGE), the Mid-America Commodity Exchange (MidAm) (affiliated with the Chicago Board of Trade), the Winnipeg Commodity Exchange (WCE) and the Toronto Futures Exchange (TFE).

The Bermuda Commodities Exchange was incorporated on July 22, 1996, pursuant to the Bermuda Commodities Exchange Act. It deals in the insurance risk market, specifically The Guy Carpenter Catastrophe Index (GCCI).

Although there are several other futures exchanges in North America, they do not account for sufficient trading activity to warrant inclusion here.

Pacific Rim Exchanges

Futures trading in Japan has enjoyed a long and colorful history. Its origins can be traced back to the middle of the Tokugawa era in the 1640s. At that time, the existing government had part of the rice that was manufactured collected as rent, which was then ground and stored in the granaries of Osaka. The Samurai of each feudal clan administered the process and disposition of the stored rice. In 1696, the Dojima Rice Market (predecessor of the Dojima Rice Exchange) was initiated. Cash settlement trading, as well as original physical rice trading, was actively conducted at this location. Rice traders who were asked by their clans to commercialize rice produced in their territories created the exchange in response to these requests.

Beginning in the early 1870s, rice futures were traded at the location of the present Tokyo Grain Exchange (TGE). In 1893, the Exchange Law was enacted. Cotton and silk yarn, rayon and sugar were listed for trading. The Hokkaido Grain Exchange (HGE) was initially established in 1893 as the Otaru Rice, Herring and Fertilizer Exchange, and reopened in 1951 as Agricultural and Fishery Products Exchange. It merged with TGE in 1995. Trading on all commodities exchanges in Japan was suspended during World War II. During the period of recovery after the war, the new Commodity Exchange Law was passed and a number of exchanges were established thereafter.

There are many futures exchanges in Japan. Two of the largest include the Kanmon Commodity Exchange (KCE) (originally established as the Kanmon Grain Exchange in 1805 and restructured in 1953) and the Kansai Commodities Exchange (KANEX). The KANEX was formed in 1997 by the merger of the Kansai Agricultural Commodities Exchange (which was previously founded in 1993 through the merger of three historic exchanges—the Osaka Grain Exchange, the Kobe Grain Exchange and the Osaka Sugar Exchange) and the Kobe Raw Silk Exchange. The Osaka Securities Exchange was established in 1949 and its predecessor, the Osaka Stock Exchange, was formed in 1878. The exchange trades futures and futures options as well as equity options.

Other Japanese exchanges include the Chubu Commodity Exchange (C-COM) created from the merger of the Nagoya Grain & Sugar Exchange, the Nagoya Textile Exchange and the Toyohasi Dried Cocoon Exchange; the Osaka Mercantile Exchange (OME), formed by the union of the Kobe Rubber Exchange and the Osaka Textile Exchange; the Maebashi Dried Cocoon Exchange (MDCE); and the Tokyo Commodity Exchange (TOCOM). TOCOM was established through the consolidation of the Tokyo Gold Exchange, which began trading in

1983; the Tokyo Rubber Exchange, which was initiated in 1952; and the Tokyo Textile Exchange, established in 1951.

The Tokyo Grain Exchange (TGE), which conducts all trading electronically, began trading in 1952 in the building that housed the Tokyo Rice Exchange (which was closed before World War II). It merged with the Tokyo Sugar Exchange in 1993 to become the largest agricultural commodities futures market in Japan. The Tokyo International Financial Futures Exchange (TIFFE), established in 1989, operates under a fully automated computer system as well as Japan's standard *Itayose* method of trading.

Malaysia hosts the Commodity and Monetary Exchange of Malaysia (COMMEX), founded in December 1998 by the merger of the Kuala Lumpur Commodity Exchange (KLCE), which was originally founded in 1980, and the Malaysia Monetary Exchange, which was originally founded in 1996. In 1995, the Kuala Lumpur Options & Financial Futures Exchange (KLOFFE) was formed and began trading futures with the launch of the KLOFFE's stock-index futures contract. With the introduction of KLOFFE, Malaysia became the third Asian economy after Hong Kong and Japan to offer domestic equity derivatives products.

The New Zealand Futures & Options Exchange Ltd. (NZFOE), founded in 1985, is a fairly active exchange, but not nearly so active as the North American and European Exchanges.

Rubber futures have been traded in Singapore since the 1920s. The Singapore Chamber of Commerce Rubber Association initially provided clearing facilities for futures transactions. These were subsequently taken over by the Rubber Association of Singapore, which was privatized and became the RAS Commodity Exchange in 1992. RAS was renamed the Singapore Commodity Exchange Limited (SICOM) in 1994. In addition to the SICOM, commodities are traded through the Singapore International Monetary Exchange Limited (SIMEX), founded in 1984.

HOW THE DIFFERENT MARKETS ARE TRADED

The traditional method of futures trading is known as the "open outcry" system. In a process that may seem archaic, disorganized or even primitive, traders gather in trading pits or rings to transact their business. While the system differs slightly from market to market, the general idea is the same. Orders from customers are called in to brokers who, in turn, send orders to the exchange's trading floor. Orders are time-stamped and recorded appropriately and then passed to a floor broker or pit trader either by hand signal or order ticket. Pit brokers openly bid or offer contracts by voice and hand signal. The bid—and offer—process via voice or open outcry was, until the late 1990s, the prevalent method of futures trading. Traders transacted their business face-to-face or nearly face-to-face.

The electronic revolution has forever changed the nature of futures trading. The open outcry system is rapidly disappearing in favor of an electronic system in which bids and offers are matched by computer. The role of the floor broker or pit broker is diminishing. This is particularly true on the newer exchanges such as those in Europe, where the human middlemen in the trading process are disappearing.

While there are those who feel that such a system is more equitable and diminishes the possibility of either illegal or unethical activities by floor brokers, others feel that the all-electronic exchange is too computer-dependent and could create problems in the event of computer failures. This remains to be seen. Progress is, however, unstoppable and undeniable, and the open outcry system will disappear within a few years, as virtually all world futures exchanges move to an electronic order matching system. Although there will be growing pains and system failures from time to time, I believe that the benefits far outweigh the potential liabilities.

Futures markets in different countries have their own specific procedures and methods of trading. In some exchanges, the method of trading is not conducive to relatively simple market entry and exit or to speculative activity. Unless those exchanges modernize, it is unlikely that they will survive in today's highly competitive and increasingly electronic markets since these current practices limit liquidity and market life, and threaten their very existence.

Issues of Concern to Traders

Given the rapid growth of futures markets, contracts and exchanges throughout the world, it is a given that some will fail while others will achieve considerable success. The growth process will take its toll. As the markets expand and proliferate, it will become more critical for futures traders to evaluate the viability of each market as a trading vehicle. The simple fact is that of the many futures exchanges and contracts now being traded, perhaps as few as fifty are worthy trading vehicles. Traders must be very selective in deciding what markets to trade. There are a number of major questions to consider in selecting markets to trade:

- *Liquidity.* Is the trading volume sufficient to permit relative ease of market entry and exit for speculators as well as bona fide hedgers?
- *Speed of order execution.* Can orders be processed, executed and reported back to the trader promptly and efficiently?
- *Government regulations.* Are government regulations prohibitive or excessive with regard to position limits, taxes, foreign traders and so on?
- *Exposure.* Does the exchange participate in actively promoting and publicizing its markets so as to attract more traders?

Before trading in any foreign market you should consider these questions as well as the specific rules and regulations unique to the particular exchange. Above all, make certain that your funds are secure both with your broker and the exchange. After all, a winning trade that you can't get out of, or collect on, is really a losing trade.

Working with a Broker—the Do's and Don'ts

The process of selecting a broker and brokerage firm to handle your orders on the international markets only slightly differs from the procedure you would follow in selecting a broker to handle your domestic futures transactions. Above and beyond the customary due diligence with regard to the financial stability of the brokerage firm and the ethical reputation of the broker, you will also need to consider the ability and efficiency in transacting your orders in the foreign markets.

Be particularly cautious and thorough in determining on which exchanges the firm can place orders and how quickly such orders can be executed. Another major concern is the cost of executing orders in foreign markets. You will likely be required to open a separate account for the purpose of paying commissions and you may be required to sign additional disclosures regarding the risk of trading in foreign markets.

Price Orders and Order Entry

As you are already well aware, the types of orders accepted at different exchanges vary considerably and could be substantially different from that to which you are accustomed. Therefore, prior to attempting futures trading in any of the foreign markets, be clear as to the types of orders you may use as well as any idiosyncrasies of the markets you trade.

Currency-Rate Changes and Their Effect on Trading

A major factor that must always be considered in trading the foreign markets is the effect of currency fluctuations on your trading systems. As you know, exchange rates can vary from moment to moment, often dramatically. The effect on your results could be substantial. In order to minimize these effects, you might want to consider establishing an account in the country of the markets you will trade. Prior to doing this, however, be sure to familiarize yourself with local tax considerations, as well as with laws governing futures trading accounts by foreigners.

The Impact of Time Differences on Trading

Clearly time difference will affect the ability of traders to participate in many of the foreign markets. Unless traders are willing to stay awake during nighttime hours, active day trading is not feasible. However, the use of trading systems for position trading will allow them to enter orders prior to market openings. Therefore traders will not need to be concerned about the differences in trading hours. For those brave insomniacs who are still intent on day trading foreign markets during their own evening hours, there are numerous markets that may be traded.

Summary and Conclusions

Many new futures exchanges have opened their doors since the early 1980s; however, futures trading in most of these markets is not yet viable due to either poor liquidity or insufficient price volatility. Of the new exchanges, the most promising are the LIFFE in London, the ParisBourse SA in France, the EUREX in Germany, several of the Japanese exchanges and the SIMEX in Singapore.

In comparison to trading activity in the United States, LIFFE stands out from the others as the next most viable market for traders. A wide variety of products is offered in the major market categories. At this time, many exchanges are still in their infancy. The natural process of growing pains must run its course before trading in these markets can be considered worthwhile or even viable.

Chapter 3

FUTURES TRADING IN EUROPE AND THE AMERICAS

The European and North American futures exchanges are currently the most actively traded as well as the most viable exchanges in terms of liquidity and variety of contracts offered. Contracts include grains, soybean complex commodities, livestock, tropicals, currencies, stock-index futures, interest rates, cotton, milk, cheese, lumber, metals interest rates and commodities in the petroleum complex. The method of trading is primarily open outcry, although fully electronic trading in some markets is growing rapidly and may soon replace the open outcry system entirely.

FUTURES TRADING IN GREAT BRITAIN

Just as commodity futures trading traces its roots back to the late 1600s in Japan, cash commodity trading in London began in the 1600s also. The Royal Exchange in London was the locus of trading and barter in a variety of commodities. Cash transactions as well as barter were the primary avenues of exchange. Although the facility housing the Royal Exchange was destroyed in the Great Fire of London in 1666, commodity trading continued to flourish in London and its vicinity. Traders frequently transacted their business in coffeehouses that eventually grew into organized exchanges.

In the early-nineteenth century, the market was dominated by grain traders, shipping merchants and financiers. Participation in the Royal Exchange grew to such large proportions that it became impossible to conduct business in only one location. Groups of traders set up shop in the nearby coffeehouses. The Jerusalem Coffeehouse off Cornhill became a favorite of the metal trading community. The tradition of the trading "ring" was born at this location. A trader with metal to sell would draw a circle in the sawdust on the floor. When he was ready to trade he would cry out "change"—at which point all those wishing to participate in trading activity would assemble around the circle and announce their bids for the product being offered.

As the trading activity and volume continued to grow, merchants often engaged in the forward contracting of entire cargoes booked to arrive many months into the future. In order to protect against the risk of potentially severe price changes in commodities between the time of purchase and future sale, trading eventually evolved into the "terminal" market. Participation in this type of trading allowed merchants to hedge their physical purchases and/or sales by providing price insurance. Records of such futures transactions date back to the late 1800s.

After World War II, soft commodities in London were traded in two locations. The individual terminal markets for coffee, cocoa and sugar were located in Mark Lane. Also traded in this location were the primarily domestic markets. Together these two markets comprised the Grain and Feed Trade Association (GAFTA). Freight futures were traded at the Baltic Exchange.

Today futures trading in Great Britain is conducted primarily in London, as it has been in various forms for several hundred years. A major step toward attracting futures trading activity from all over the world was taken in 1982 with the formation of the London International Financial Futures Exchange (LIFFE). In 1986, the aforementioned terminal markets located in Mark Lane merged to become the London Commodity Exchange (LCE).

After the merger, LCE trading volume grew. Several new futures products were launched. The LCE's merger with the Baltic Futures Market established the exchange as the leading soft commodity and agricultural exchange in Europe. The LCE had become an attractive organization to other exchanges. In November 1995, it was announced that the LCE would be merging with LIFFE. On September 16, 1996, the newly merged market opened for business, retaining the moniker of the LIFFE.

The London International Financial Futures Exchange (LIFFE)

Growth of the LIFFE has been dramatic. In relatively short order, the exchange has grown to become the world's third largest exchange in trading volume. Its merger with the LCE in 1996 added 15,000 contracts in trading volume to its previously held 600,000 contracts. The amazing growth of the LIFFE reflects a growing demand and trend toward trading in financial futures. LIFFE is a forward-thinking exchange with state-of-the-art open outcry trading as well as electronic trading.

The Impact of LIFFE on Futures Trading in Europe

Until the LIFFE began trading financial futures in London, European futures trading was minimal compared with that in the United States. However, by focusing only on financial futures, the LIFFE was able to fill a vital need. As European economies grew and fluctuations in currencies and interest rates grew more volatile, the need for a viable market in European interest-rate futures also grew. Hence, the LIFFE's timing in introducing its financial futures vehicles was propitious. The vast majority of trading in European interest-rate instruments and stock-index futures occurs at the LIFFE. The demand for futures trading has grown by over forty percent a year since its inception. It earns £1,000M in invisible earnings for Britain and provides 25,000 jobs.

In May 1999, the LIFFE achieved a record level of open interest in its benchmark Euribor futures contract of over one-million lots (1,016,404). A volume market share of eighty-four percent in Euribor futures and ninety-nine percent in Euribor options also confirms LIFFE's dominance of the Euro-denominated, short-term, interest-rate market.

LIFFE offers the most extensive range of derivative products of any exchange in the world. It provides futures and options contracts across six different currencies and across various currencies and product lines: bonds, short-term interest rates, equity indices and individual stocks and commodities. LIFFE's products are supported by additional trading facilities that meet the particular needs of the market—for example, inter-contract spread, basis- and flex-trading facilities. The dynamics of the open outcry environment allow for a large number of strategy trades to be implemented across as well as through product lines.

One of the cornerstones of LIFFE's success has been its use of state-of-the-art technology support and enhancements on a wide range of Exchange functions. LIFFE continues to develop its open systems to ensure continued access to the Exchange from around the world.

LIFFE is a hybrid exchange. Its contracts are traded on open outcry and electronic trading platforms. Its new state-of-the-art electronic trading system, LIFFE CONNECTTM, provides a powerful combination of high-performance capacity and open-system design that enables the Exchange to distribute its products globally, in a manner that gives members, and through them, other users, unparalleled flexibility and choice of trading environments. With this technology it as easy for nondomestic users to take advantage of LIFFE's contracts, including sterling, dollar, ECU, lira, Swiss franc and Japanese yen-denominated contracts, as it is for users in London. Their existing systems make LIFFE a uniquely efficient market in which to trade.

LIFFE continued its strong growth in 1999 and into the first quarter of 2000. LIFFE traded an average daily value of £223 billion in March 2000 or £14 trillion for the first quarter of 2000. Its position as the largest exchange in Europe in value of contracts traded was therefore maintained.

The LIFFE Euribor contract was up forty-five percent in volume on a yearly basis. Trading in equity products also increased. The FTSE 100-Index futures contract was up twenty-two percent on a yearly basis and equity options were up twenty-three percent on a yearly basis.

As you can see, the LIFFE continues its trend as a leading world exchange. In addition the LIFFE has opened most of its Pan-European Stock Index Futures to U.S. investors.

LIFFE has received approval from the United States Commodity Futures Trading Commission by a "no action" letter authorizing five more of its pan-European stock index futures to be offered for sale in the U.S.

U.S. investors will soon be able to trade the following five LIFFE futures:

- The FTSE Eurotop 300 Index, FTSE Eurotop 300 (ex-UK) Index and the FTSE Eurobloc 100 Index futures
- The MSCI Euro Index and the MSCI Pan-Euro Index futures

John Foyle, LIFFE's Deputy Chief Executive, hailed the CFTC's decision as a move that will allow U.S. investors to "have access to a wider choice of pan-European stock index future products." The majority of LIFFE's pan-European equity futures products are now available to U.S. investors. CFTC approval for the FTSE Stars Index Futures also is expected in 2000.

FIGURE 3.1

MARKETS TRADED AT THE LIFFE

Currencies

Euro
Japanese Yen
Swiss Franc

Foods

Cocoa
Coffee
Potatoes
Sugar

Equity Options

BIFFEX (Dry Freight Futures)
Eurotop
FTSE-100 and 250

Grains & Oilseeds

Barley
Wheat

Indexes

DAX Index
FTSE Eurotop Index

Interest Rates

BOBL—German Government Bond *(Bundes obligationen)*
Bonos—Spanish Government Bond
BTP—Italian Government Bond
EuroBund—German Government Bond
Euribor
EuroDollar
EuroLibor
EuroLira
EuroMark
EuroSwiss
EuroYen
Gilt
JGB—Japanese Government Bond
Short Sterling

Stock-Index Futures

FTSE-100 Stock Index

THE LONDON METALS EXCHANGE (LME)

The London Metal Exchange (LME) also had its roots in the opening of the Royal Exchange during the reign of Queen Elizabeth I. Trading in cash metals was brisk. At first, traders dealt only in physical metals for the domestic market. However, as Britain became a major exporter of metals, European merchants began to expand their participation in the Exchange's activities.

In the early part of the nineteenth century, the United Kingdom was self sufficient in copper and tin. Quoted prices often remained fixed for many months. However, with the Industrial Revolution came a substantial increase in demand, changing the price structure of virtually all commodities forever. Almost overnight, the UK became the most technologically advanced country in the world, importing vast amounts of raw commodities from abroad in order to feed the machinery of industrialization. The result of increased demand was a marked change in the stability of prices.

London metal traders, who bought products from as far away as Chile and Malaya, could no longer depend on the stability of prices for goods booked to arrive via ship many months later. Traders and their clients were often exposed to considerable price risk as a result of the time lag between the completion of a purchase agreement and the actual arrival of the goods. Intercontinental lines of communication via telegraph somewhat diminished the risk of price exposure. Furthermore, the development of steam-powered ocean cargo vessels facilitated the timely arrival dates of commodities.

Traders and end users could more correctly anticipate the time of arrival of a cargo. This allowed them to forward contract delivery of goods on a fixed date. Both buyer and seller would agree on a fixed price to be honored at the time of delivery—no matter what the actual price might be on the delivery date. Both the buyer and the seller were protecting against a major change in price during the voyage. At times the benefit was to the buyer and at times to the seller. Although some traders defaulted on their forward contracts, the system appeared to work well. For the most part, such forward contracts were honored and executed as agreed upon.

In 1869, the opening of the Suez Canal further shortened the delivery time of tin from Malaya. The new delivery time of three months for tin matched the delivery time for copper from Chile.

This gave rise to LME's unique system of daily trading dates for up to three months forward contracting.

As the total tonnage of deliveries grew to meet increasing demands of British industry, more merchants were attracted to the market. It soon became necessary to secure a permanent location where they could conduct their transactions daily. Their move to the Lombard Exchange and Newsroom proved to be inadequate.

In 1877, the London Metal Exchange Company was formed. Telegraph lines were installed to aid trading and price reporting. Membership numbers increased substantially. After growing to over three hundred members, the exchange needed new quarters and moved to a building on Whittington Avenue, which was its headquarters for the next ninety-eight years. Next came a period of fourteen years at Plantation House, after which the Exchange moved to it most recent home on Leadenhall Street in 1994.

The London Metal Exchange is center of the world's trading in base metals. Ring (open-outcry) dealing brokerage firms meet to trade industrial nonferrous metals. Markets traded are copper, primary aluminum, aluminum alloy, lead, nickel, tin and zinc. Floor trading is the focus of the daily business; however, a significant proportion of LME business is also traded inter-office. The LME offers 24-hour trading services, and its daily value of metals traded averages about US$10 billion.

FIGURE 3.2
MARKETS TRADED AT THE LME

Aluminum (including Primary Aluminum)
Copper
Lead
Nickel
Tin
Zinc (including Special High Grade)

Today the Exchange has a membership of over 100 firms. Of these, 15 participate in ring dealing, the open outcry sessions, which occur twice a day. Other Broker Members (about twenty-seven) participate in the continuous trading of futures and options between offices.

The Exchange is highly international in its membership with ninety percent of its Clearing Member firms wholly or partly owned by overseas companies. With approximately ninety-seven percent of its business coming from abroad, the LME share (by weight) of world terminal market nonferrous metals is over ninety-five percent of all copper and virtually all aluminum, lead, nickel, tin and zinc.

The LME is not a cash-cleared market. Its unique floor and inter-office trading procedure is combined with a clearing system operating between principals that is based on bank guarantees and other forms of collateral. Both floor and inter-office trading are covered by a matching system run by the London Clearing House, whose role is to act as a central counter party to trades executed between Clearing Members and thereby reduce risk and settlement costs.

FUTURES TRADING IN SPAIN

The Spanish Financial Futures Market (MEFF RF) began operations in March 1990; a year after OTC (over the counter) derivative products were introduced in Spain. In December 1991, MEFF Holding was created to merge the trading operations of derivatives on debt in the Spanish Financial Futures Market, and the derivatives market on the stock-exchange index and shares in the Spanish Equity Derivatives Exchange (MEFF RV). Each of these markets has a two-fold function: as an exchange for trading and as a clearinghouse for clearing and settlement through an electronic trading system developed by MEFF Holding. These exchanges, and others that participate in the Spanish securities markets, are regulated and monitored by the Comision Nacional del Mercado de Valores (CNMV).

The MEFF RF has consolidated its position to become the fourth largest futures and options exchange in Europe and it is in the top twenty internationally. Trading volume for interest-rate futures in 1999 declined to 3.6 million from 10.6 million in 1998 and 14 million in 1997.

In 1993, the MEFF became a Designated Investment Exchange approved by the Securities and Investments Board (SIB) and a Recognized Overseas Investment Exchange by the British Treasury. In 1995, the Commodity Futures Trading Commission (CFTC) authorized the promotion of MEFF products in the United States, allowing North American clients to trade directly in the Spanish market. With the clause 30 exemption of the CFTC, the same authorization is given to MEFF members.

MEFF is a totally electronic market designed to integrate trading, clearing and settlement in a single system, providing the market with the latest technological innovations. The characteristics and sophistication of MEFF's electronic trading system has attracted interest and resulted in export orders from other markets, including the Citrus Fruit and Commodity Futures Market of Valencia, the Portuguese Futures and Options Exchange in Oporto, Portugal and the Caracas Stock Exchange in Venezuela.

FIGURE 3.3

MARKETS TRADED AT THE MEFF RF

Currencies

Spanish Peseta/German Mark

Spanish Peseta/U.S. Dollar

Interest Rates

Bonos—Spanish Government Bond (including Three-Year, Five-Year and Ten-Year and E-5, E-10 and E-30)

BUBOR (including One-Month and Three-Month)

Notional Government Bond (including Three-Year, Five-Year and Ten-Year)

FUTURES TRADING IN FRANCE

Commodity futures markets were established in France in 1885 and closed in 1939. The cocoa futures market was reopened in 1962, and financial futures trading began in 1986 as the MATIF (Marché a Terme International de France). The MATIF traded several agricultural contracts and a full range of instruments for the active management of risks associated with changes in interest rates, share prices and several commodities.

In 1999, the four major French markets—SBF, MATIF SA, MONEP SA and Societé du Nouveau Marché—merged to become the ParisBourse SA. With approximately 170 million contracts traded in 1999, the ParisBourse SA is one of the world's leading futures markets. Its primary product, the Notionnel futures contract, rapidly became a world benchmark for the markets and the world's number-two bond futures contract in terms of trading volume. The merger creating the ParisBourse SA has created an exchange that promises to rival the major U.S. exchanges as well as the LIFFE.

Income for 1999 was forty-two percent higher than in 1998, as a result of record trading on the ParisBourse. The 58 million trades surpassed the 1999 total by thirty-nine percent. This was the largest increase for any of the European exchanges. The 1999 total capitalization of ParisBourse stocks stood at 1.5 trillion, EUR (Euros), which was the highest figure for any continental European exchange.

The ParisBourse now supplies electronic trading systems to 17 markets across five continents, making it the world leader in this area.

The ParisBourse SA is yet another example of the trend toward consolidation and mergers in world exchanges. In most cases such unions and joint marketing efforts have been successful not only for the exchanges but they have also proven beneficial to the traders by providing a central location and often lower commissions.

FIGURE 3.4

MARKETS TRADED AT THE PARISBOURSE SA

Foods

Coffee

Potatoes

Sugar

Grains & Oilseeds

Corn

Rapeseed (Canola)

Wheat

Indexes

CAC-40 Index

Dow Jones

Euro (ECU) Bond

Notionnel Bond

Interest Rates

CAC-40

EBond, Thirty-Year

ENote, Two-Year

Euribor

Euro All Sovereigns

Euro Five-Year Bond

Euro Notional Bond

French Government Bond, Medium-Term

French Treasury Bond

KO—Four-Year Bond

Notionnel Bond (GLOBEX)

PIBOR, Three-Month

Stock-Index Futures

CAC-40 Index

Dow Jones Euro STOXX 50

Dow Jones STOXX 50

FUTURES TRADING IN BELGIUM

The Belgium Futures and Options Exchange (BELFOX) is located in Brussels. At present trading vehicles at this exchange are limited to the following three areas.

FIGURE 3.5

MARKETS TRADED AT THE BELGIUM FUTURES AND OPTIONS EXCHANGE

Currencies

U.S. Dollar/Belgium Franc

Equity Options

B-Gold Index

BXF (Futures of BEL 20 Index of the Brussels Stock Exchange)

Indexes

BEL 20 Index

Gold Index

Interest Rates

BGB—Belgian Government Bond

BIBOR, Three-Month

Liquidity and trading volume are limited, overshadowed by the more active European exchanges.

FUTURES TRADING IN AUSTRIA

Since 1991, a fully automated screen-based trading and clearing system for financial futures and options has been operated by Wiener Borse AG (WBAG)—formerly the Vienna Stock Exchange and the Austrian Futures and Options Exchange (OTOB). The exchange trades futures and options on the Austrian, Russian and multinational CECE Composites Indexes; options are also traded on Austrian stocks.

The Wiener Borse trades a variety of stock indexes:

Czech Traded Index (CTX)
Hungarian Traded Index (HTX)
Polish Traded Index (PTX)
Russian Depository Receipts Index (RDX)
Russian Traded Index (RTX)

Trading volume is relatively thin and not suitable for most traders.

FUTURES TRADING IN THE EUROPEAN ECONOMIC UNION

With the advent of the European Economic Union and unified European currency, several European futures exchanges have merged into one central location. Located in both Frankfurt, Germany and Zurich, Switzerland, the European Futures Exchange (EUREX) was initially established by a letter of intent between the Deutsche Terminborse (DTB) and the Swiss Options and Financial Exchanges (SOFFE) in December 1996 and began trading in May 1998. The number of EUREX members continues to grow, totaling 312 as of December 1998, trading a total volume of 248,222,487 contracts in 1998.

In 1999, the EUREX set a new world record in trading volume. Over 379 million contracts were traded in 1999, with the EuroBund future as its highest-volume product; 144 million contracts were traded. This corresponds to an increase of about fifty-three percent in trading volume.

At the EUREX during the first quarter of 2000, 121.5 million contracts were traded. This was more than forty-five percent above the same period for 1999. In the first quarter of 2000

EUREX total volume was larger than was traded for the entire business year 1996.

The Schatz futures contract—a two-year fixed income interest rate future—set a new record with about 3.4 million contracts traded. This was one hundred sixty-two percent above the figure for 1999.

The Bobl (bond) future reached its second highest volume in March 2000, trading 5.9 million contracts above the 1999 total.

The EUREX Bund (German bond) future retains its distinction of being the world's most actively traded futures contract. Approximately 14.5 million Bund contracts were traded at EUREX in March 2000, the third-highest volume ever. Stock index futures traded over 7.2 million contracts, setting a new record in March 2000.

The EUREX exchange, although still relatively young in comparison to the U.S. exchanges and the LIFFE, has succeeded in surpassing the world's largest exchanges (in trading volume) in only one year. Trading volume at the EUREX has increased dramatically. This is especially true of Bund futures (currently trading approximately 600,000 to 1,000,000 contracts, on active days).

Record trading volume at EUREX was assisted by the continued upmove in futures and options on the EUREX Dow Jones Euro-Stoxx 50 contract. Record volume of about 2 million contracts traded was attained, surpassing the previous, December 1999 peak of 1.4 million contracts. Trading in the Dow Jones Euro Stoxx futures contract was about two hundred nineteen percent above the March 1999 figure. Options trading volume, at 540,000 contracts was up six hundred fourteen percent!

DAX futures, with over 1.5 million contracts traded, set a new record in monthly volume (previous high was 1.4 million contracts traded).

FIGURE 3.6

CONTRACTS TRADED AT THE EUREX

Currencies

U.S. Dollar/DMark

Equity Options

LEPO on Swiss Equities

Indexes

Dow Jones Euro Stoxx 50
Dow Jones Stoxx 50
DAX Index (German Stock Index)
MDAX Index
SMI Index
VOLAX Index

Interest Rates

BOBL—German Government Bond (*Bundes obligationen*)
COMI
CONF
Euribor
EuroBund—German Government Bond
EuroMark (including One-Month and Three-Month)
Jumbo Pfanbrief-Future
Schatz
Swiss Bond

Stock-Index Futures

DAX MIDCAP
DAX Xetra (Electronically traded DAX)
Swiss Market Index

FUTURES TRADING IN SLOVENIA

The Commodity Exchange of Ljubljana (CEL), established in Slovenia in 1994, began trading in March 1995. It uses a traditional open outcry system of trading with after-market electronic trading. The CEL trading floor is small by U.S. standards, providing room for 240 floor brokers and exchange employees. The exchange maintains an Internet web site where simultaneous monitoring of trades occurs.

In addition to the markets listed in Figure 3.7 that follows, the CEL has plans to expand trading to include wheat, apples, other agricultural products, wood, freight and a variety of financial futures and options.

FIGURE 3.7

FUTURES CONTRACTS TRADED AT THE CEL

Foods

Maize for feed production
Barley for feed production

Currencies

Deutschemark
Euro (ECU)
Italian Lira
Japanese Yen
U.S. Dollar
U.S. Dollar/German Mark

Equity Options

BTC
KID
KRKA

Grains & Oilseeds

Barley
Maize

Interest Rates

Short-Term Interest-Rate Futures

Stock futures based on the stock price of seven Slovenian corporations

FUTURES TRADING IN THE RUSSIAN FEDERATION

The Russian Exchanges are currently trading. In the fall of 1990, the Russian Commodities and Raw Materials Exchange organized the first trading floor in Russia at The Russian Exchange (RE), which was the first one located there since the 1917 Revolution. It is unclear as to exactly which products will be traded at all of the exchanges, but they intend to trade stock-index futures, currency futures and interest-rate futures.

FUTURES TRADING IN SOUTH AMERICA

Trading began very early in South America. Organized markets in Venezuela can be traced back to 1805 and, after a number of attempts, a formal marketplace was established in 1840. In Argentina, the Buenos Aires Stock Exchange (BCBA) and the Bolsa de Cereales de Buenos Aires or the Buenos Aires Grain Exchange (BAGE) was formed in 1854—just one year after the Argentine Constitution was adopted. The BAGE in its various forms has existed as a cash and forward market since that time, and today is perhaps the most viable of exchanges in South America.

In 1917, Brazilian exporters, businessmen and commodity producers founded the São Paulo Commodities Exchange, Bolsa de Mercadorias de São Paulo (BMSP), as the first Brazilian exchange for forward trading. In time, it established a rich tradition in the trade of agricultural commodities, especially coffee, live cattle and cotton. Margin requirements on the above contracts are approximately US$1,000, with contract size of 100 *tonnes*. In 1986, the Bolsa Mercantil & de Futuros (BM&F) was established and trading sessions began the next year. In 1991, the BMSP and BM&F merged to create the Commodity and Futures

Exchange (Bolsa de Mercadorias y Futuros), which maintained BM&F as its title. In 1997, the Brazilian Futures Exchange, Bolsa de Vaolores Regional (BBF) of Rio de Janeiro, which was founded in 1983, also joined BM&F.

The Bolsa de Mercadorias y Futuros has entered into a trading alliance with five major world exchanges.

The Chicago Mercantile Exchange, the Singapore Exchange Derivatives Exchange, the Montreal Exchange, the ParisBourse, and the BM&F alliance created an international network of exchanges that can offer a broad range of products that can be traded through a single electronic platform.

The GLOBEX Alliance allows each of the exchanges to trade online through a common electronic trading system. Products to be traded will be determined in the second quarter of 2000. The major products offered will be interest rates, foreign currencies, equities, stock indexes, agricultural commodities and energy futures.

The trading hours on the BAGE may seem somewhat peculiar to traders accustomed to other futures markets. As of April 1999 the trading schedule was:

Sector 1

Wheat:	14:30–14:50
Soybeans:	14:55–15:15
Wheat:	15:20–15:40
Midday Break:	*15:40–16:15*
Soybeans:	16:15–16:35
Wheat:	16.40–17:15
Soybeans:	17:30–18:15

Sector 2

Corn:	14:30–15:00
Corn:	15:20–15:40
Midday Break:	*15:40–17:00*
Corn:	17:00–17:30
Sunflower:	17:45–18:15

FUTURES TRADING IN CANADA

Canada is a country of vast agricultural and mineral resources. Financial exchanges date back to the early 1800s. Yet, in spite of the significant amount of commodities produced in Canada, futures trading remains relatively light.

Montreal has been a place of commercial exchange from its very early days, but it wasn't until 1832 that the first stock transactions took place, at the Exchange Coffee House, in the *Auberge du Marché* on Saint-Paul Street. Several years later, early brokers formed an association and became members of The Board of Produce Brokers, which determined the value of stocks, bonds and agricultural products. In 1863, stockbrokers and agricultural product brokers formed two distinct bodies, The Board of Brokers and The Corn Exchange. Then in 1872, only two years before its incorporation, The Board of Brokers became known as the Montreal Stock Exchange. Futures are also traded in Winnipeg and Toronto, but overall there is not much activity in the Canadian futures markets.

FUTURES TRADING IN THE UNITED STATES

Although futures trading may have its roots in the Japanese markets of the 1600s, the United States has, for many years, been the futures trading volume leader of the world. In the late 1990s, the European exchanges have, with their increased trading activity, challenged the U.S. markets for first place; however, the U.S. markets remain among the top three active market leaders in the world.

The leading U.S. exchanges are the Chicago Mercantile Exchange (CME), the Chicago Board of Trade (CBOT), the New York Board of Trade (NYBOT), the New York Mercantile Exchange (NYMEX/COMEX), the Kansas City Board of Trade (KCBOT) and the Minneapolis Grain Exchange (MGE). Literally thousands of books have been written about trading the U.S. markets. Therefore, they will not be covered extensively in this book.

Summary and Conclusions

Commodity trading in Europe has had a long and colorful history. Futures trading, although present in rudimentary form as early as the 1800s, did not achieve its modern status until the mid-1900s. Since the 1980s, great strides have been made both in overall trading volume and in new contracts launched. The leading European exchange, the LIFFE, is the third largest futures exchange in the world. The newest exchanges, the ParisBourse SA and the EUREX, are quickly becoming leading futures exchanges as well in terms of total trading volume.

Among the most liquid and tradeable, they are efficient and offer the latest technological advances in trading. In some cases, their operations and procedures are even superior to those at the U.S. exchanges.

Canadian futures trading is relatively subdued by comparison, in spite of the large amount of agricultural and mineral products produced in that country. On the other hand, the U.S. exchanges are among the most active in the world, in spite of rapid growth by the European exchanges. The markets of South America are not sufficiently active to warrant serious trading, although with some promotional efforts and modernization, they could attract more activity in the future.

Chapter 4

FUTURES TRADING IN ASIA, THE PACIFIC RIM, AFRICA AND THE MIDDLE EAST

Inasmuch as Japan is known as the birthplace of commodities trading, one would expect that the Asian futures markets would be among the most active in the world. Yet the reverse is true. Even today, despite worldwide increases in futures trading volume, the Asian and Pacific Rim markets remain relatively quiet in comparison to those of Europe and North America.

FUTURES TRADING IN ASIA

Futures trading originated in Japan in the 1640s. Whereas the European fairs had developed the structure and rules presaging a modern futures market, they were, nevertheless, cash markets. No attempt was made to take the next step and develop an actual futures contract. Evidently, the market fairs did not present a set of circumstances that made the trading of futures contracts beneficial to producers, commercial end users and speculators.

In Japan, however, the feudal system did just that. Japanese landowners found that they could use certificates of receipt against their rice crops as a sort of currency. As these certificates found their way into the economy, various individuals discovered that the value of the certificates could rise or fall as the price of rice fluctuated. Thus was born the Dojima Rice Market—the world's first futures market—where speculators traded the certificates of receipt, which were actually contracts for the future delivery of rice.

The practice of transacting these certificates of receipt, however, was little more than gambling because there was no allowance for physical delivery of the rice. If there is no provision for delivery, then a futures contract has little relationship to the underlying cash value of the commodity, and its value as an open exchange can fluctuate wildly and unpredictably. As a consequence, the Japanese government prohibited futures trading for a while in the seventeenth century. Later, with increased regulation that made physical delivery possible, the government allowed futures trading exchanges to reopen.

FUTURES TRADING IN CHINA

The system of government in China has not been conducive to the development of free trade and enterprise. However, significant changes and liberalization of agricultural distribution and production methods during the late 1980s and 1990s have resulted in the growth and development of futures exchanges that have been initiated under the control and supervision of provincial governments.

The exchanges have developed quickly even in the absence of viable, standardized and liquid cash markets. Given the often-independent role of provincial governments, there has been considerable duplication in the futures markets from one location to another. Due to severe limitations on trading imposed by the Chinese government, the Chinese futures exchanges are still essentially closed to Westerners. However, this should, and could, change dramatically by the year 2005, so a working knowledge of the Chinese markets may prove valuable in the not-too-distant future. The China Zhengzhou Commodity Exchange (CZCE), for example, has a very large trading floor that accommodates 300 members and 460 trading desks. Annual trading volume has increased steadily since 1993. In 1995, the CZCE merged with the Kansai Exchange.

The China Securities Regulatory Commission (CSRC), the People's Bank of China, and the Securities Commission of State Council are the primary regulatory agencies. The CSRC is primarily responsible for the regulation and supervision of the Chinese futures markets. Early attempts at futures trading were essentially disorganized and problematic. In response to this, the CSRC and the People's Bank have taken steps to reorganize and systematize the markets. One of their first actions has been to make the registration of futures brokers mandatory. Brokers must meet a variety of requirements, including a minimum capital worth.

Trading of certain commodity markets deemed to result in "excessive speculation" has been temporarily banned. Reorganization plans and efforts also include a temporary moratorium on the establishment of new exchanges. Relicensing of existing exchanges has been made contingent upon their ability to meet a variety of recertification requirements.

Foreign-owned/joint-venture brokers and speculative transactions by state-owned enterprises are banned. However, businesses that are essentially profit-making enterprises are permitted access to the international futures markets for the purpose of hedging. They are required to obtain prior approval and they are subject to regular audits of their finances and procedures. In mid-1995, the CSRC formed a joint agreement with the Hong Kong Securities and Futures Commission in order to further streamline Chinese futures trading.

Established in 1976 as the Hong Kong Commodity Exchange, the exchange originally traded futures on agricultural commodities including cotton, sugar and soybeans. In 1980, gold futures were introduced. In the mid-1980s, the Hong Kong Commodity Exchange changed its name to the Hong Kong Futures Exchange. Its first financial product, the Hang Seng Index futures, was launched in 1986. An international electronic trading link with the New York Mercantile Exchange began on

June 13, 1997, allowing members to trade NYMEX/COMEX contracts through ACCESS during Asian trading hours.

FUTURES TRADING IN HONG KONG

Hong Kong has a long tradition as a major center of commodities trading. Commodity Trading Ordinance (CTO), the first official trade regulatory body for the colony, was established in 1975. Shortly thereafter, the Hong Kong Commodity Exchange (HKCE), its first futures exchange, was established. Since the early 1990s, primarily due to a lack of participation and trading volume, most futures trading has been discontinued. As in the case of listed derivatives, the OTC (over the counter) market there for commodities is poorly established.

Hong Kong has instituted strict regulations for trading in derivatives. The Securities and Futures Commission (SFC) and Hong Kong Monetary Authority (HKMA) are the main regulatory authorities of these markets. The SFC, under the CTO, has been given the responsibility for regulating the markets, which includes broad authority over the derivatives markets. Until 1993, most of the contracts in the OTC market were not legally enforceable under the Gambling Ordinance. However, since then, these provisions have been amended and are legally binding.

FUTURES TRADING IN INDIA

Commodity futures trading has a long tradition in India. The country's first organized exchange, Cotton Exchange of Bombay, was established in 1921 and, five years later, the Seed Traders Association Ltd. of Bombay was introduced. These exchanges traded in options as well as futures, but options trading was banned in 1939. In implementing remedial measures to control the quick rise in commodities prices, the government adopted various price control measures during the 1940s. These measures resulted in *de facto* closures of the futures markets of the country. This impasse was broken by the Forward Contracts (Regulation) Act (FCRA) of 1952. This Act still governs the functioning of the derivatives market in India. Later, the Forward Markets Commission (FMC) was formed to supervise and regulate the derivatives markets, which gradually lost most of their earlier power for self-regulation.

Over the years the scope of derivatives trade has been increasingly limited. More and more commodities have been removed from the scope of the derivatives markets. The perception that excessive speculation in these exchanges resulted in increased prices of commodities was the major factor behind these restrictive measures. This trend was reversed, albeit partially, during the late 1970s when futures trading in a limited number of commodities was allowed, and subsequently this list has been broadened somewhat.

In spite of active futures trade of commodities, the scope of derivatives trade in commodities remains quite limited. Furthermore, as a matter of policy, Indian entities cannot access the offshore futures exchanges and OTC markets even for the purpose of hedging, although successive committees appointed by the government have recommended commodity coverage of the futures market in India be increased.

India's foreign trade in commodities constitutes a small percentage of the world trade. Further, there has been decline in the world share of many of India's commodity exports and imports, which though small by international standards, constitute a substantial proportion of India's overall foreign trade.

FUTURES TRADING IN THE PACIFIC RIM

Futures trading in the Pacific Rim countries has had a relatively sparse history in comparison to the United States and Europe. With the modernization of third-world countries and with the growth of international trade in the twentieth century, steps have been taken to organize futures trading and to provide effective structures, rules and regulations that will attract the business of speculators and commercial interests. In addition, political instability in some Pacific Rim countries has been a limiting factor in the development of stable futures exchanges. There are a number of notable exceptions, however.

FUTURES TRADING IN AUSTRALIA

There are two major financial regulatory bodies in Australia. The Australian Securities Commission (ASC) administers Corporation Law (CL) and Securities Law (SL), and the Reserve Bank of Australia monitors all aspects of operation by Australian banks, including their dealings in derivatives. Futures exchanges in Australia are private entities with delegated regulatory functions. All financial service providers and intermediaries in the Australian futures markets, including trading advisers, must be licensed in order to conduct their business. The CL exempts futures contracts from gambling and wagering laws that might otherwise prevent futures contracts from being legally binding.

An agreement between the New York Mercantile Exchange (NYMEX) and the Sydney Futures Exchange (SFE) allows its members to trade in energy futures at the NYMEX directly through the SFE. Apart from domestic OTC commodity forwards and swaps, generally executed through foreign institutions as hedging instruments, Australian traders are permitted to access the overseas futures exchanges and OTC markets. Cross hedging by Australian entities in overseas-listed and OTC markets is also quite common.

Providers of derivatives in Australia, either acting directly or through licensed entities, are required to register under the Financial Corporation Act. Various OTC derivatives are exempted from futures regulations if an authorized financial institution (such as a registered bank or a merchant bank) is a party to the transaction.

Sydney Futures Exchange

The Sydney Futures Exchange (SFE) has grown considerably. In March 2000, trading at the SFE totaled 4,107,137 futures and options contracts. This was the second highest monthly turnover in SFEs 40-year history.

The high turnover was stimulated by equity market volatility, uncertainty over interest rates and the rollover of many SFE contracts from the March quarter into June quarter.

The continuing high trading volume is also a reflection of the capacity and reliability of SFE's electronic trading platform, SYCOM®.

The SFE electronic trading system, SYCOM® IV, was introduced, in part, to integrate trading on the NZFOE (New Zealand Futures and Options Exchange) with the SFE. Trading hubs serving the NZFOE market are available in Auckland, Wellington, Sydney, Melbourne and London.

Futures Trading in Indonesia

Indonesia did not have an organized futures market until the mid-1990s. Prior to that time, there was trading in standardized forward contracts. In order to hedge the risk of production and manufacturing needs, Indonesian corporations are permitted to trade in the international futures exchanges and in the offshore OTC markets. In the absence of well-developed organized derivatives markets, the major regulatory body for futures trading is the Ministry of Finance and Capital Market Supervisory Agency (BAPEPAM).

Indonesia is set to launch an electronic commodity futures exchange in the year 2000. It plans to begin with coffee and crude palm oil and later become a multicommodity exchange, which will include soybeans, corn, gold and aluminum as well as currencies and interest rates. The plan is to have the exchange fully online so that people around the world will be able to trade electronically.

FUTURES TRADING IN JAPAN

The first recorded example of actual futures trading in Japan occurred in the 1640s. This country has the most diversified commodity futures trading framework in the Asia and the Pacific Rim. Unfortunately contract duplication among the various exchanges often results in poor liquidity in some of these markets.

Several government agencies regulate the Japanese financial markets. Futures and options are regulated by the Commodity Exchange Act, while OTC transactions are governed by the rules of the National Federation of Bankers Association. Membership in Japanese exchanges is divided into two categories—Futures Commission Merchants (FCMs) and General Members. FCMs, licensed annually by the Ministry for International Trade and Industry (MITI), are permitted to trade for their personal accounts as well as for client accounts. Association members are required to execute their transactions through FCMs.

In 1963, Japan was the home of sixteen commodity exchanges. Today there are only nine major exchanges. The Kobe Rubber Exchange (KRE) and Osaka Textile Exchange merged in 1997 to form the Osaka Mercantile Exchange (OME) and the Maebashi Dried Cocoon (MDCE) and Yokohama Raw Silk (YRSE) exchanges plan to merge soon as well. The mergers have created more competition as well as an increased interest in futures trading by consolidating previously disconnected entities into a central exchange. This has attracted more foreign business and has increased domestic trader confidence in the viability of and liquidity of exchange-traded contracts.

The Osaka Mercantile Exchange hopes to increase its non-Japanese trader participation, especially among neighboring countries such as Korea, China, Singapore and Taiwan, which have trading ties to the rubber and textile industries. The goal is to globalize participation in the Japanese exchanges by facilitating the ability both of Japanese investors to trade on the foreign markets, and that of foreigners to trade into the Japanese markets.

Distinct differences exist in the way that some Japanese markets are traded in comparison to European and North American exchanges. Several of Japan's commodity markets use a "session trading" format system called *Itayose*. A "call master" indicates the provisional price of the contract and initiates trading. All trades are carried out at a single price for each delivery month. The members, in response to the provisional price, place buy and sell orders. The price is then raised or lowered until the number of buy orders and the number of sell orders are in balance. Once the price is determined, members have to wait for the next session to place orders. The number of sessions varies from four to six per day depending on the contract and the exchange. No trades are permitted between or after sessions.

On the Tokyo Grain Exchange (TGE), for example, this is done consecutively by delivery month for each contract. The nearest contract month is traded first until the price is fixed. Then the next nearest contract month is traded. This process continues until the farthest contract month price for that session is set or fixed. When the initial price for a given month for a contract is displayed, traders place their orders. The price is then lowered incrementally in order to draw out additional buy orders. If the number of buy orders increases, then the price is raised accordingly in order to draw out more sell orders. Again this process continues until the number of buy orders and the number of sell orders are in balance. When this occurs, the provisional price is fixed, and that price is the only price at which *all* buy and sell orders are executed for a particular contract month for the given market during the session.

While this process is familiar to Japanese traders, European and North American traders who trade in the traditional open outcry or more recent electronic exchanges are often confused by this seemingly convoluted procedure. I believe this process will become obsolete as the Japanese markets become more westernized.

Japan's Big Bang

The Japanese markets have been undergoing a major change that has been termed the "big bang." This is the largest reformation of business and financial sectors in Japan's history. By overhauling the banking, finance and insurance industries, Japan seeks to transform its markets into self-regulating entities that are both flexible and compatible with their counterparts in the United States, Europe and other Asian markets.

The end result of "big bang" reforms will be favorable for domestic as well as international futures trading firms, which have been mired in archaic and excessive government regulations for many years. These changes are currently set to take place by 2001. It is unclear at this time whether such changes will occur in one fell swoop or incrementally over an extended period of time. Although the Japanese have been discussing deregulation of the markets for many years, such changes have yet to be seen.

The Tokyo Commodity Exchange (TOCOM)

There are two major differences between the trading methods of the TOCOM and those of the U.S. and European exchanges.

First, as previously stated, the clearing system (*Itayose*) adopted by Japanese commodity futures exchanges is different from that in the United States and Europe. In Japan, no independent clearinghouse exists for commodity futures trading.

Instead, commodities exchanges function as intermediaries between members for settlement. Unlike U.S. and European clearinghouses, a Japanese commodities exchange does not become a counterpart for each member through its clearing process. In practical terms, however, it functions quite like in-house clearinghouses in the United States.

Second, TOCOM also offers a continuous computerized trading. The continuous method is used for trading precious metals and aluminum, while rubber and cotton yarn are still traded using the traditional *Itayose* method.

Trading activity at the TOCOM has increased dramatically in some areas while it has declined substantially in others. In February of 1999, trading in wool yarn futures was halted. Trading activity in gold and silver have increased since 1984 with over 16 million contracts of gold traded in 1999; 966,000 in silver; 13 million in platinum; 5.8 million in platinum; and a one-hundred percent increase in aluminum to 710,000. Under-standably, large increases in trading volume were seen in gasoline and kerosene. The TOCOM, by virtue of its important contract listings, should continue as a viable exchange.

Futures Trading in Malaysia

Malaysia is a major producer and exporter of raw commodities such as crude oil. Due to its high production of various commodities, Malaysia had to participate in the futures markets in order to hedge its risks. The Commodity Trading Act (CTA) was passed in 1985, and futures trading has gained considerable momentum since. The Central Bank of Malaysia (CBM), Bank Negara Malaysia (BNM), and the Commodity Trading Council (CTC) of Malaysia are the primary regulatory agencies of the domestic futures markets. The regulatory agencies have established rules for clearinghouse membership. In 1995, Malaysia adopted strict rules to regulate the national OTC derivatives markets which must be approved by the BNM.

In 1998, the Commodity and Monetary Exchange of Malaysia (COMMEX) was founded by the merger of the Kuala Lumpur Commodity Exchange (KLCE) and the Malaysia Monetary Exchange. The Kuala Lumpur Options & Financial Futures Exchange (KLOFFE) offers its primary trading vehicle, KLOFFE's stock-index futures contract.

In early 2000, the Kuala Lumpur Stock Exchange (KLSE) signed a Memorandum of Understanding with the Commodity and Monetary Exchange of Malaysia, designed to facilitate the consolidation of the exchanges into one holding entity.

KLSE is the parent company of the Kuala Lumpur Options & Financial Futures Exchange, trading KLSE Composite Index futures, and COMMEX Malaysia trades Crude Palm Oil (CPO) futures and three-month Kuala Lumpur Interbank Offered Rate (KLIBOR) futures (interest rates).

KLSE Executive Chairman, Dato' Mohd Azlan, hailed the merger as "a cost-effective way of achieving optimum utilization of resources and economies of scale leading to greater cost efficiency—thus improving competitiveness."

"(Consolidation) . . . will make our markets more attractive to all investors, bringing benefits to all market participants, including exchanges and investors."

The KLSE and COMMEX merger is yet another example of the consolidation trend that has been so prevalent throughout the world.

FUTURES TRADING IN NEW ZEALAND

The New Zealand Futures Exchange (NZFE) commenced trading in January 1985. In 1990, it changed its name to New Zealand Futures and Options Exchange (NZFOE) and, in December 1992, the business assets of the NZFOE were sold to the Sydney Futures Exchange. In September 1995, the Sydney Futures Exchange Limited (SFE) established a link with the world's largest commodity exchange—the New York Mercantile Exchange (NYMEX/COMEX)—enabling contracts listed at these exchanges to be traded through SYCOM. These include gold, silver, light sweet crude oil and natural gas.

Futures Trading in Singapore

Commodity trading in Singapore dates back some two hundred years. The markets have been in existence since the British founded Singapore in the early-nineteenth century. Rubber, spices, timber, coffee and palm oil have been the primary trading vehicles. Modern-day traders use the markets to hedge and speculate in a variety of different markets. These activities have made Singapore an important center for international commodities trading. Singapore is already a major market for rubber futures and the world's largest natural rubber-trading center.

Prior to 1983, the futures market in Singapore was not closely regulated or monitored by government agencies. As a result, trading abuses were all too common. In order to curb market manipulation and trading abuses, the government has taken aggressive steps to establish a well-regulated, international derivatives market. Such efforts have led to the development of Singapore as a major international center for both exchange traded and OTC derivatives products.

The Singapore Commodity Exchange Limited (SICOM) was established in 1994. It originally began trading in the 1920s as the Singapore Chamber of Commerce Rubber Association, and then became the Rubber Association of Singapore in 1992, assuming its current name in 1994. Futures are also traded at the Singapore International Monetary Exchange Ltd. (SIMEX), which was established in 1984. The Futures Trading Act (FTA) and Singapore Trade Development Board (STDB) have authority over the regulation and supervision of Singapore's commodity futures markets.

FUTURES TRADING IN AFRICA AND THE MIDDLE EAST

Exchanges in Africa and the Middle East have focused their trading primarily on stock-index futures, interest rates and currencies. To a lesser extent, various agricultural commodities are also traded. The Saudi Arabian exchange, understandably, has focused on petroleum futures. In Turkey, the Istanbul Stock Exchange (ISE) trades financial futures and stock indexes. Of these markets, the Tel Aviv exchange, the Tel Aviv Stock Exchange Ltd. (TASE), is the most progressive and liquid for speculative and for trading purposes.

Unfortunately, trading volume at the South African Futures Exchange (SAFEX) appears to have dwindled since 1994, particularly in bond futures. Unless trading activity increases substantially, trading at the SAFEX will not be viable for most speculators.

SUMMARY AND CONCLUSIONS

A vast number of commodities markets and exchanges can be found in these parts of the world. But with the exception of certain key exchanges—Australia, Israel, New Zealand and Japan—most are not suitable for the kind of speculative trading that can be easily and readily achieved in the European and U.S. exchanges. This is due to the relatively limited trading volume. However, as more traders become aware of the markets, their benefits and their potential activity are certain to increase, therefore resulting in more trading and more suitability for speculative trading.

As you can see from what has been discussed in this chapter, some of the regulations and trading methods in these markets are distinctly different from that which traders in Europe and the Americas are accustomed. In order to overcome these potential limitations, considerable study, knowledge and practice will be necessary. My caveat is simple: *Do not trade any market until and unless you fully understand its characteristics and methods of operation.*

To trade without such vital knowledge is to invite losses. Frequently the worst mistakes made by traders are more a function of insufficient knowledge about market procedure than they are a function of incorrect decision making. This is why a thorough knowledge of market procedures is a necessary prerequisite to success.

Chapter 5

FUNDAMENTAL ANALYSIS OF THE INTERNATIONAL FUTURES MARKETS

At a commodities seminar many years ago, I was approached by an individual who had a keen interest in the soybean market. As he sat down, newspaper in hand, he said, "It rained in Illinois and Indiana last night. The price of beans was probably down yesterday."

He then turned to the business section, ran his finger down the futures prices until he came to soybeans, and exclaimed, "Yep! Down three cents." With a self-satisfied air, he closed the newspaper and laid it on the floor next to his chair, content with his very simple but correct fundamental analysis of the soybean market. Would that all analysis of futures markets be so simple and accurate!

His basic reasoning, of course, was correct. The weather had been dry up until that time, leading to predictions of lowered production and higher prices. The higher prices would be caused by lowered supply in the face of steady or increased demand. The recent rain would cause increased production, leading to greater supply and hence to lower prices. To the lay person, the logic seems faultless. But if fundamental analysis of the markets were that simple and easy, there would be many more wealthy traders in the world. The explosive growth of financial and stock-index futures in Europe, Asia and the Pacific Rim has opened yet a new area of fundamental analysis to traders. In short, the analysis of fundamental forces that influence prices is more complicated than ever.

To be a successful fundamental analyst requires careful consideration of a massive amount of information. Fundamental analysis has its roots in economics. Economic theory is not just one theory; rather, there are many economic theories. Similarly, there are many different approaches to fundamental analysis. The common element in all approaches to fundamental analysis is the study of the purported causes of price increases and price decreases in the hope of ascertaining changes prior to their occurrence. The success of all the approaches rests upon the availability of accurate assessments of the variables analyzed, as well as knowledge of variables that may not be known to other fundamental analysts.

The plethora of statistics available to the fundamentalist at any given point in time can be overwhelming. The fundamentalist must be selective and be prepared to evaluate a massive amount of data. As a consequence, there is no one typical fundamentalist. Rather, there are many different types who evaluate different kinds of data at different times. There are those who, by virtue of their skill and expertise, can provide accurate forecasts, and there are those who, working with the same tools, make worthless forecasts.

SUPPLY AND DEMAND

The basis of fundamental analysis is supply and demand. But even a concept so simple as that is not without its complications. Basically, a fundamental analyst assumes that anything that decreases supply will tend to raise prices, and anything that increases supply will tend to lower prices. Conversely, increased demand will raise prices, and decreased demand will lower prices.

Now we get into the hard part of supply and demand: To an economist, demand for an item means simply how much of a commodity or service buyers are willing and able to buy at a particular price, at a certain time, in a given place. Normally, there is a close correlation between price and consumption. As price goes up, consumption drops, and vice versa. Supply and demand factors apply to interest-rate and stock-index futures as they do to food and metal commodities.

Many factors must be considered when measuring demand. For instance, what is the general state of the economy? Demand for money will be less in a recession than during inflation. How will political changes affect stock-index futures? How will changes in currency rates affect interest-rate futures?

A third factor to consider when measuring demand for a product is the availability of alternative products. Economists measure the tendency to switch products by using an index they call *elasticity of demand.* It simply rates a product according to the estimated percentage of consumers who will switch to another product as the price rises.

Just as demand for a product is difficult to measure, supply of that product is not always simple to calculate either. As a rule, supply consists of the carryover stocks from the previous marketing year plus the amount being produced this marketing year plus the amount being imported. But, like demand, there is an elasticity of supply regarding the price factor. As the price of a commodity rises, more sellers are willing to sell the product, and vice versa. As the price of an agricultural product goes up, for example, more farmers switch to growing that crop. As a consequence, available supply is closely related to price. Similar relationships exist in the stock-index and interest-rate futures markets.

Supply is also determined in part by the ability to store the product. The more perishable the commodity, the less likely it can be held off the market in anticipation of better prices. Even with storable commodities, the cost and availability of adequate storage space are important factors in the determination of supply.

As you can readily see, even the seemingly simple concept of supply and demand becomes very complicated in the process of fundamental analysis of the commodity markets. Fortunately, there are some sources of information that can be helpful.

MARKET REPORTS

Governments regularly issue statistical reports that affect prices. Whether such reports are issued by the Bundesbank or the Japanese government, the fact remains that they can significantly affect the European and Asian markets which in turn can affect markets throughout the world. In addition to government reports, there are private market-reporting services for many markets, as well as detailed reports published by the exchanges that provide important statistics.

The analysts who use all this information to make forecasts for the major producers and the large brokerage houses develop an economic model into which they insert the various statistics as they become available. Often, this model is computerized so that voluminous quantities of data can be handled quickly and easily, and the forecasts can be readily updated as new data become available.

SEASONALITY

If we study cash commodity prices over an extended period of time on a month-to-month basis, we find that during certain months of the year price tends to top, whereas during other months price tends to bottom. Furthermore, during certain times of the year uptrends are common, while during other times of the year downtrends are common.

Each cash commodity market has its own seasonal price tendencies, but virtually all commodities follow a definite seasonal pattern. Because perishable commodities must be brought to market quickly, prices of those commodities tend to rise and fall as the product becomes more or less available. Agriculture commodities are not the only markets that exhibit seasonal price tendencies. Stock-index futures in the European and American markets tend to make their lows in September and October and rally during the summer months. There are also distinct patterns based on seasonality in European interest-rate futures, although there is currently insufficient historical data to make a strong case. It is most likely that these markets will move seasonally in the same direction as the U.S. interest-rate markets.

Less perishable, storable commodities like the grains generally are priced lowest at harvest time, as the available supply is relatively large in relationship to demand; but seasonal price moves of these commodities tend to be less volatile during the rest of the year than those of perishable commodities. Usually, with the grains, the price at times other than harvest reflects the price of the grains plus storage costs. Seasonal tendencies also exist in metals, stock-index and interest-rate futures.

Monthly seasonal price tendencies can be charted for each commodity when the price history of that commodity is known. By comparing monthly average prices for a commodity over the history of that commodity, anywhere on the planet can have an effect on the price of one commodity or another.

A market analyst wishing to use the concept of seasonality for trading in the international futures market, particularly a speculator who trades on a short-term basis, will find that charting seasonal tendencies of futures prices on a week-to-week or day-to-day basis is more suited to the needs of the short-term trader than is the monthly cash seasonal. In this case, seasonal futures tendencies are specific to the futures contract month.

CYCLIC PRICE CHANGES

Prices of all commodities tend to repeat up-and-down trends in a relatively predictable fashion over a prescribed period of time. The cyclic method of analysis and forecasting has its roots in the work of Edward R. Dewey, founder of the Foundation for the Study of Cycles. With the advent of computer technology and the ease of access to data, the use of price cycles has been popularized in recent years. Yet cyclic analysis does not have many followers today.

For one thing, the application of cycles to the marketplace is not nearly so simple a matter as is the demonstration of their existence. Although the process of identifying price cycles from price data is fairly easy, the intricacies of cyclic analysis are such that a commitment must be made in order for a trader to achieve lasting success in trading with this system. Even when a trader decides to use cyclic analysis as a method for trading in the markets, other timing devices and filters are necessary in order to determine when to get in and out of the market.

Much has been written about business cycles, price cycles, and the like. Suffice it to say that a proper understanding of price fundamentals requires a thorough knowledge of price cycles. The U.S. Stock Market, for example, has shown an approximate 4-year cycle. Similar cycles appear in European stock prices. It is a known fact that virtually all commodity prices exhibit cyclical patterns. The cycles in European commodity markets most likely mimic those in U.S. markets. On a large scale, these cycles include a 54-year interest-rate cycle, an approximate 10- to 11-year interest-rate cycle and an approximate 3- to 4-year stock market cycle. Many other commodities throughout the world have exhibited approximate 28-day and 14-day cycles.

Futures and cash prices demonstrate many different cyclic lengths, ranging from the ultra-long term to the ultra-short term.

On the short-term end of the spectrum, we have the approximately 4- to 5-day cycle in silver prices. On the long-term end of the continuum, we find the approximate 54-year cycle in most commodity prices; this represents about the longest cycle that commodity traders study.

Cycles are measured low to low, high to high, or low to high, and various types of measurements are possible. Price cycles can vary considerably in length, thereby making it difficult, if not impossible, to make precise predictions about the future behavior of the cycle. At times, there is even an inversion of cyclic highs and lows, with tops being made when lows should be made. This tends to occur when the market is at a major turning point.

Using cyclic analysis as a trading method requires: (1) projecting the cycles, (2) forecasting the next high or low, and (3) timing your entry into the market. Computer programs can help you find cycles by matching dates and cycle lengths and testing them in the past, as well as projecting them into the future. Once the cycle has been identified, simply counting into the future establishes a time frame or time window during which the cycle should ideally top or bottom. A suitable timing indicator then provides the signal to enter the market.

Although cyclic analysis is fascinating, using it as a specific trading system for the international futures markets is not recommended for the novice trader.

SECULAR TRENDS

Less predictable than seasonals and cycles but significant nevertheless as an influence on prices are price trends resulting from long-term changes in supply and demand. Such changes as demographic movements, long-term weather changes, changes in customs and tastes, government policies, the discovery of new uses for a commodity and large-scale changes in consumer purchasing power may move prices of a commodity into a different range than it previously traded.

Other secular trends can be created by crop substitution, revaluation of the dollar, new technology and increasing or decreasing the available crop acreage. Secular trends must be taken into account in any long-range prediction of price movement no matter where the markets are traded.

Government Programs

The government is an ever-present but often fickle influence on commodity prices. Because of its tendency to react much too slowly and to respond all too often to political issues, the government can often exacerbate rather than solve market problems. Nevertheless, government programs have a significant influence—in some cases the most significant influence—on the prices of commodities. Through loans to farmers, acreage allotments, direct cash incentive plans, programs to dispose of surplus crops and programs to take land out of production altogether, the government intervenes in myriad ways with the market economy.

The role of government as a force in all market sectors is an ever-present factor. European and Asian governments are just as likely to intervene in market turns as are governments in North America. In addition to the effect of government economic policies and actions, market can also be markedly affected by government regulatory practices on the futures markets themselves.

Government Reports

Market and price reports are released periodically by most governments. They also publish many other reports that may have a strong effect on commodity prices. The various reports on wholesale prices, consumer prices, trade deficits, unemployment, money supply, stockpiles of goods—the list goes on—all have a more or less direct and significant effect on prices in all futures markets.

Political Influences

Political decisions anywhere in the world may affect commodity prices significantly. In many developing countries, the government may elect to support the price of a particular commodity in order to enhance its value on the world market. Other countries may adopt protectionist attitudes, which result in tariffs and other trade barriers, to protect local producers from outside competition.

OTHER FORCES AND FACTORS AFFECTING COMMODITY PRICES

There are other forces and factors that affect commodity prices.

International News

Many commodities that have an international source—sugar, petroleum, copper, platinum, coffee and cocoa, for example—are especially vulnerable to news of war or international tensions. News of war can lead to hoarding as well as to a greater demand for raw materials for defense and stockpiling. Moreover, there is the possibility of imports being cut off. On the other hand, the prospect of losing major export markets can significantly depress the prices of domestically produced commodities.

Currency Fluctuations

Now more than ever before, a critical factor in the profitability of business operations is the exchange rate between currencies.

When the dollar is strong against foreign currencies, exports from the United States are more expensive and therefore less desirable. As the dollar declines, American goods become more competitive on the world market and exports tend to increase. As foreign markets continue to grow, demand for some commodity might increase, leading to a rise in prices domestically. It is possible to envision the unlikely scenario of commodity prices rising domestically while actually becoming more competitive internationally.

GENERAL BUSINESS CONDITIONS

People are more willing to spend their money during optimistic times. Demand tends to be high for commodities when the economy is healthy, unemployment is low, the experts are predicting prosperous times ahead, and business is expanding. But demand falls when the threat of recession arises, unemployment creeps up, business slows, and people become nervous about the future. Consumers become less willing to spend. Inasmuch as such factors can vary substantially from one country to the next, the effect on international futures trading can be significant.

PRICE ANALYSIS

The individual who is serious about analyzing price by the fundamentals faces quite a job. He or she must first determine the general business climate, whether it is inflationary or recessionary, whether unemployment is rising or falling. Next, check the trend of commodity prices by looking at the various price indexes.

After checking the general situation, the specific circumstances regarding individual commodities must be checked: What is the seasonal price pattern? What is the long-term price trend?

What about government programs? What are the prospects for demand domestically? What about foreign production? Currency exchange rates? Foreign political situations? Are there weather circumstances that may be significant?

Fortunately for many fundamental analysts, there are computer programs that factor in much of the above information and develop price forecasts. Even with computer help, however, anyone who has the desire to be a fundamental analyst must feel overwhelmed at times by the scope of the information that must be processed and the number of variables that must be considered.

Summary and Conclusions

Large brokerage houses and large producers and users generally have the resources to maintain the staff and equipment to carry out adequate analysis of all the fundamental forces that move the market. The average futures trader will find it more difficult, if not impossible, to develop a viable and thorough program of effective fundamental analysis. Even the most sophisticated of systems will not be perfect. There will always be unexpected variables that the analysis failed to consider. I have always maintained that the markets work perfectly as they respond to the multiplicity of forces that act upon them. It is our inability to find, parse, and correctly weight the impact of these factors that limits our results and the success of our fundamentally based forecasts.

Chapter 6

TIMING: EVALUATING TECHNICAL INDICATORS

As we all know, the quintessential issue in futures trading is *timing*. No matter how valuable a forecast may be, timing is the critical variable. There is a distinct and vast difference between a market forecast and market timing; between a "feeling" or "hunch" and actual market timing. Timing is quasiscientific. A hunch or feeling is emotional. Although they may be based on some internal logic, they are not sufficiently quantifiable to be used by the disciplined futures trader. Eliminate them from your bag of tricks. They will not serve you well.

Whatever markets you trade, it is in your best interest to follow the rules and risk-management principles of a time-tested system. Whether the system is based on technical patterns or fundamentals, using a systematic approach is vital to your success. It will help minimize emotional decisions and limit losses. An added benefit of following an organized set of trading principles is that you will learn from your mistakes. Whether you trade bonds at the London International Financial Futures Exchange (LIFFE) or the Sydney Futures Exchange (SFE), a loss is a loss and an error is an error. The essence of a trading method system is to assure the discipline that will minimize errors.

To paraphrase E. L. Thorndike, the "father" of American learning psychology, there are millions of things a person can do wrong but only a handful of things that he or she can do right. In this chapter, we will take a good look at traditional technical analysis to see what will work well for you in the international markets.

We will look at examples of several types of indicators, and explore their advantages and disadvantages. I will *not* discuss the methods of calculating these indicators. This information is available in virtually any good book on technical analysis. (Although I may ruffle some feathers by making negative comments about your favorite indicators, I can only be objective within the scope of my experience and research as a trader.)

"TRADITIONAL" TECHNICAL ANALYSIS AND THE FUTURES MARKETS

The futures market is essentially a laboratory for the study of group psychology. In fundamental analysis of the futures market, price is determined by the interplay of supply and demand. This concept seems straightforward enough until we encounter such complications as *elasticity*. What creates elasticity in supply and demand? Simply put—human nature.

Consumers differ greatly in their perceptions of what constitutes a good price, or when something is a bargain, or, for that matter, when they can afford it. For instance, two individuals making identical salaries may be totally at odds when it comes to a decision about whether or not they can afford a new car. Obviously, in purchasing decisions much more is involved than simple supply and demand. As an example, an individual who just received a fifteen-percent increase in salary might be inclined to shop for a new car, but if this same person hears a rumor that the company is having problems and might be laying off twenty percent of its workforce, the decision to buy the new car will likely be deferred.

Similarly, in the futures market, any two individuals may perceive the same fundamental information and arrive at opposite conclusions on prices. In fact, it is that phenomenon that creates a futures marketplace. Since the activity of speculating in futures contracts requires a buyer and a seller, there must always exist opposing forecasts of price moves for there to be a liquid market or one in which transactions can occur quickly and easily. Fortunately, varying interpretations of reality know no national boundaries.

My experience with traders all over the world tells me beyond a doubt that they react in essentially the same way to market risk and market opportunity. Therefore, many traders believe that the patterns of group behavior in the futures market can be recorded and studied, and that predictions regarding futures behavior can be made based on recurring patterns. In other words, it might be possible to overlook fundamental information and focus entirely on the patterns of price movement because these patterns reflect the behavior of the participants, and people's behavior tends to repeat itself. Most traders, including myself, tend to repeat their behavior and, therefore, chart patterns, which reflect trader behavior, tend to be relatively predictable.

PROS AND CONS OF BASIC TECHNICAL CHARTING METHODS

What follows is a discussion of various technical timing indicators and their application to the international markets. In each case I have discussed the pros and cons and I have included a chart to illustrate their application(s).

Moving Average Indicator (MA)

Whether you use one, two or three moving averages, the concept is generally the same. Either the market price must close above or below its MA to signal a buy or sell, or the MAs themselves must change their relationship to one another in order to signal a trade. Figure 6.1 shows two MA signals on a monthly chart of the CAC-40 Index.

PRO: Traditional MA indicators tend to work extremely well in uncovering major trends both on an intraday and longer-term basis. Simply stated, they tell you to go long (buy) when the shorter MA crosses above the longer MA and vice versa for short positions. You will make money using them when a major trend develops. As long as markets are liquid and tradeable, the odds are that, in the long run, such methods will work. They seem to be effective in the international markets as well as in the U.S. markets as long as there is sufficient trading volume and liquidity. This is one key to the effective use of multiple moving averages in the futures markets.

CON: Traditional MA indicators give many false (i.e., losing) signals. They will often get you into a move well after it has started. When a change in trend occurs, they will often get you out after you have given back a considerable amount of your profit. This is true no matter which markets you trade in, and is a major drawback of moving averages in all markets. However, there are ways to overcome this limitation. When not uncovering major trends, traditional moving averages tend to be very inaccurate and they can lead to periods of drawdown as well as many consecutive losing trades. "Drawdown" is defined as the dollar amount of deterioration that a trading system experiences before it becomes profitable. The performance of traditional MA-based signals in essentially sideways markets is marginal. This is a limitation even in trending markets.

FIGURE 6.1

MONTHLY CAC-40 FUTURES (PARIS) WITH NINE- AND EIGHTEEN-MONTH MOVING AVERAGE SIGNAL

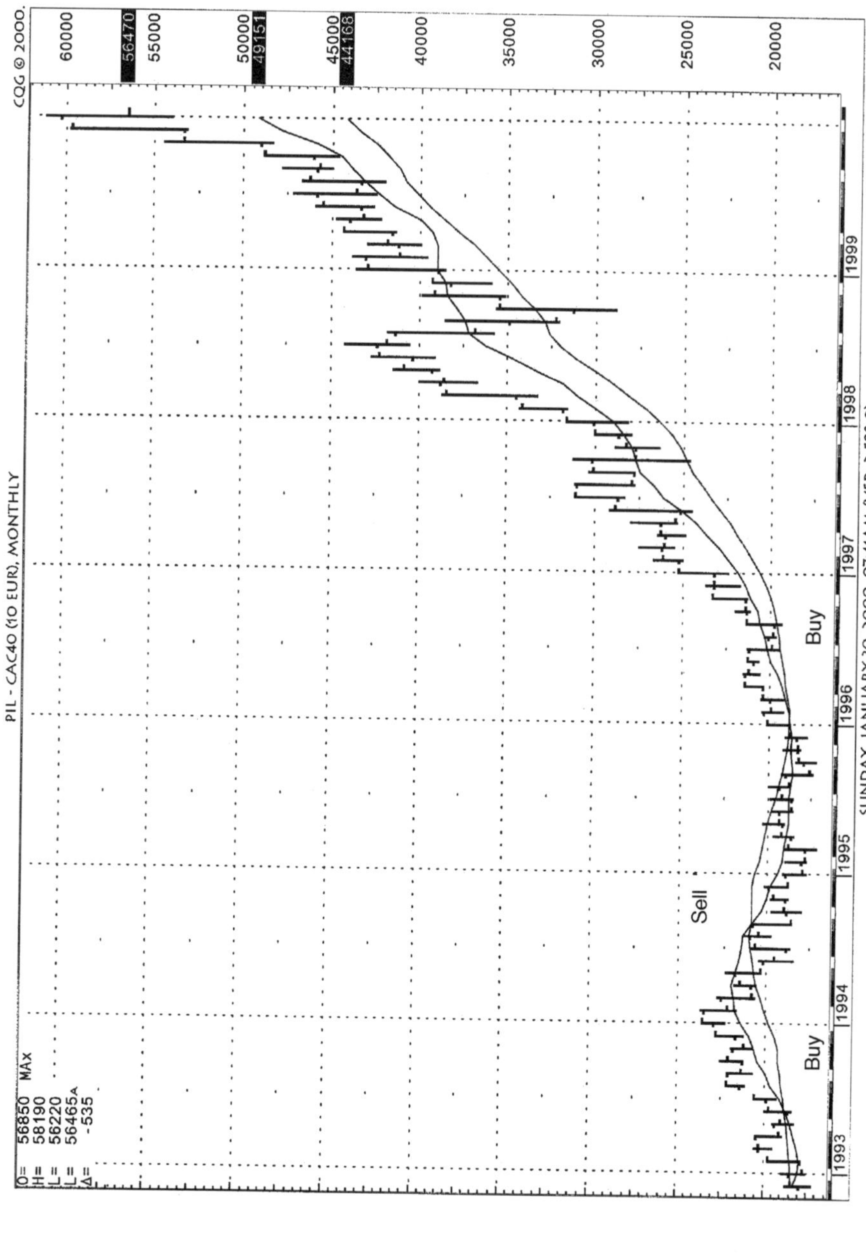

Figure 6.2, for example, shows a triple MA approach for short-term trading in FTSE futures. It is a ten-minute chart. I have marked the "ideal" buy and sell signals on the chart. As you can see, such a combination of moving averages can yield numerous trades, even within the time frame of one day, all of which may ultimately prove costly in terms of commission and slippage. Traditional MA-based systems tend to trade too often, no matter which market is being traded. They create too much "heat" (losses) and often very little "light" (profits).

CONCLUSIONS: Some of the limitations of using traditional moving averages when trading the international futures markets can be decreased by using:

- A weighted, exponential, smoothed or displaced MA.
- A different MA length to exit a trade from what you use to enter a trade.
- Different MA lengths for stop losses.
- Another indicator to confirm or deny MA signals.

OTHER TYPES OF MOVING AVERAGE INDICATORS

There are numerous variations on the theme of moving averages. These include MA-based oscillators such as MACD (moving average convergence/divergence), the MAC (moving average channel) and various high/low MA combinations. All apply to most international futures markets as long as they yield an open, high, low and closing price (or ending price) for the time frame being traded.[1]

---

[1]A more thorough discussion of the moving average channel (MAC) method can be found in the following book: Bernstein, Jake, ***The Compleat Day Trader***, New York: McGraw Hill, 1995. (The MACD was specifically designed for S&P trading by Gerald Appel, while the MAC is my brainchild.) It appears to have merit when used on stock indexes other than S&P.

FIGURE 6.2

TEN-MINUTE INTRADAY FTSE-100 FUTURES (LONDON) WITH TRIPLE MA BUY AND SELL SIGNALS

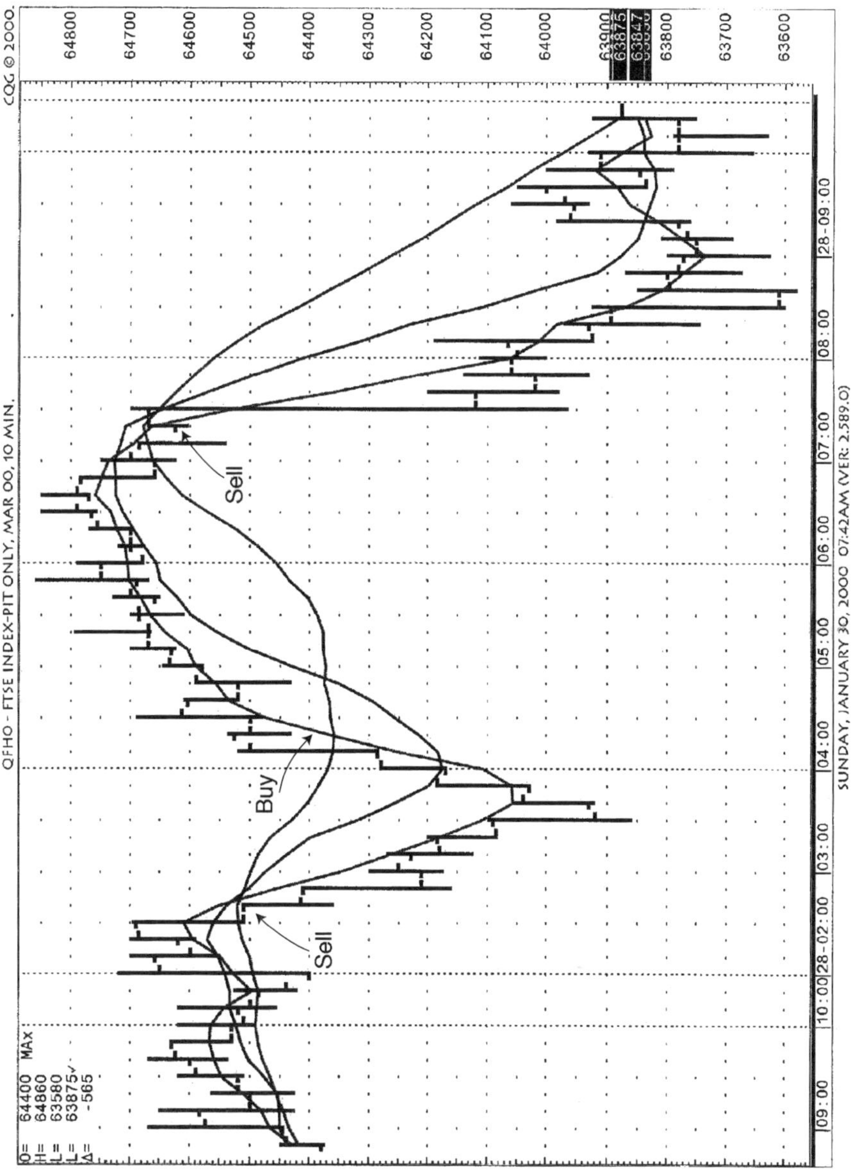

Moving Average Channel (MAC)

Several years ago I developed a moving average technique that was distinctly different from the traditional approach. Unlike using a moving average of closing prices, my moving average channel (MAC) method uses two moving averages, one of the high and one of the low, to construct a channel that determines support and resistance as well as buy and sell signals. Many years have passed since I introduced this technique, and time has validated it as a very useful one, not only for position traders, but for short-term traders as well.

The MAC is a simple MA-based method. It signals a long position when there are two consecutive price bars above both the N day moving average of high prices and the N day moving average of low prices. I prefer to use 10 and 8 respectively for these values. In other words, I use a ten-day MA of highs and an eight-day MA of lows on my daily charts. Figure 6.3 shows the use of an hourly MAC on the FTSE sixty-minute chart. Note the buy and sell signals as marked.

Figure 6.4 illustrates another 3-high/3-low use of the MAC relationships on daily London Gilt. It shows how the channel acts in relation to price bars. Each price bar represents one unit of time that can be either a weekly, daily, monthly or intraday price bar, depending upon your time frame. In examining the chart, note the following important relationships between price, price trend and the MAC:

1. Bull trends are defined as those in which price is above or returning to within the MAC.
2. Bear trends are those where the price is below or returning to within the MAC.
3. Markets turn from **bullish to bearish** when price bars begin to appear outside the bottom of the MAC. Let's call the **bottom** of the MAC the Moving Average of **Lows** (MAL).

FIGURE 6.3

SIXTY-MINUTE MAC SIGNALS ON FTSE-100 FUTURES (LONDON) CHART

(NOTE THE BUY AND SELL SIGNALS AS MARKED.)

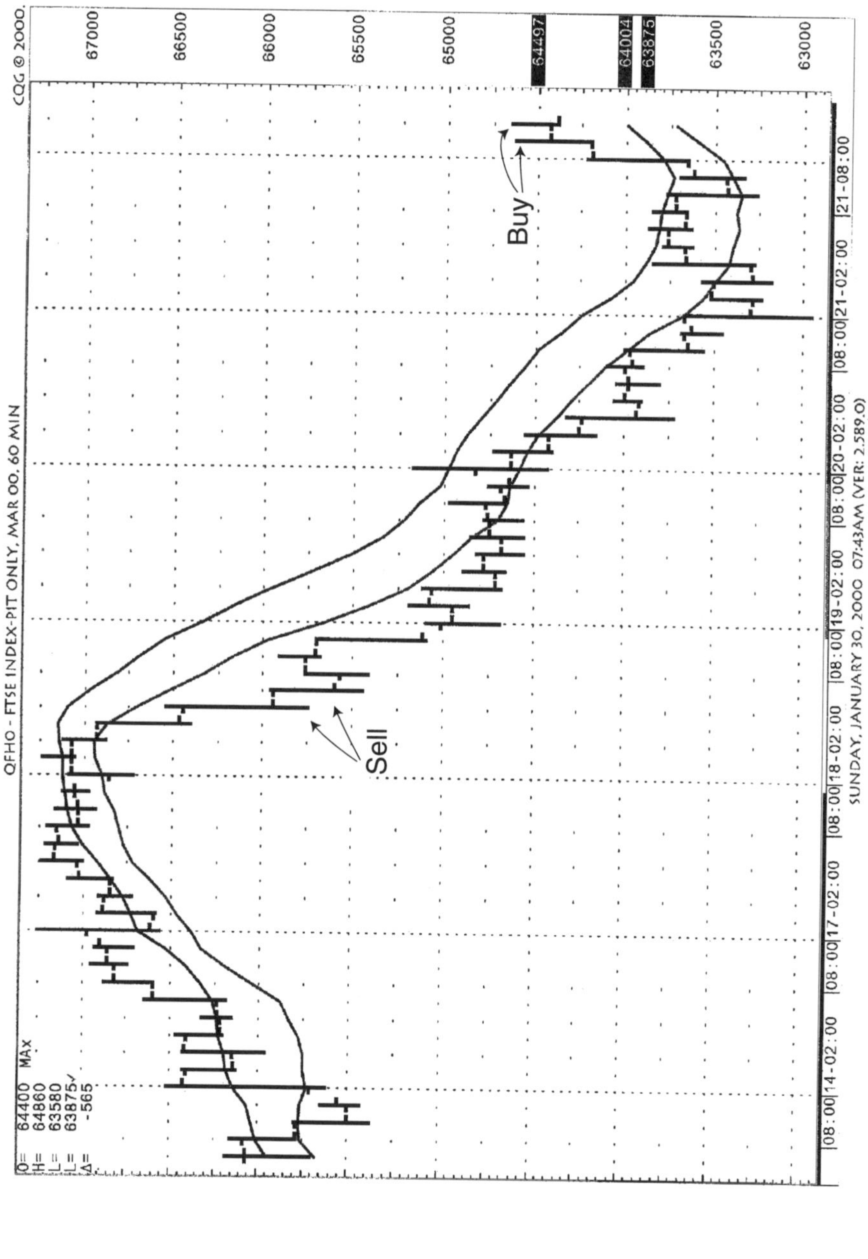

FIGURE 6.4

LONG LONDON GILT CHART WITH THREE HIGH-LOW MAS

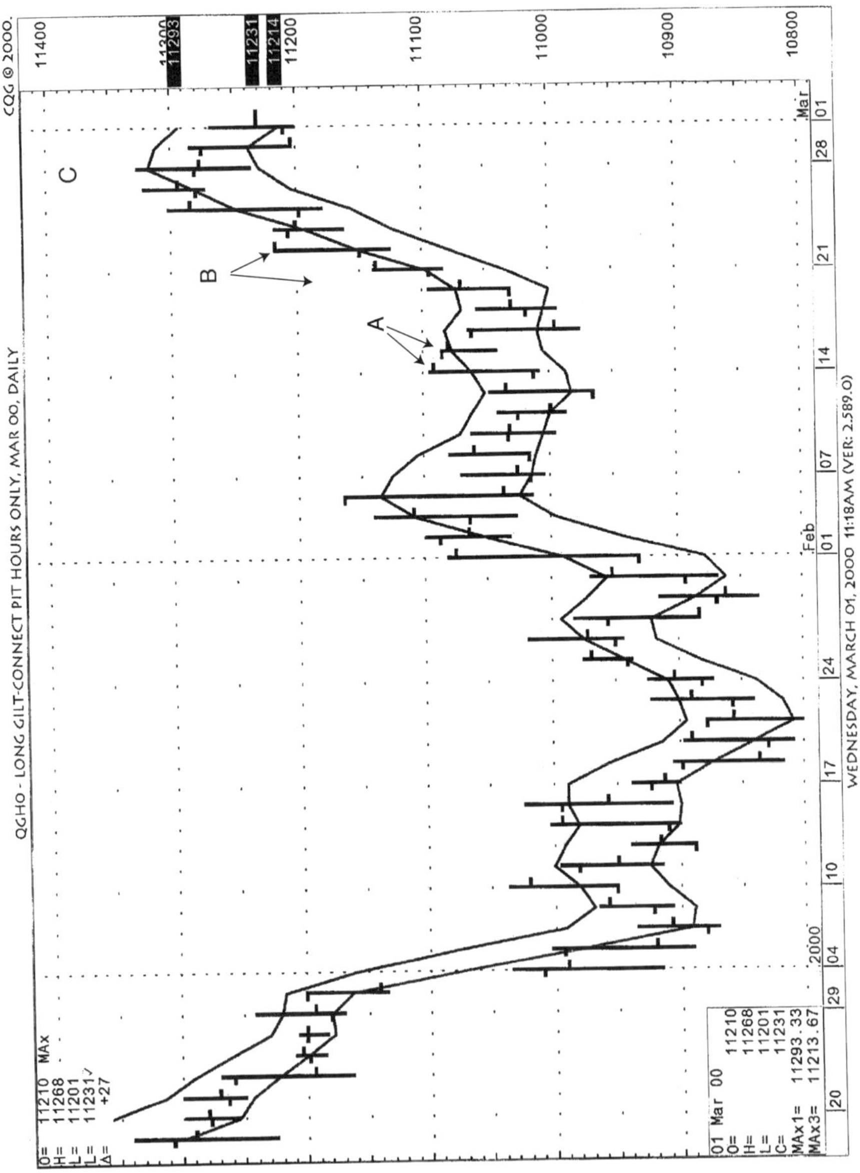

4. A market turns from **bearish to bullish** when price bars begin to appear outside the top of the MAC or the Moving Average of **Highs** (MAH).
5. Strong bull trends are evidenced by the fact that no portion of the price bar touches the MAH for extended periods of time.
6. In bull trends, a return to the MAL often results in support and, therefore, an opportunity to go long consistent with the trend.
7. In bear markets, a rally to the MAH often constitutes a rally to resistance and an opportunity to go short consistent with the trend.

Still another approach to using MAs on the international markets is to use a 3-high vs. a 3-low MA channel (similar to the 10/8 MAC but with 3 and 3 for the values). This produces a channel that serves as support (3MA of the low) in an uptrend and resistance (3MA of the high) in a downtrend.

Study Figure 6.4. I've marked the channel high and low, the price bars and the signals.

In addition to the basic signals I've just described, there are several other ways in which buy and sell signals can be determined. One is to buy when there have been successive price bars above the channel or to sell when there have been two successive price bars below the channel.

At point A, the market closed above its MA channel high two days in a row. This was an entry signal on the long side. The market rallied strongly and topped at point C but there was no sell signal. At B anothor long was triggered. This is only one appreciation of the MAC method.

This approach has considerable merit and I urge you to pursue it. There are many applications of the MAC for short-term, intermediate-term and long-term traders, all of which are related to the use of the channel for determining technical support and resistance levels. Since there is still a great deal of research that should be done on this method, you may want to strike out on your own. I think you'll find the results very rewarding.

The accompanying chart (Figure 6.5) shows the 3/3 MA channel on a chart of the daily London Gilt (LIFFE).

PROS: These variations on the MA tend to be more accurate and more sensitive than simple MA combinations of the closing price. The MAC in its various applications can also be used to determine concise support and resistance levels. This approach can be very helpful to the day trader as well as to the position trader who wishes to trade actively in the direction of the trend. From what I've seen and as you can see from some of the examples I have included, both of the MA channel approaches appear to have merit in the international futures markets.

CONS: There is a tendency, as with many MA-based systems, to give back too much profit once a change in trend has developed. This is true of all lagging indicators.

CONCLUSIONS: Here are some suggestions as to how one might overcome the limitations of MA-based indicators:

- Use a shorter combination of MA lengths for exit. Hence, exit will be triggered before the MAs indicate a reversal in trend.
- Use another indicator to confirm the MA signals.
- Use another indicator that is not MA-based for exiting positions.
- Develop a trailing stop loss plan that will enhance exit while not significantly diminishing system accuracy.
- Remember to use MA indicators only in active markets. Some of the international markets are not yet actively traded. To use such indicators in markets that have low volume or poor liquidity will result in numerous false signals. This would also hold true for virtually any technical system or method.

FIGURE 6.5

DAILY LONDON GILT WITH 3 HIGH/LOW CHANNEL SIGNALS (*ARROWS SHOW SELL POINTS AT RESISTANCE.*)

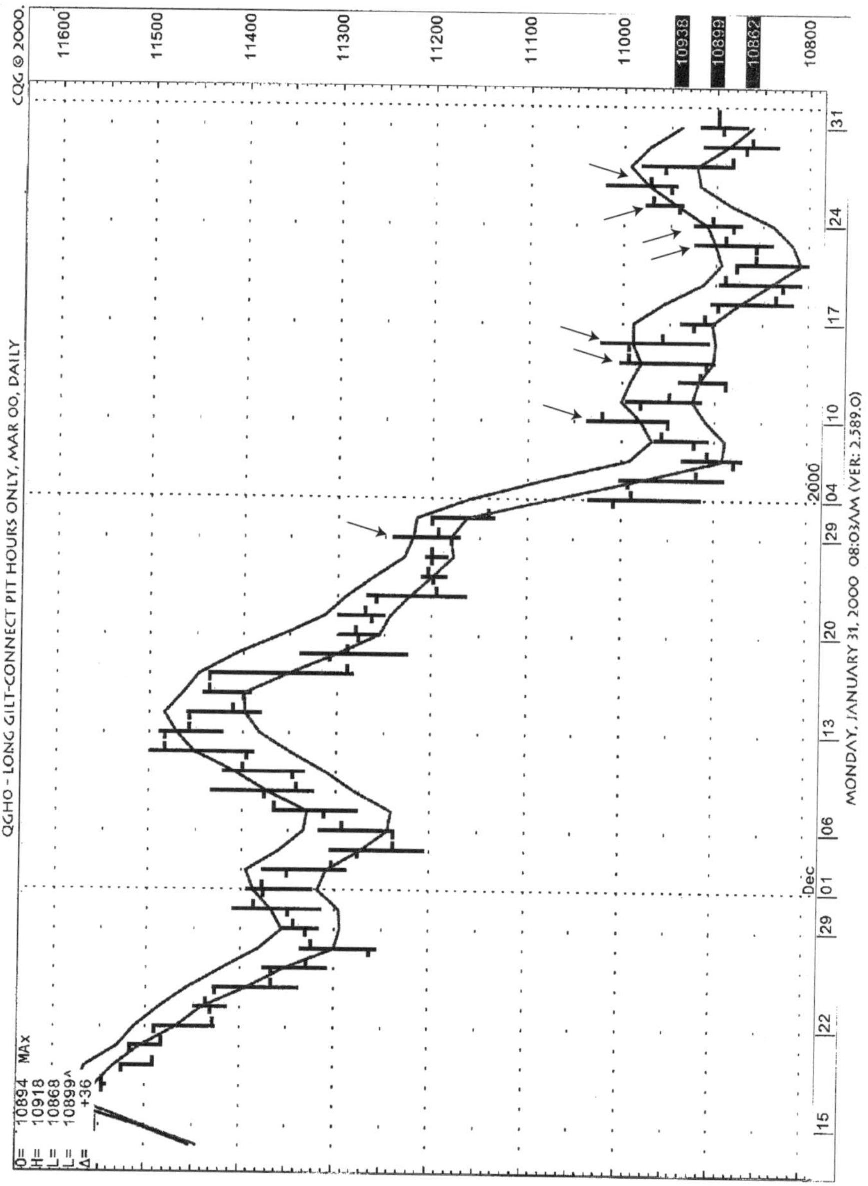

THE STOCHASTIC INDICATOR (SI) AND RELATIVE STRENGTH INDEX (RSI)

Dr. George Lane popularized the stochastic indicator (SI). RSI is essentially similar to the SI.[2] The difference is that SI has two values while RSI has only one. Computing a moving average of the first SI value derives the second SI value. Both indicators are often used to identify theoretically "overbought" or "oversold" conditions. The terms "overbought" and "oversold" refer loosely to levels at which traders feel prices are unlikely to continue higher (overbought) or unlikely to continue lower (oversold). SI and RSI may also be used as timing indicators. As long as a market yields high, low and closing price data, the SI can be applied. It is applicable to all time frames, provided there is sufficient trading activity to yield valid signals.

PROS: The SI has considerable "sex appeal" as a timing indicator—it looks good on a chart and tends to identify tops and bottoms quite well.

The RSI is also useful in timing, provided you use the appropriate crossover areas. See Figures 6.6 through 6.8 for examples of SI and RSI.

Figure 6.6 shows the eighteen-period stochastic signals on sixty-minute FTSE-100 futures. Buy signals occur when both SI values have been below 25 and then cross above it. Sell signals occur when both SI values have been above 75 and then cross below it. If a sell occurs and both SI values cross back above 75, then another buy signal occurs and vice versa for sell signals.

Figure 6.7 shows the SI on CAC-40 at the ParisBourse.

Figure 6.8 shows the RSI signals on daily London FTSE futures. Note the close correlation between tops and bottoms and oversold and overbought levels.

---

[2] George Lane, Investment Educators, 719 South Fourth Street, Watseka, IL (815) 432-4334.

FIGURE 6.6

SI SIGNALS IN SIXTY-MINUTE FTSE

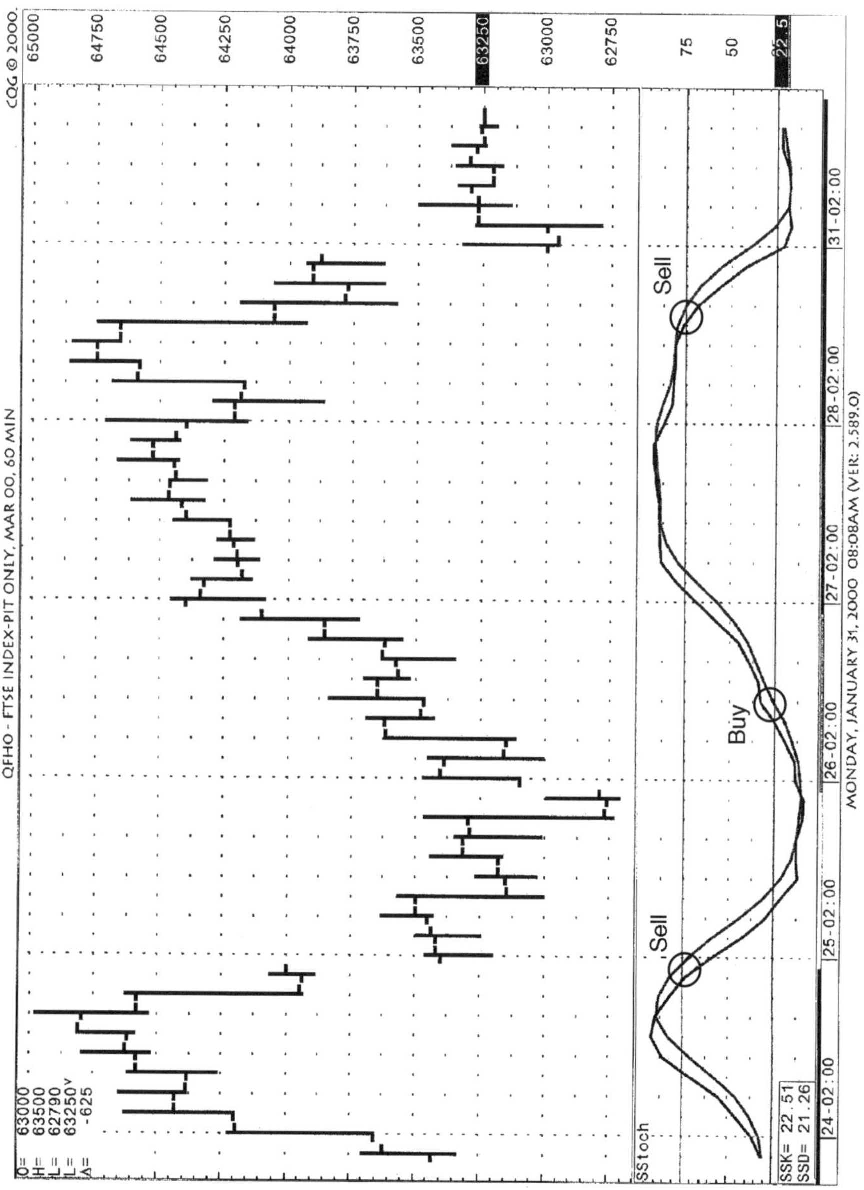

FIGURE 6.7

STOCHASTIC INDICATOR ON CAC-40 DAILY AT THE PARISBOURSE

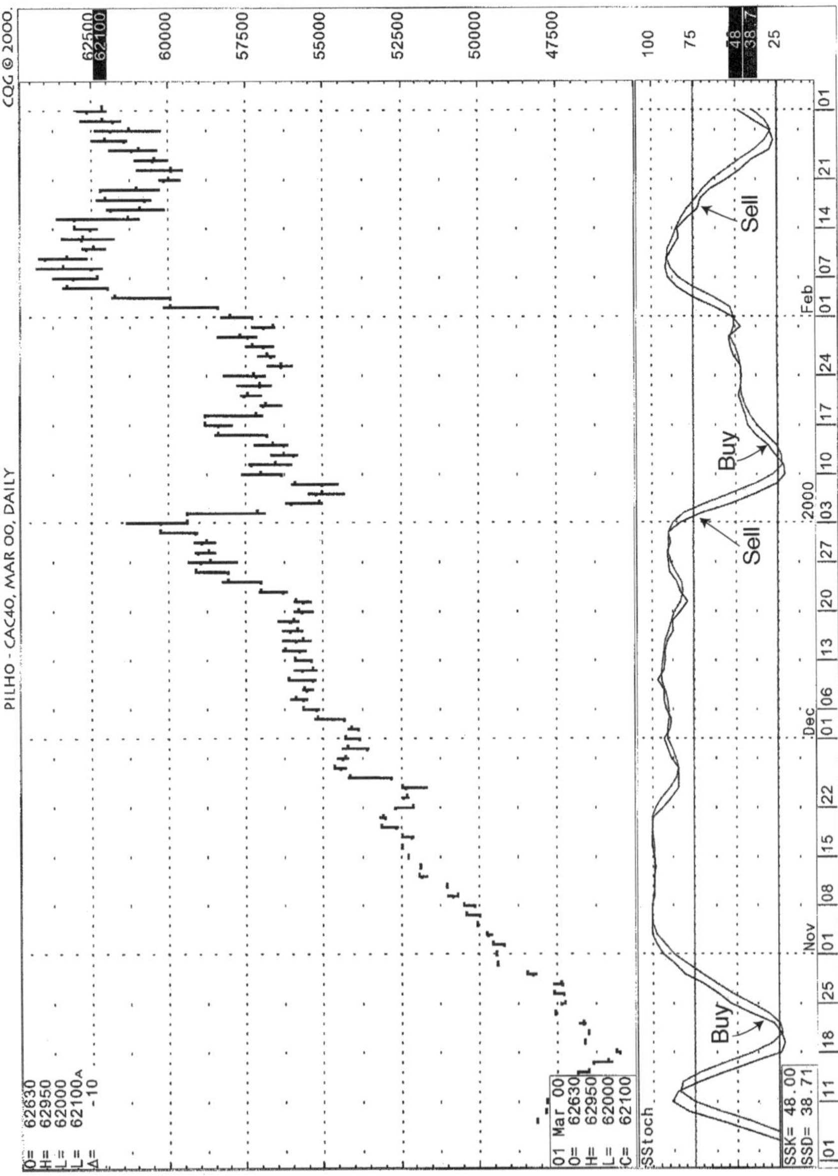

FIGURE 6.8

RSI SIGNALS ON DAILY LONDON FTSE FUTURES

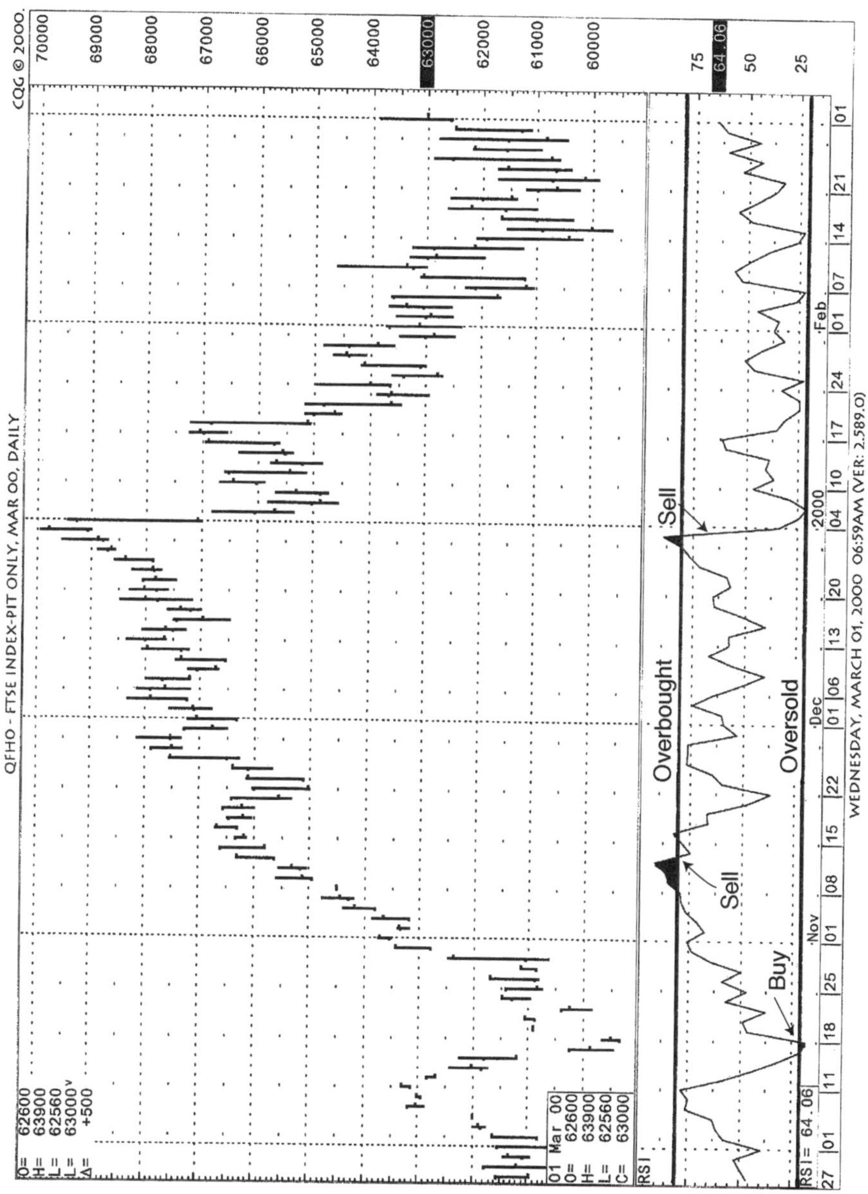

CONS: Be cautious when using *overbought* and *oversold* indicators. No matter what market you use them in, they can get you into trouble. Both indicators tend to continue in what is called "overbought" territory or "oversold" territory for a long time. As prices move higher and higher, the indicator remains "overbought," and vice versa as prices move lower. The problem is that traders often equate the term *overbought* with a market top and *oversold* with a market bottom. *This is not always the case.* Many times a market will push higher and higher while traders continue to fight the trend based on an overbought RSI or SI reading. The same will hold true in downtrends.

CONCLUSIONS: Don't use the SI and RSI for determining overbought or oversold conditions—no matter what the market. Use them as timing methods when readings cross above or below certain values. You might also consider using RSI and SI with other timing indicators. Another way to use the RSI and SI is to exit trades using a shorter-length indicator than was used for entry.

Finally, I have developed my SI "POP" method that may be helpful in trading moves that occur in overbought and oversold territory.[3]

To this day, the SI, along with its numerous applications, is one of the most widely followed, yet still grossly misunderstood and misused indicators in the stock and futures market. I say "misunderstood" and "misused" because many traders erroneously believe that because the SI reads high (i.e., eighty percent or higher), the given market is priced too high and a top is imminent. Conversely, they are also under the mistaken impression

---

[3]This method is covered in depth in my book *Short-Term Trading in Futures*. (Bernstein, Jake, MBH, P.O. Box 353, Winnetka, IL 60093, 1999.)

that an SI reading of twenty percent or lower means that prices are too low and that a bottom is imminent. The opposite is, in fact, true—namely, when the SI reaches eighty percent or higher, buying is often the right thing to do. In fact, when the SI reaches twenty percent or lower, selling short is often profitable. I researched this concept and out of that research I developed what I call the "stochastic POP" (SP) method.

George Lane was impressed with this approach and adopted it as part of his methodology. Here's how the SP works: If at the end of whatever time bar you are using, the fourteen-period slow smoothed SI reads seventy-five percent or higher, you buy. You hold your position until the %K or %D lines cross in the opposite direction. A sell signal occurs when the fourteen-period smoothed SI reads twenty-five percent or lower. You hold your short position until %K and %D reverse their relationship. Figure 6.9 shows a number of SP signals on a sixty-minute EuroBund chart. By varying the input lengths of the SI, you can generate more trades or less trades depending upon the activity level you wish to maintain as a trader.

I have done considerable research on the SP indicator, both in historical testing and in real-time trading. After many years, I have developed still another adaptation of stochastics which, although not yet thoroughly tested, may be even better than the current applications. Here's how it works: When the stochastic reads above fifty percent and then falls below forty-five percent, sell short. Your stop loss is either a crossing of the stochastic lines or a move back over the fifty-percent line, at which point you would reverse to a long position.

As always, the true value of a trading approach or method is its performance ability in sideways or "whipsaw" markets. The sixty-minute EuroBund (Figure 6.9) has clearly been a sideways trend for many weeks. Note my comments.

FIGURE 6.9

STOCHASTIC POP ON SIXTY-MINUTE EUROBUND

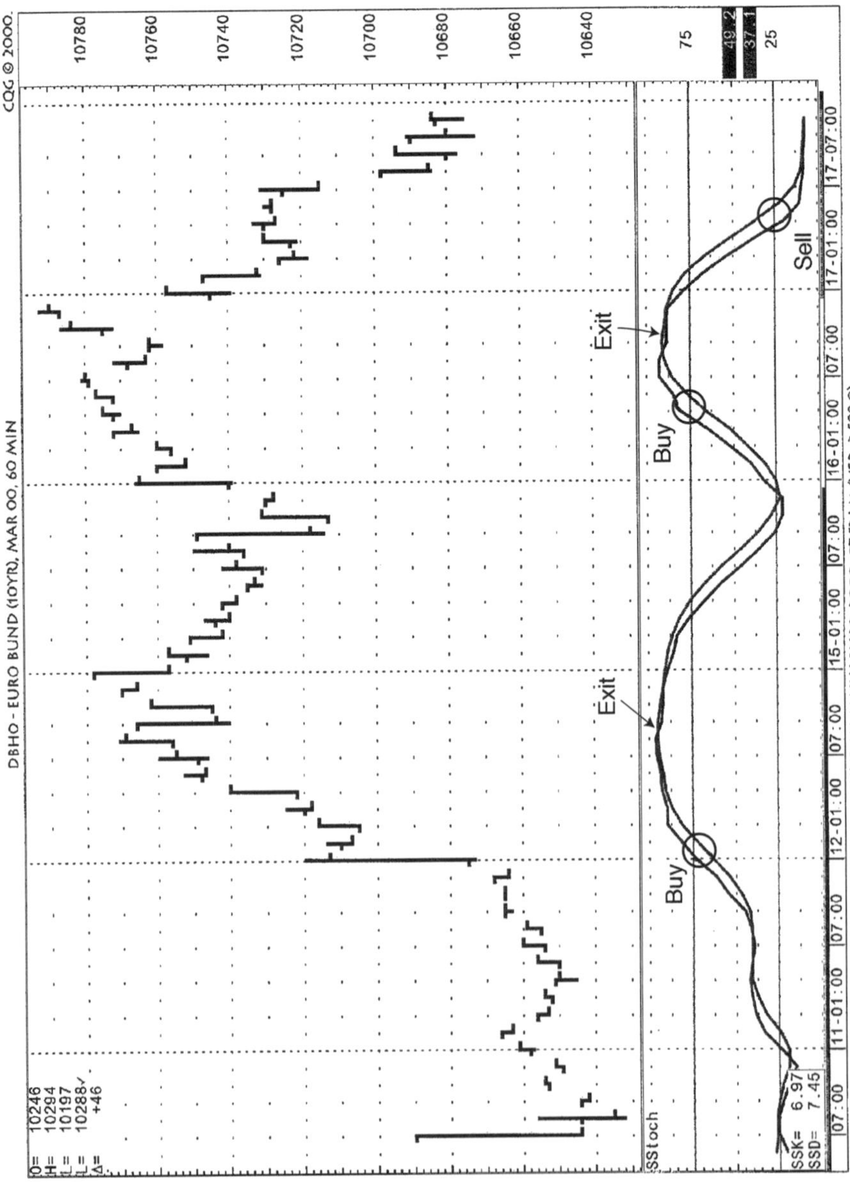

The reverse holds true for buy signals. When the SI has been below fifty percent and rises above fifty-five percent, you buy. Figures 6.10 and 6.11 illustrate this method. As a position-trading approach and as a short-term trading approach, this method appears to have great potential.

These two "nontraditional" stochastic applications show great promise. You may want to spend a little time studying and developing them to your specific needs. There are many variations on the theme and there are specific methods and procedures that you can build into them for more effectively managing risk in order to maximize overall performance. Note that SP signals may be used in all time frames. As you can see, stochastics can be a powerful timing and trading tool; however, it's important to apply it properly.

PROS: The SI correlates to tops and bottoms and follows market trends closely. SI is objective and can be used to identify cycles.

CONS: Overbought and oversold levels on the SI do not necessarily indicate buy and sell points since overbought and oversold conditions can last for a long time.

CONCLUSIONS: The SI is used to corroborate timing of other indicators by the SI and should not be used to determine market tops and bottoms.

CHART PATTERNS AND FORMATIONS

These methods are based on the traditional analyses as proposed by Edwards and McGee, as well as other methods such as those developed by W. D. Gann, George Bayer and R. N. Elliot. There are many different chart formations and various outcomes possible for each. They require a good deal of study and are, at times, quite intricate. Specifically, the chart methods use such things as support and resistance trendlines, pennants, flags, channels, gaps,

FIGURE 6.10

THE 45-55 STOCHASTIC METHOD ON EUROBUND

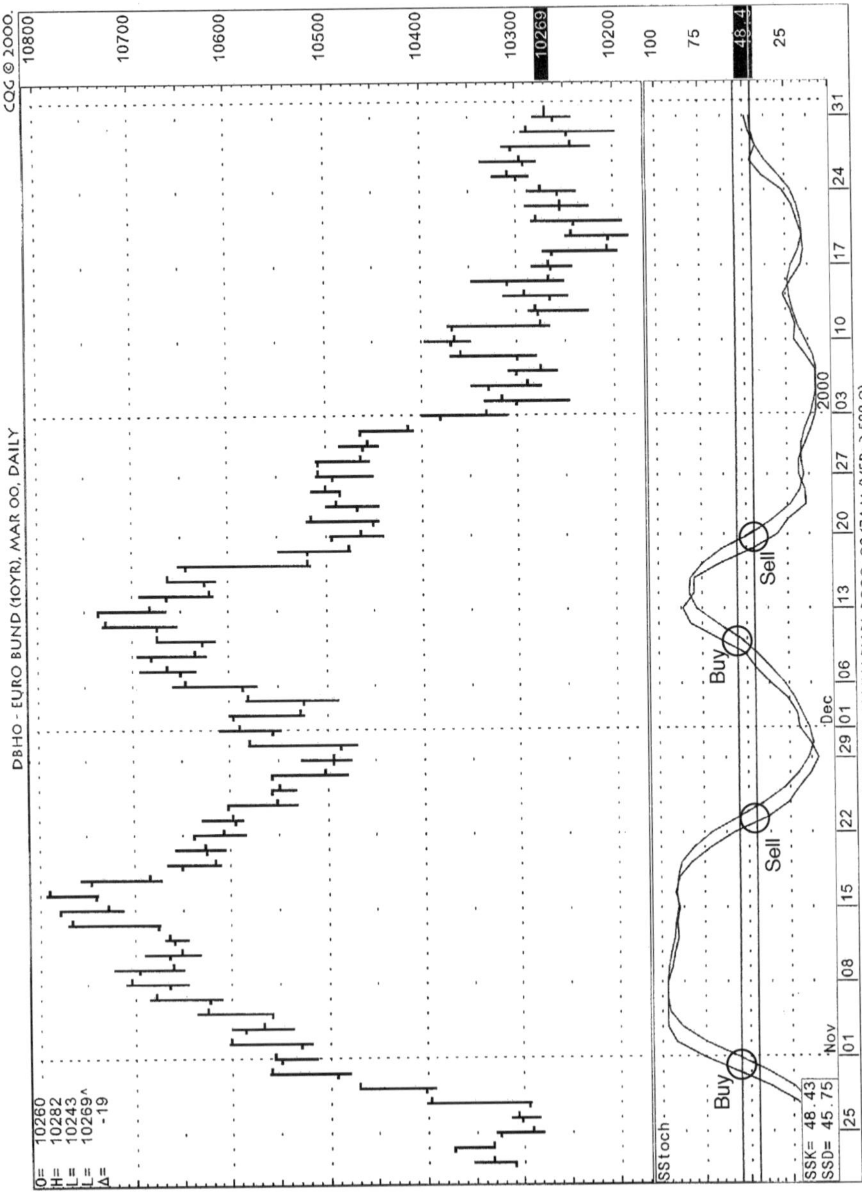

FIGURE 6.11

THE 45-55 STOCHASTIC METHOD ON DAILY JAPANESE BOND (LIFFE)

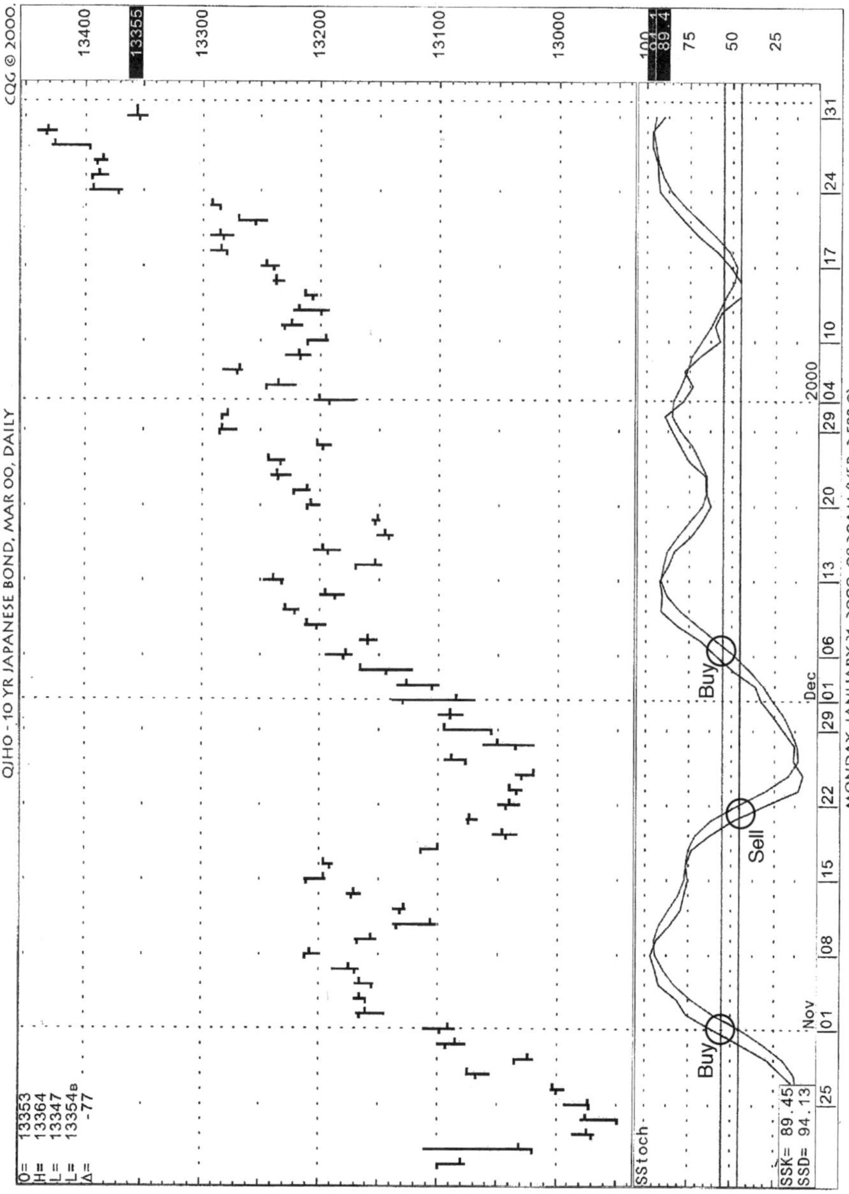

breakouts, "head and shoulders" formations etc., in order to determine potential buy and sell signals. Other methods, such as those of R. N. Elliot, use wave formations and wave counts in order to determine market trends, buy signals, sell signals, tops and bottoms. Inasmuch as these methods are all designed to assess trader emotion, they are all applicable to the international markets.

PROS: These methods are highly visual. You can draw lines on a piece of paper and see what should be done. They don't necessarily require a computer; they are usually quite logical, and can be easily learned. Frequently, the prescribed actions are specific, once you have completed the necessary interpretation of chart patterns. Hence, they have a good deal of face validity. My experience with these approaches to the international futures markets suggests that they have validity. However, they are subject to some degree of interpretation and should be used cautiously.

CONS: In most cases, these methods are highly subjective and difficult to test for accuracy. The Gann and Elliot methods, for example, have been known and used by traders for many years; however, there is considerable disagreement, even among experts, as to what patterns exist at any given point in time and, in fact, how these patterns should be traded. I have only limited personal experience with the use of Gann and Elliot methods and defer to those who are more conversant in such techniques. If, however, they are based on solid principles that reflect the behavior of traders, then they should work well in the international futures markets since the psychology of traders is the same throughout the world.

CONCLUSIONS: A way to effectively use traditional charting patterns is to use them in conjunction with other timing methods that are more objective and operational. As a rule, I suggest not using these methods in markets that are thinly traded or that tend to trade in narrow ranges for long periods of time. In such markets, these methods (as well as most others) will not be effective.

The Parabolic Method

The parabolic method is based on a mathematical formula derived from the parabolic curve. It provides the trader with two values each day: a sell number and a buy number. These serve as sell stops and buy stops.

Penetration of the buy number tells you to go long and close out any shorts, while penetration of the sell number means to close out longs and go short. Figure 6.12 is an example of a parabolic indicator plotted on a daily price chart. The buy and sell signals are marked with an "X."

Note that the parabolic value can be changed. Figure 6.12 shows a parabolic value of .02015. Other values may prove more effective, and should be adjusted in relation to the various markets, since the characteristics of different markets vary. Your results may, therefore, be more profitable if you use a parabolic value that reflects the inherent characteristics of the market you wish to trade.

Pros: The parabolic method is totally objective. It can be used as a mechanical trading system with risk-management methods. Since it provides a buy and sell stop, it is therefore capable of changing orientation from long to short very quickly in a relatively brief period of time.

Cons: Using this method, you can get "whipsawed" badly in sideways or highly volatile markets. The parabolic method can catch some very large moves; however, it has many of the same limitations inherent in the use of traditional moving averages.

Conclusions: Use the parabolic method in conjunction with other indicators that are not necessarily based on price, for example, volume and/or open interest. Use shorter-term time frames for exiting parabolic trades. Also, since the parabolic method in its pure form is an "always in the market" system, you may be able to adapt it by specifying certain conditions in which it goes into a neutral stance (i.e., no position). Clearly the parabolic indicator can be useful in trending markets. My work with the parabolic method on the international markets has been very reassuring.

FIGURE 6.12

PARABOLIC INDICATOR PLOTTED ON A DAILY PRICE CHART OF JAPANESE TEN-YEAR BOND

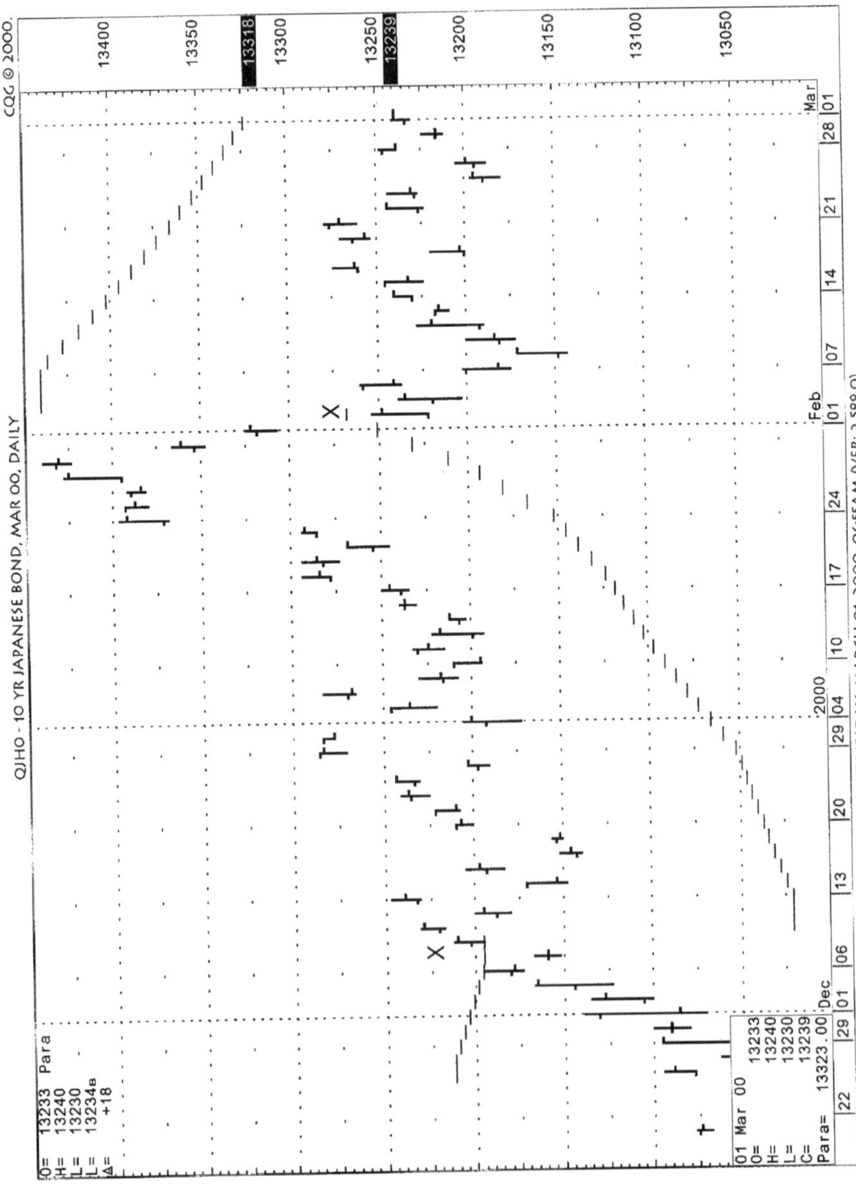

ADX and DMI Indicators

The Average Directional Movement Index (ADX) and Directional Movement Index (DMI) are unique indicators based on reasonably solid theories about market movement. They are calculated with relative ease and may be used either objectively as part of a trading system or as trend and market strength indicators. For this reason, I believe they can yield good results when used on the international markets.

Pros: These methods tend to follow trends closely and effectively to pinpoint market turning points.

Cons: They tend to lag somewhat behind market tops and bottoms. As a result, they can give late signals that will cost you money, since your signals will come late. You may, therefore, buy when prices are making a top and sell when prices are making a bottom.

Conclusions: Use these indicators in conjunction with other indicators that are based on different theoretical underpinnings of the markets.

Use a derivative of the ADX or DMI as part of your method. In other words, compute a moving average of the ADX or the DMI and use the moving average to achieve more accurate timing.

Cyclical Indicators

Cyclical methods are based on the fact that price history repeats. Sufficient academic theory and research supports the existence of economic cycles and market cycles, which seems to hold true for all markets that are freely traded. The Foundation for the Study of Cycles has documented a considerable body of evidence to support the cyclical approach to trading. In addition, Jay W. Forrester at MIT has developed a highly intricate and statistically valid method of evaluating long-term economic cycles.

PROS: Cycle trends and cyclical patterns are relatively easy to find and can be subjected to major mathematical testing and evaluation. Price cycles exist in virtually every market and in many different time frames.

CONS: Cycles are not completely consistent. At times, cycle lows and highs are skipped; other times, cycles can bottom late or early or top late or early. Hence, timing is an issue of major importance. There is also some doubt as to whether cycles even occur on a very short-term basis. Dyed-in-the-wool proponents of cycles would argue that cycles exist in all time frames, although there is still insufficient statistical evidence to support this contention.

This does not mean, however, that cycles are totally useless for short-term or day trading. It is possible to extract cyclical tendencies that, when used with timing, can prove effective in day trading, position trading and short-term trading for all markets.

CONCLUSIONS: Use timing indicators with cycles. Do not make the mistake of thinking that cycle lengths are written in stone; they can be skewed. Tops can come *very late* or *very early*, as can bottoms.

SEASONAL INDICATORS

Seasonality also has a lengthy research history. It is based on the valid and fundamentally sound idea that prices repeat their patterns within the course of a year. This results from a variety of causes, including the supply and demand, weather, and consumption.

Seasonal patterns can be found in spreads and in ratios as well as in monthly, weekly and daily data. What is more, we know for a fact that certain markets have shown a high probability of closing in a given direction on certain dates of the year and at certain times of year. (Date-specific seasonal tendencies have occurred with very high degrees of accuracy in the stock market and in stock-index futures.) All of this is good news for day traders.

While seasonals have a long history of reliability, their predictability and statistical validity is a function of data length. Many of the international markets have limited data histories. As a result, it is not possible to determine valid seasonal patterns, unless the markets track closely with markets currently traded in the United States that have long data histories. Among these I include the grain and soy complex markets, the currencies, interest-rate futures and petroleum futures. Where such markets are traded in countries other than the United States, the seasonal patterns should closely reflect those that are found in the U.S. markets.

PROS: Seasonals are often specific and capable of being tested historically as well as validated mathematically. They can also be adjusted relative to current conditions to determine if the pattern is likely to develop in the present year. Seasonals can be used with or without intraday timing.

CONS: Seasonals have gotten a bad reputation in the last ten years because of slick and dishonest sales practices by various futures options firms. This should not dissuade you from using seasonals, provided the information is based on sufficient data. Since seasonals are based on statistical probability, the longer the data history, the more reliable will be your conclusions.

CONCLUSIONS: Use daily seasonals with intraday timing indicators or with trend indicators as a filter. The use of a filter (or a confirming indicator) tends to eliminate trades that are less likely to be profitable while retaining trades that are more likely to result in a favorable outcome. Also use only seasonals that are based on lengthy historical data. Avoid seasonals that are based on less than fifteen years of history. If you use futures options with seasonals, then use at-the-money or close-to-the-money options. Generally speaking, however, I advise against the use of futures options for the purpose of day trading.

Remember: Seasonal indicators are not perfect—they do result in losses no matter how high their historical reliability may have been.

MOMENTUM/RATE-OF-CHANGE INDICATORS

Momentum (MOM) and Rate-of-Change (ROC) indicators are actually one and the same in the final analysis. Although they are derived by using different mathematical operations, their output is the same in terms of highs, lows and trends. Both MOM and ROC have been ignored and underrated as trading indicators and as valid sources of information for trading systems. Nevertheless, I believe they work very well in the international markets and have excellent potential when adapted to use as the core part of trading systems.

To calculate the one-day momentum (MOM), simply subtract today's price from yesterday's price. Therefore, if today's price is $52 and yesterday's price is $52, today's one-day momentum is +0. To calculate a two-day momentum index, subtract the price two days ago from today's price. For calculating three-, four- and/or five-day momentum, follow the same procedure.

Momentum is a rate-of-change indicator, since it provides you with an idea of trend strength. When momentum is moving down very quickly, it is an indication that prices are changing rapidly on the downside; when momentum is rising rapidly, it is an indication that the market is trending strongly higher. Momentum can be used as a trading indicator by applying some simple rules. I must stress at the outset, however, that momentum is merely an indicator of market strength and/or direction. It is not a system, but a trading technique that you will need to work with and refine.

Figure 6.13 shows momentum on an intraday Italian bond chart. As with most oscillators, MOM is good at finding trends; however, it gives many false signals as it "flutters" above and below zero. Regardless of this limitation, MOM can be used very

FIGURE 6.13

MOMENTUM ON INTRADAY ITALIAN BOND

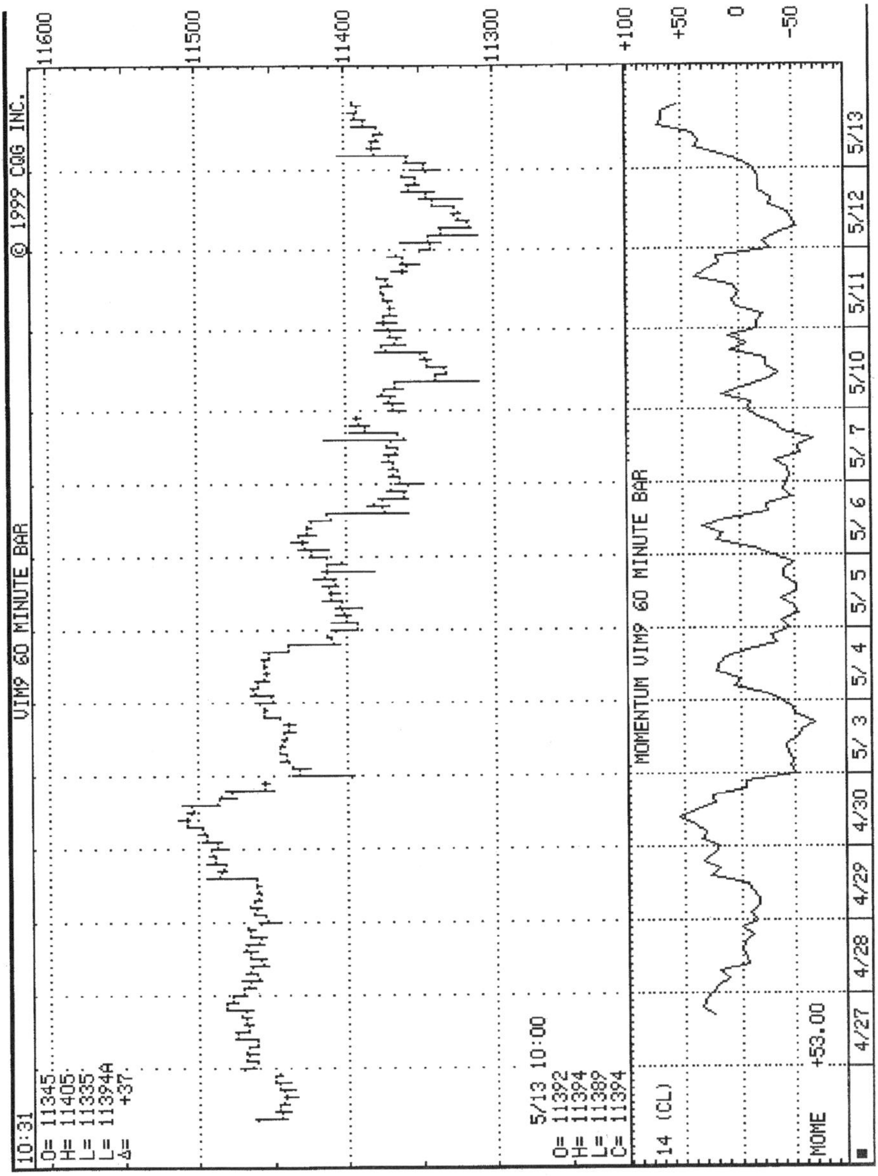

effectively for position and day trading by comparing it to its first derivative, a moving average of itself. This is a simple procedure.

MOM/MA Indicator

I find this indicator very helpful, and its use is simple. The entry and exit signals are shown in chart form on Figure 6.14 which shows MOM/MA on a five-minute FTSE chart.

As you can see, when MOM crosses above its MA, a buy signal has occurred. At this point, you go long or reverse to long from short. When MOM crosses below its MA line, it gives a sell signal, and you should sell short or reverse to short from long. The simple illustrations (Figure 6.14 and Figure 6.15) below show how the MOM/MA triggers entry, exit and reverse signals. Note that MOM/MA is specific and not subject to interpretation.

To decrease the number of false signals, it's a good idea to wait for at least two consecutive crosses of MOM and MA before considering a signal to be valid. Note also that MOM/MA can be used in all time frames and with spreads. By adding a risk-management method as well as specific rules, MOM/MA can be used as a trading system.

Figures 6.16 and 6.17 illustrate the momentum indicator and its variation, the momentum moving average (MOM/MA).

The rules of MOM are straightforward:

- When MOM crosses from negative to positive, a long position is indicated.
- When MOM crosses from positive to negative, a short position is indicated.
- When MOM and price show divergence, buy or sell signals can be generated based on such patterns.
- Use a derivative of MOM (i.e., MOM/MA) vs. MOM as a crossover-timing indicator.

FIGURE 6.14

MOM/MA ON FIVE-MINUTE FTSE

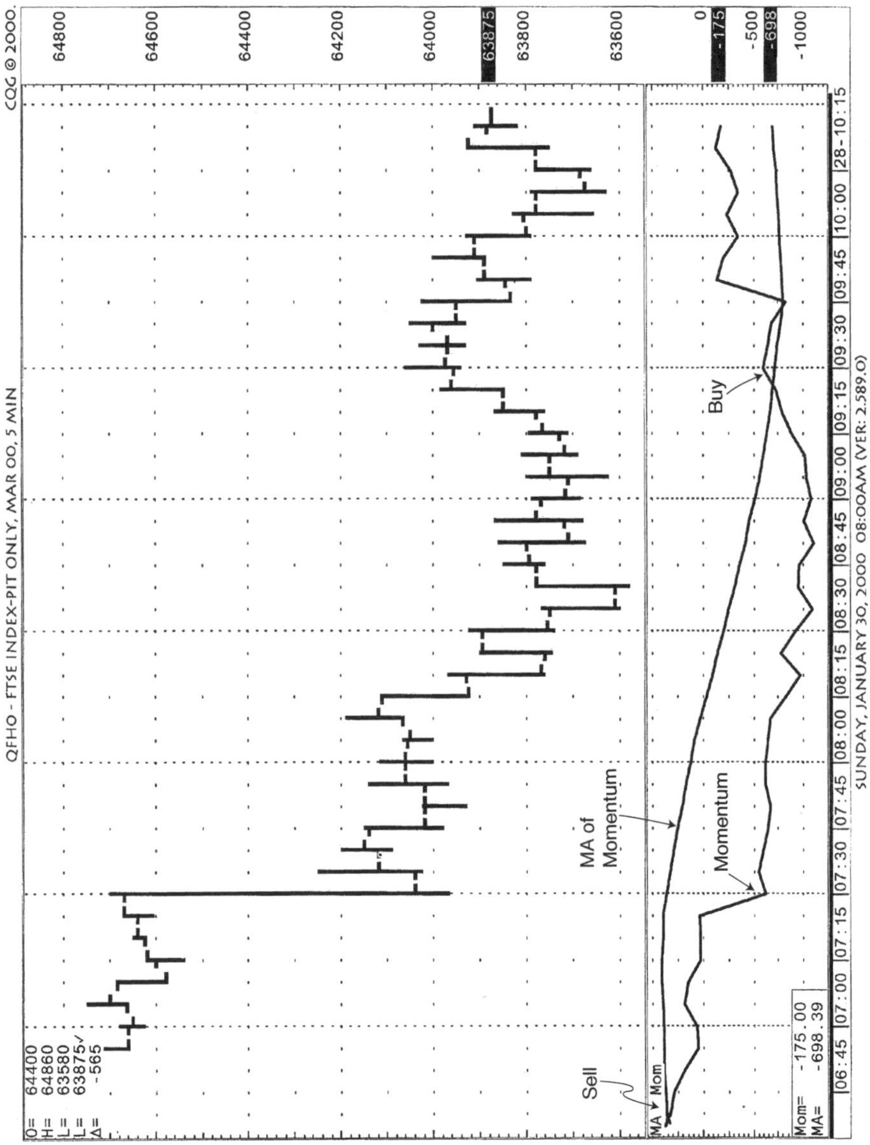

FIGURE 6.15

MOM/MA SIGNALS ON WEEKLY LONG GILT

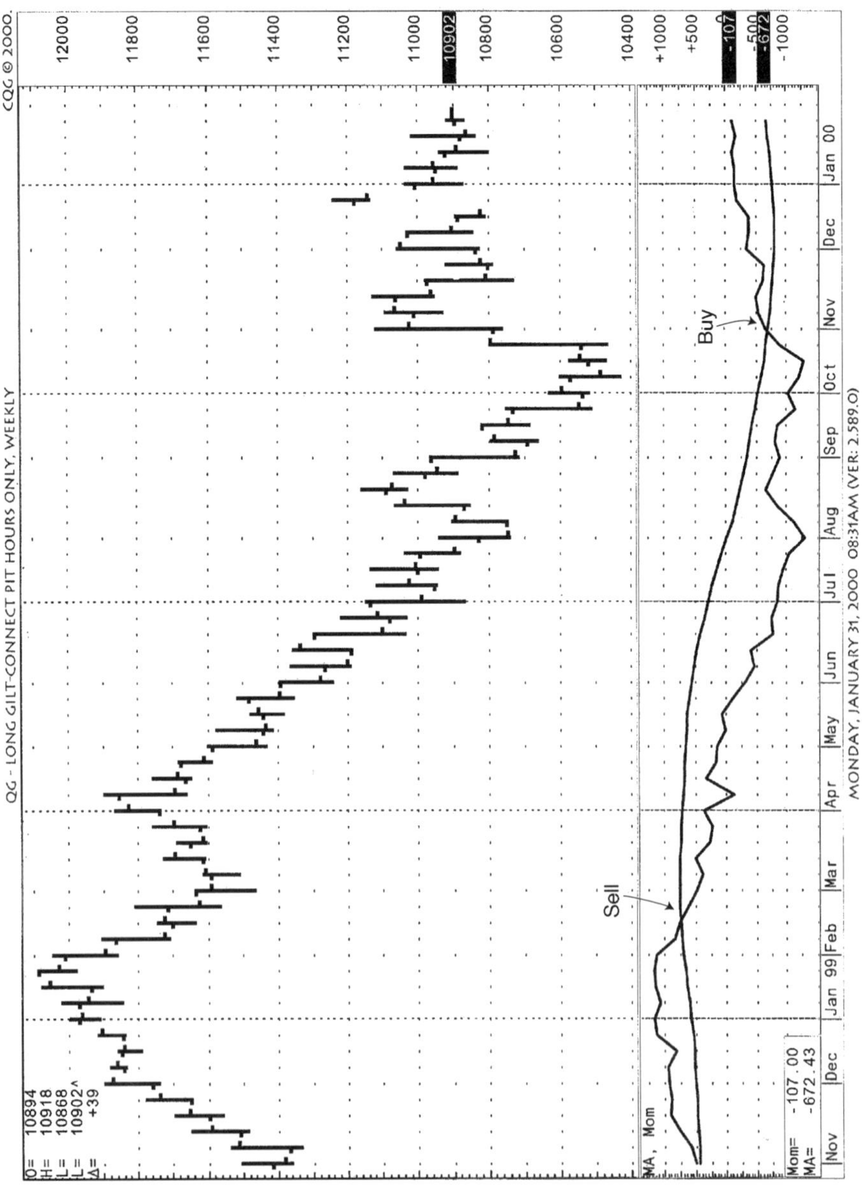

FIGURE 6.16

TEN-YEAR JAPANESE BOND MOM/MA SIGNALS

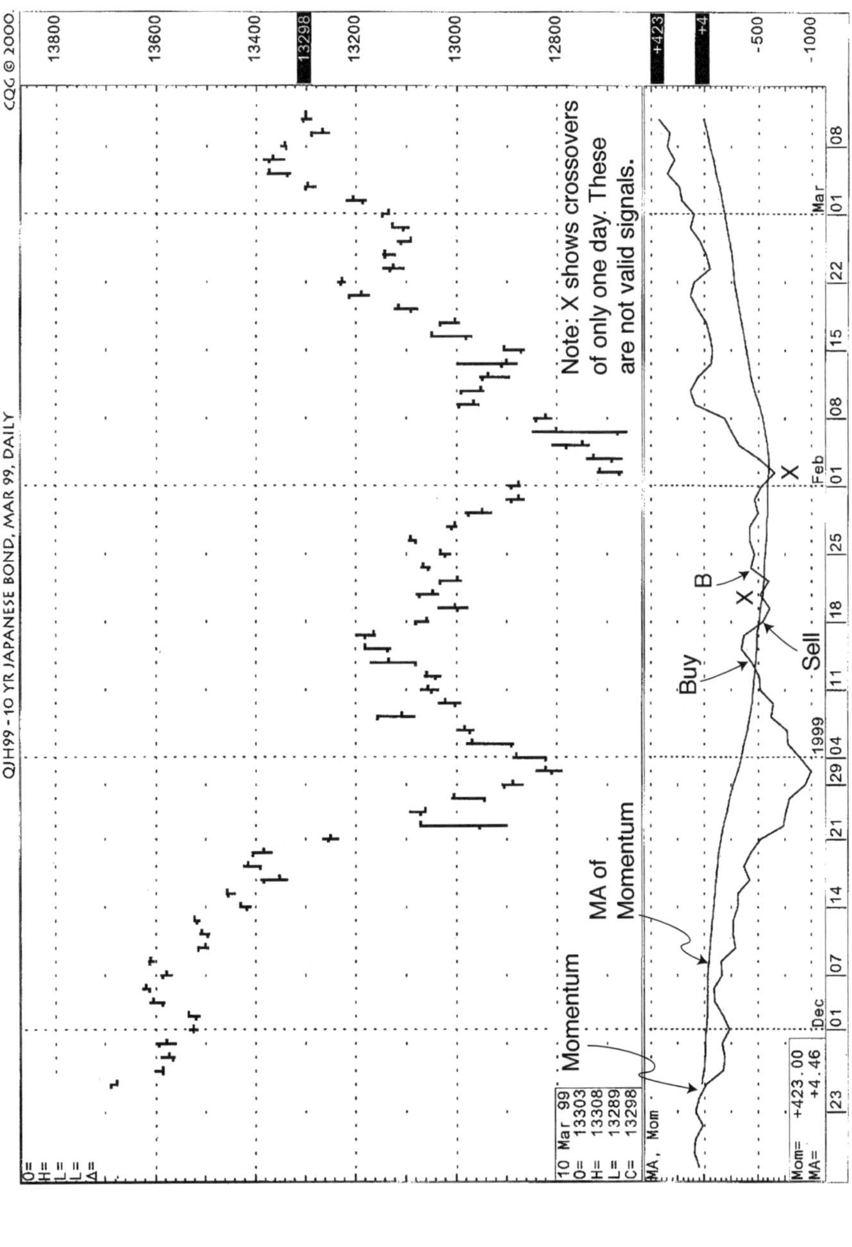

FIGURE 6.17

WEEKLY MOM/MA SIGNALS IN EURIBOR (EUREX)

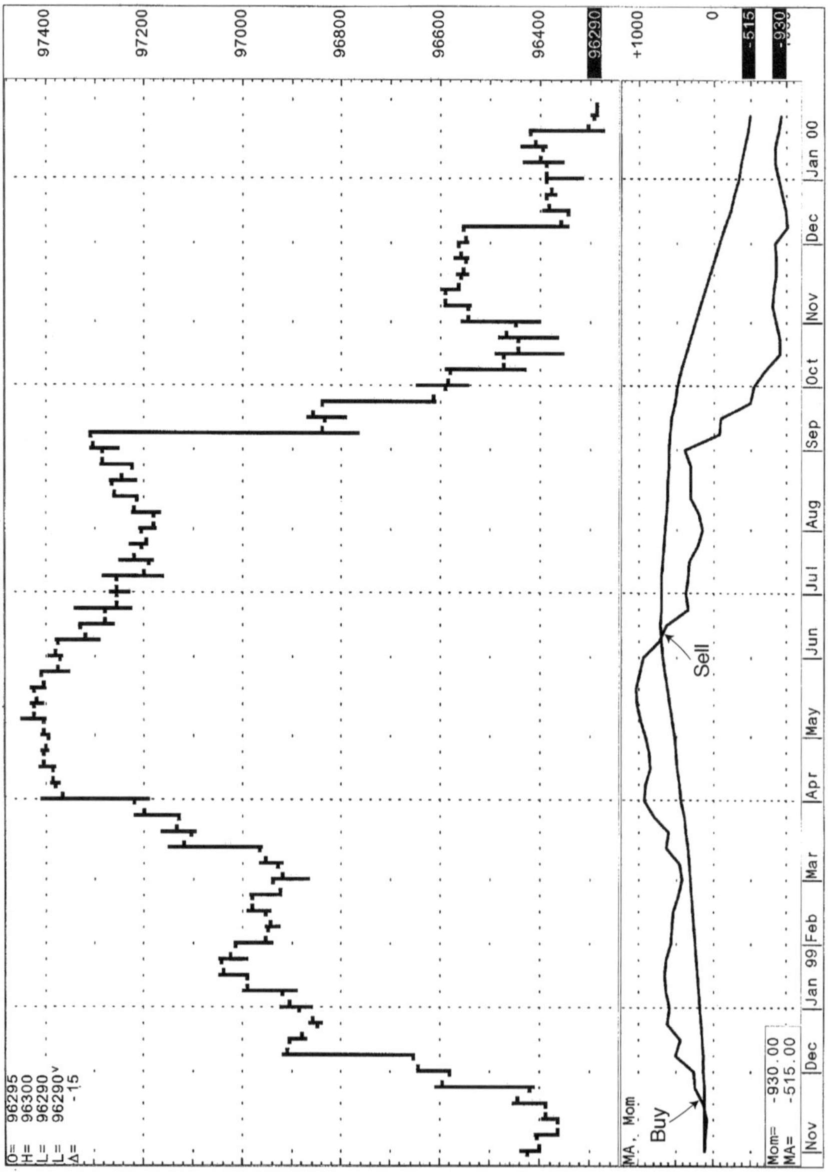

PROS: These indicators are highly adaptable to market conditions as well as to a variety of applications. They can be used either as confirming indicators or as the core of timing systems. They can be developed into specific trading systems with risk management. They can also be used for the purpose of timing intraday spread entry and exit.

CONS: They are lagging indicators. As a result, they tend to be a little late at tops and bottoms.

CONCLUSIONS: MOM and ROC indicators can be plotted against their own MAs in order to reduce the lag time. Another way to improve the reliability of the signals is to require that the oscillator remain above its zero line for at least two or three time periods before you take action. The signals shown in Figures 6.14 through 6.17 have been filtered for this requirement. As you can see, it eliminates whipsaw-type signals.

Open vs. Close Indicator

I have found that the relationship between opening and closing prices can be very helpful in determining market trend, strength and weakness. This is true on U.S. exchanges as well as on the foreign futures markets. The relationship is best examined using a moving average of opening prices vs. a moving average of closing prices. Theoretically, when markets are in bullish trends, the daily *closing prices tend to be higher than the opening prices* a majority of the time. The opposite tends to hold true in bear markets where *closes tend to be persistently lower than opens*. Figure 6.18 shows the Italian Government Bond futures (LIFFE). I have marked an arrow on every day that closed lower than the opening price. Note the large majority of days (sixty-three percent) on which this occurred, particularly when the market was in a downtrend. Conversely, Figure 6.19 shows the same relationship with close greater than open in a bull trend (however, the oscillator at

FIGURE 6.18

ITALIAN GOVERNMENT BOND FUTURES (LIFFE)

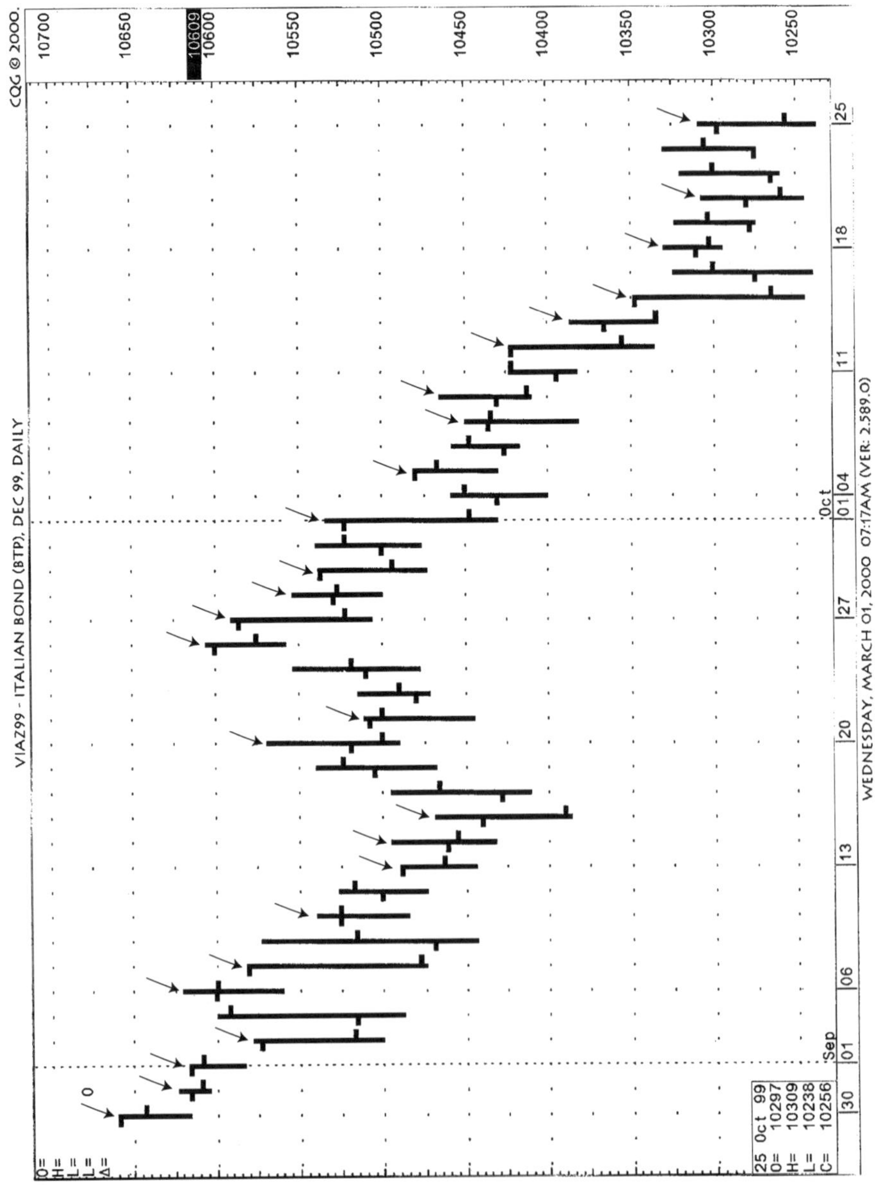

FIGURE 6.19

ITALIAN GOVERNMENT BOND WITH ARROWS SHOWING CLOSE GREATER THAN OPEN

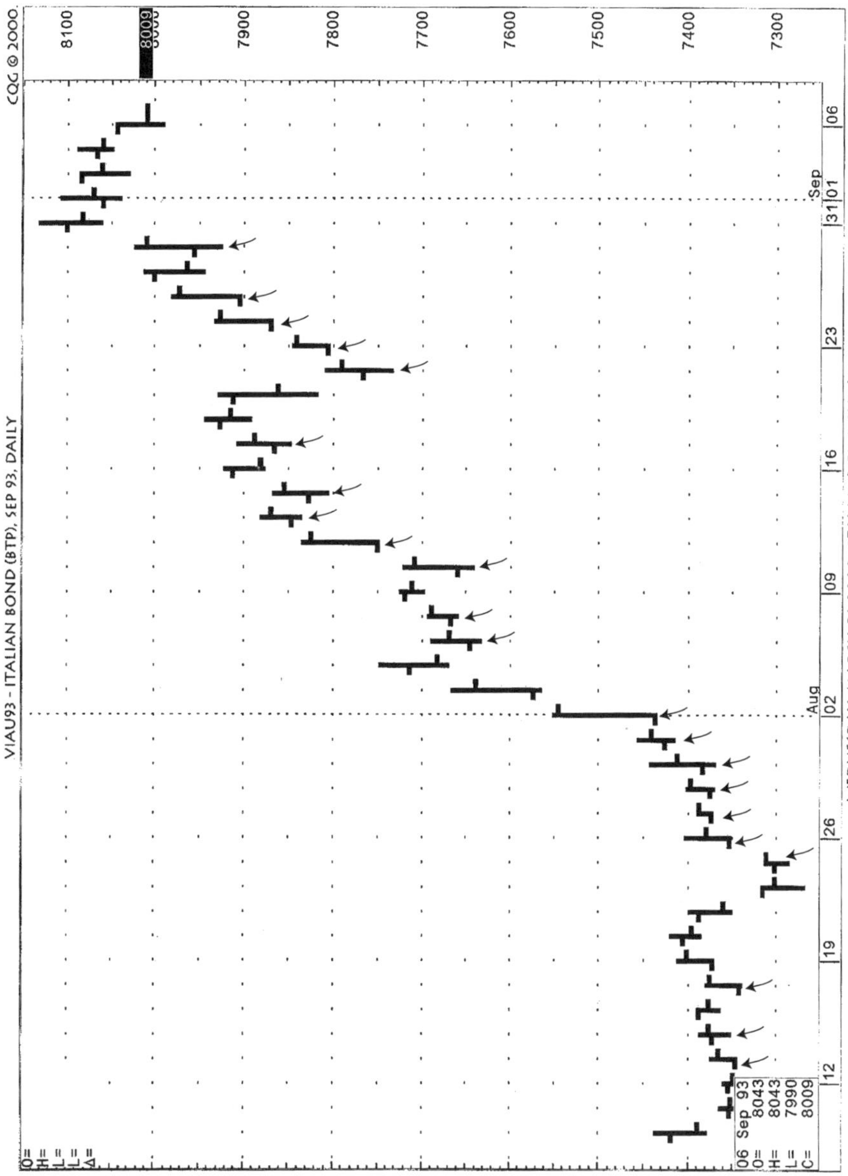

the bottom replaces the days on which the close/open relationship occurred). By subtracting the average of open vs. close, you arrive at an oscillator. When the oscillator is above zero, the trend is assumed to be bullish; when it is below zero, the trend is considered bearish. (See Figure 6.19 as an example.)

PROS: The open vs. close indicator is good for catching longer-term as well as shorter-term moves. It produces some false signals, but tends to catch the big moves when they occur. By setting the open vs. close indicator lengths correctly, you will be able to avoid many of the false signals.

CONS: There are some false signals; however, this is common to all technical indicators.

CONCLUSIONS: The open vs. close relationship is one of the most important patterns that exists in the futures markets. I find its importance to be paramount in virtually all international markets. Those who have an interest in researching trading systems and methods would do well to consider the open/close relationship a good starting point.

ACCUMULATION DISTRIBUTION INDICATOR

Larry Williams and J. J. Waters[4] developed the accumulation distribution indicator (ADI). An excellent indicator of longer-term market movement, it measures the accumulation and/or distribution of contracts or shares. When used with its moving average (which is my adaptation), it yields excellent signals in many markets.

PROS: The ADI method is good for catching longer-term moves as long as you set the variables correctly. Used within the right time frames, it appears to be very effective in most markets.

---

[4]Their article entitled "Measuring Market Momentum" appeared in the October 1972 issue of *Commodities Magazine*.

Cons: There are some false signals; however, this is common in all technical indicators. By setting the ADI lengths correctly, you will be able to avoid many of the false signals.

Conclusion: The ADI has excellent potential as a longer-term indicator in the international futures markets. It is not recommended for short-term applications.

Market Sentiment Indicators

These indicators are based on the concept of contrary opinion. The idea here is that the majority will be wrong most of the time. There are several indicators or sources from which contrary opinion can be deduced. These include *Market Vane*, the *USDA Commitment of Traders Report*, odd lot short sales (for the stock market) and my own *Daily Sentiment Index* (DSI). Some measures of market sentiment are not objective (i.e., examining newspaper headlines and stories for their bullish or bearish content) because they do not provide a definitive evaluation of bullish or bearish consensus. In order to determine if prevailing opinions are primarily bullish or bearish, a numerical evaluation is best. The theory of market sentiment is simple; when bullish sentiment is too high, prices tend to top, and when bullish sentiment is too low, markets tend to bottom. When market sentiment is ninety percent or more, a top tends to develop within days. When market sentiment drops to ten percent or lower, a market bottom is often close at hand. This relationship appears to be just as true for the European futures markets as it does for the U.S. markets. Based on my historical sentiment data on the European markets, it appears that these statistics can be very helpful in finding market tops and bottoms.

Pros: Market sentiment and contrary opinion have a lengthy history of validity and reliability. They can be used in an objective way, preferably combined with timing and other technical tools.

In addition, they can be used with fundamental analysis and as inputs in neural network systems. Neural network systems are advanced software programs that use artificial intelligence to determine market trends, buy signals and sell signals. Market sentiment indicators are often leading indicators. By using moving averages of daily sentiment data, market sentiment can also be used for short-term and intermediate-term swings.

CONS: These indicators can, at times, pick tops and bottoms too early. In some cases, the information is not timely since there is a lag between the time it is collected and the time it is made available to traders. To the best of my knowledge, my *Daily Sentiment Index* is the most timely. It is usually issued within several hours of market closings for the day. A sample of the DSI for European markets is shown in Figure 6.20.

CONCLUSIONS: Use these indicators in conjunction with market trends and timing. Use moving averages of market sentiment data to develop a timing approach.

FIGURE 6.20

DSI FOR EUROPEAN MARKETS

European Daily Sentiment Index (DSIE) for: FRI APR 16, 1999

MARKET	% Bullish
Notionnel	32
Japan Bond	75
FTSE100	68
DAX	72
Gilt	21
Bund	45
Italian Bond	62
Short Strlng 35	
EURIBOR	63
CAC40	63
Euro	15

Next update MON 11AM

Summary and Conclusions

In this chapter, I have provided an overview of the key timing and trend indicators most often used by contemporary traders. While some methods and systems appear to make sense on the surface, they do not lead to profits when tested or traded.

In trading the international futures markets, you will have many methods, systems and indicators from which to choose. You must take the time to study which of the methods is most appropriate for the market(s) you wish to trade. I have attempted to narrow the field and direct your focus to those approaches that have the most merit.

Chapter 7

MANAGING RISK

Successful futures traders advocate a strict approach to risk management. In this chapter I touch on some money management issues and principles that will help keep your risks lower.

Speculators often learn early in the futures trading game that risk management is the key element to success or failure. I rank risk management even higher in importance than your trading system or trader experience, although I hasten to add that the success of any trading system or risk-management method is, to a certain extent, a function of trader expertise.

Notwithstanding the importance of experience, risk management is an issue with which all traders must deal. Seemingly outstanding trading systems have been rendered less than worthless for lack of solid risk management, and mediocre trading systems have shown excellent profits as a result of effective risk management.

PRESERVATION OF CAPITAL

To put it succinctly, you must preserve your capital by cutting your losses if you want to survive in the futures game. This may seem obvious enough, but I assure you that it is easier said than done. Many traders find it virtually impossible to manage their money. In today's highly volatile international markets, risk management is more important than ever.

Proponents of capital preservation have advanced the concepts of maximization of return on each profitable trade and minimization of loss on each losing trade. Having a maximum amount you are willing to risk when you enter a trade or setting a risk limit based on technical indicators will help you achieve your goals. Although this is simple, sound reasoning, it may well be found to be incorrect and even presumptuous. The practice of using stop-loss placement as a function of predetermined dollar risk is misguided. It is not necessarily consistent with the objectives of a technical system. It is a requirement imposed by psychological and financial needs as opposed to technical indicators. Even if one optimizes stop-loss procedures by basing them on market history, the logic may not necessarily be any more solid. A reasonable alternative is to let each trade take its natural course and allow the indicators to get you in and out, but with a fail-safe level established for each trade that will get you out if the indicators fail. Each speculator must find his or her particular solution to this dilemma.

MAXIMIZATION OF CAPITAL

The second function of successful money management is the maximization of capital. Some traders feel that they must be in the market at all times or that they must trade every day if they are to maximize their capital. I suspect that operating on this basis alone is a good way to minimize capital. Capital maximization is achieved by:

- Conserving trading capital for only the most promising situations.
- Allotting capital on the basis of performance and potential.
- Trading only the required amount of capital, with the excess employed in other areas of speculation or investment.

PROFIT DISPERSAL

Although it is hard to believe, this is a frequent problem. Traders often make profits quickly and give them back even more quickly because they don't have a well-prepared plan for distributing their profits. I view the marketplace as a treasure chest: When it is open, one must grab all one can get before the heavy lid slams shut. The idea is to take it quickly and to keep it out of the treasure chest.

At times, you may have to force the lid open and this will take time, energy and money (for the proper tools). Yet, the goal is always the same—to take out more than you put in. Therefore, I urge all traders to regularly remove some profits from the market, placing them in investments that guarantee a slow but steady rate of return. Routinely removing profits from the market will help you in two ways:

- First, you'll have funds to put back into the market in the event that you need to refinance your account.
- Second, you'll have funds for other purposes.

LOSS MANAGEMENT

There are two basic approaches to loss management. One method limits losses by setting a predetermined dollar amount per trade. Using this approach, a trader decides to risk only a certain amount on each trade or on each market. This approach, however, imposes an artificial limit on the market and on your trading, and therefore seems impractical to me.

It makes more sense to manage losses by market behavior. After all, isn't it ultimately the market that must be followed? Before you decide to go with a strict maximum dollar-per-trade approach, consider loss management by market behavior as an alternative.

Before deciding which approach better suits you, consider the following:

1. Loss management by market behavior (that is, using timing signals and trading objectives only) may require you to take more risk per trade.
2. A maximum dollar-per-trade approach may limit your loss on each trade, but it may also remove you from situations that could ultimately turn out to be profitable.
3. A maximum dollar-per-trade approach may allow you to trade more markets at once, thereby allowing you to diversify your trading.

DOUBLE UP OR CUT BACK?

It is not uncommon for traders to double up after one or two losing trades. This practice was, perhaps, originally adapted from the blackjack card game. The mere fact that this practice may be derived from gambling puts it in a bad light among traders. However, I suggest that under the right circumstances it might not be bad to double up.

For example, if you have a system that rarely takes more than three successive losses, you can double your position after the third successive loss. But if you do so you must remember that you are taking more risk and you will not necessarily be guaranteed a profit. Ultimately, a trading system with a high number of winning trades will benefit from such a procedure, though it takes stamina and fortitude to implement.

On the other side of the coin, there is the practice of cutting back when things are not going well. There's nothing wrong with this approach. In fact, it's not a bad way to preserve capital while you try to figure out what's going wrong.

DIVERSIFICATION

I won't spend a great deal of time on this aspect of money management for limiting loss. The fact is that many traders fail to diversify. Your success or failure should not depend entirely upon the performance of your trading approach in only one or two markets. I suggest that you monitor and trade in a variety of markets. Avoid the thin markets, but monitor at least 14 to 18 markets regularly and diversify your trading accordingly.

Note that many markets move together. The various interest-rate and stock-index markets tend to trend in similar directions. Try to diversify into different markets as part of your strategy.

Consider Multiple Positions

I find that a particularly useful strategy is to trade in multiple contracts (if you can afford to do so) but in a manner distinctly different from the old pyramiding approach. In the typical pyramiding approach, the initial entry consists of the smallest number of contracts. As the market moves in your direction, more and more contracts are added, leading eventually to an upside-down pyramid with the largest number of contracts at the highest price.

This leaves the trader vulnerable; a small reversal can bring the house down. This is not, to my way of thinking, the way to trade. I advocate building a real pyramid instead. Begin with your largest position and add successively smaller units along the way.

Another procedure particularly suitable for the day trader is to begin with multiple contracts. As the market moves in your favor you can take a profit quickly on half of your contracts, keeping the remaining contracts for a more optimistic target. I prefer this approach because it allows one to take some profits and let some profits ride.

Be Sure to Be Well-Capitalized

Avoid any type of trading until you are well-capitalized. Though this should be an obvious caveat to all traders, it's one that tends to be ignored by the overly zealous. By today's standards, any account of less than $10,000 has little chance of success. Increase your initial trading capital and you'll have more staying power. Don't begin trading with an amount so small that you are beaten before you start.

The markets are more volatile than ever. And, volatility is here to stay. It is imperative to begin with sufficient capital.

Stop Losses: A Double-Edged Sword

Risk management, simply defined, is the act of limiting losses. A number of time-tested and highly reliable techniques are part and parcel of effective risk management. Among these are the use of stop losses, futures options, spreads, position size and asset allocation.

To a certain extent all of the above are inseparable. For example, if you are a trader carrying a position that is way too large considering your available risk capital, you may attempt to compensate for the risk exposure by using a very small stop loss. This is a counterproductive methodology and a sure invitation to losses. Similarly, if you spread a position to avoid taking a loss, you may think you are limiting your loss, but in reality you are actually doubling your risk exposure. Risk management is like all other things in life. There are hundreds of things you can do wrong and only a handful that are right. The key is to find those that are right and to do them consistently.

What makes stop losses difficult, if not impossible, to use is the fact that they're a double-edged sword. You know that their use is necessary if losses are to be minimized, yet you also know that you've been stopped out of positions many times, only to see the market go your way after you've been stopped out. What should you do? There's no doubt that stops are necessary, but using stops effectively and placing them carefully are keys to success. Note that different exchanges have different rules and regulations regarding stops. Be certain that you know these rules before you trade any of the international markets.

Smaller Stops = Smaller Profits = More Losses

Perhaps one of the best lessons I learned about stop losses is that they have to be large enough to permit the market reasonable movement. Stop losses that are too close to the market are not recommended other than under very special circumstances. Many day traders, for example, are fascinated with the idea of using extremely small stop losses in order to limit risk. The end result of this approach may be that the accuracy of their trading may be very low, because stops will be hit very frequently.

A stop loss must be large enough to allow the market its reasonable movement. If, for example, FTSE-100 futures have shown an average daily range of 150 points, then a stop loss of 50 points may be much too small, inasmuch as the random behavior of the market will stop you out more often than not. Regardless of how exact or precise your trading system may be in picking concise price points, no trading system is immune to random market behavior.

Side-by-Side Comparison

Figure 7.1 (on page 133) illustrates my point about stop loss levels. It displays the historical performance of a trading system I developed quickly using Omega TradeStation™. The tabular presentation shows historical backtesting of the same market entry and exit rules with eleven different stop loss levels. Here are my conclusions:

1. As stop loss increases, so do net profits per trade.

2. As stop loss increases, so does system accuracy until it peaks and can no longer increase.
3. As stop loss increases, drawdown remains fairly stable. Hence more risk per trade does not increase drawdown.
4. As stop loss increases, the largest losing trade increases minimally.
5. As stop loss increases, overall profits for the system nearly double.
6 Stop loss increases to a point of diminishing returns and system performance peaks.
7. The smallest stop losses produce the worst results.
8. The largest stop losses produce the best results.
9. As stop losses increase, the number of successive losing trades decreases considerably.

As you can see, small stop losses do not do what you'd expect them to do. Big stop losses work better.

THE LAW OF DIMINISHING RETURNS

In economic theory the law of diminishing returns states that the amount of return one derives from additional inputs of effort or resources peaks at a point and then levels off. Very similar to the law of diminishing returns in economics (which states that beyond a certain point, increased investment will not result in increased returns), the protective value of a stop loss decreases as the stop loss amount is increased. The protective value of a stop loss decreases when the stop loss gets too high. Hence, stop losses must somehow be optimized. This is a relatively simple procedure to perform with mechanical trading systems. These systems can be backtested with different stop losses and stop loss scenarios.

FIGURE 7.1

SYSTEM BACKTEST USING ELEVEN DIFFERENT INITIAL STOP LOSS LEVELS

Initial Stop	Total Profit	Average Trade	% Correct	Draw-down	Largest Loss $	Largest Win	Consec. Losers
500	34,715.00	257.15	39%	–7,155.00	–875.00	+15,775.00	7
750	46,910.00	350.07	44%	–5,965.00	–1,645.00	+15,775.00	7
1000	48,730.00	363.66	49%	–6,650.00	–1,825.00	+15,775.00	6
1200	52,940.00	395.07	51%	–5,955.00	–1,825.00	+15,775.00	5
1400	57,395.00	431.54	52%	–2,175.00	–2,175.00	+15,775.00	5
1600	57,815.00	434.70	53%	–5,655.00	–2,175.00	+15,775.00	4
1800	56,475.00	424.62	53%	–5,635.00	–2,175.00	+15,775.00	4
2200	58,470.00	442.95	53%	–5,145.00	–2,175.00	+15,775.00	4
2800	57,480.00	435.45	53%	–5,480.00	–2,775.00	+15,775.00	4
3500	57,590.00	436.29	53%	–6,180.00	–2,875.00	+15,775.00	4
4500	60,720.00	460.00	54%	–6,165.00	–2,765.00	+15,775.00	4

Naturally, critics will argue that history does not always repeat itself exactly and that using such a procedure to optimize stops is subject to the problems that are always associated with system optimization. To a certain extent these criticisms are valid, but such testing for stop losses is a viable methodology that can tell you a great deal about the optimum size of a stop loss for certain patterns or systems.

In some cases a larger stop is worse than a smaller stop, but the idea of testing for stop loss size is important. If you find that the ideal stop loss is too rich for your account, then you can either avoid the trade or research another method of risk limitation. Remember that systems won't always work this way. The point is that sometimes less in terms of a stop loss is not more when it comes to the bottom line.

Risk Management Through Margin Control

Another way to manage risk is to redefine the rules of margin. Instead of putting up the exchange minimum margins, it is often preferable to give yourself a large cushion, particularly if you're going after longer-term moves.

Some will argue that this destroys the attraction of the futures game inasmuch as it removes the leverage. While there may be some truth to that, leverage is a double-edged sword—it can help you and it can hurt you. Unfortunately it hurts most people in the futures market. If you use leverage wisely, then you can use it to your advantage.

Trailing Stop Losses

The trailing stop loss has been a favorite among traders for many years. Simply explained, the trailing stop loss "trails" market moves. As your profit continues to mount, the stop loss is continuously changed to reflect the increased profit. The goal is to protect the profit from a reversal in trend.

While this sounds like a reasonable and rational methodology, it is also a flawed approach as most often used by traders. The reason it is flawed is that, once again, traders do not allow the market sufficient space for random movements. Most often, traders are stopped out of their positions with trailing stops because the trailing stops are too close to the market.

When the market responds emotionally to news, even news that is unrelated to the underlying trend, many traders with trailing stops are stopped out. It is not the trailing stop concept that's at fault; rather it's the size of the trailing stop that's the culprit.

Figure 7.2 displays the results of another experiment based on trailing stops. It was developed on the same system as Figure 7.1, but for ten different levels of trailing stop losses using a fixed initial stop loss.

FIGURE 7.2

TRAILING STOP LOSSES

Trail % Stop Loss	Total Profit	Average Trade $	% Correct	Draw-down $	Largest Loss $	Largest Win $	Consec. Losers
10	35,760.00	262.94	54%	–5,860.00	–2,775.00	+5,735.00	3
20	32,190.00	236.69	54%	–6,195.00	–2,775.00	+5,735.00	3
30	31,420.00	231.03	54%	–6,195.00	–2,775.00	+5,735.00	3
40	32,255.00	238.93	55%	–5,975.00	–2,775.00	+5,735.00	3
50	28,930.00	215.90	55%	–5,750.00	–2,775.00	+5,735.00	3
60	35,645.00	268.01	55%	–5,910.00	–2,775.00	+5,735.00	3
70	44,815.00	336.95	54%	–5,780.00	–2,775.00	+5,735.00	3
80	54,420.00	412.27	55%	–5,780.00	–2,775.00	+5,735.00	3
90	57,560.00	436.06	53%	–5,780.00	–2,775.00	+5,735.00	4
100	56,610.00	428.86	51%	–5,780.00	–2,775.00	+5,735.00	7

SUMMARY AND CONCLUSIONS

Managing risk is perhaps the single most important consideration in futures trading regardless of which markets are being traded or where such trading takes place. This chapter emphasized the role of stop losses, trailing stop losses and diversification as the essential elements of effective risk management.

Chapter 8

TRADING PSYCHOLOGY AND THE INTERNATIONAL MARKETS

In this chapter I touch on what is one of the most critical issues in successful futures trading: that of using psychology to your best advantage. There are many issues to consider and, depending on your nature and behaviors, some may be more relevant to you than others. I suggest you read them all and consider them carefully in light of your own self-understanding.

The futures trading game is now an international phenomenon. No matter when you trade or where you trade it, psychology is always hard at work, lurking under the surface, ready to "undo" you. Remember that no matter which market you trade, the importance of trader psychology cannot be underestimated.

THE BEHAVIOR OF TRADERS

Traders are a strange and wonderful lot indeed. When I made my first trade in the summer of 1968, I had no idea that there are perhaps as many different approaches to the markets as there are traders. I've also discovered that even though traders may tell us they want to make money in the markets, their behavior often tells us otherwise.

I've distilled some of my more salient observations of trader behavior into a few pages. I hope you enjoy them, but most of all I hope you benefit from them. Here, then, in no particular order, are my thoughts.

Traders Are Often Too Willing to Take Tips that Have No History Behind Them While They Ignore Solid Trades with a Long History of Reliability

Traders work hard to gather reliable information and develop trading systems. They plan their trades. They are methodical in setting a risk point. They have the discipline to follow their systems. Yet all it takes is one urgent call from a broker or one piece of dramatic news, and all their good intentions vanish.

Traders react impulsively to news, not knowing their odds of success, their risk, or the history behind the trades. They lose money on the trade that they took impulsively and yet they fail to learn from the experience. It seems that the human mind is always looking for an "easy shot." When something comes along that seems easy, discipline appears to deteriorate in spite of all intelligent reasons to maintain it.

Traders Tend to Be a Very Insecure Group of People When It Comes to the Markets

What is it that causes traders to err? Lack of knowledge? Lack of capital? Lack of a systematic approach? Yes, at times it is one or all of these. But what it all adds up to is this: Traders tend to wallow in insecurity, no matter how good their trading systems may be. Only the exceptional trader is totally immune to the errors that result from insecurity. Having a solid trading system combined with a disciplined approach can go a long way toward eliminating most trader insecurity.

Traders Love Forecasts

Forecasts tend to polarize a person's thinking. They tend to restrict possibilities and give traders tunnel vision. They create a mind-set that is not easily overcome.

Bad Price Fills Are the Bane of a Trader's Existence

Traders frequently complain about their price fills. While there is certainly an element of truth to the complaints, there is also the fact that the overwhelming majority of traders have no idea about how to place orders effectively or which orders are most suited to their purpose. By merely using the right order at the right time, a trader can save thousands of dollars by saving a few ticks here and a few ticks there.

Those "Nasty" Floor Traders!

Traders are also universal in their dislike and mistrust of floor traders. They accuse them of virtually everything from stealing ticks to fixing prices. Floor traders are just as fallible and human as are all traders. The only difference is that they have more experience and know how to "milk" markets for the few ticks they attempt to extract from their trades.

Traders Hate Buying on Strength and Selling on Weakness

A costly lesson I've learned in over 30 years in the futures business is the value of buying on strength and selling on weakness. This is the ultimate way of trading with the trend. Yet traders shy away from this effective strategy because they're always afraid of buying too high or selling too low. The average trader is always trying to find a "deal." While this may work with a street vendor in a flea market, it's not a winning strategy in the futures markets. There are ways to buy at support in bull markets and ways to sell at resistance in bear markets, but most traders don't have the discipline to follow these methods consistently or effectively.

Traders Hate Taking Losses— Even Small Ones

This is no surprise to you, is it? This is by far one of the worst traits of traders. All too often those little losses, which were not taken when they should have been, turn into account-devouring monsters that can make equity disappear in a matter of days. Many traders would rather allow a small loss of several hundred dollars to turn into a monster than admit to the small loss at the right time.

Traders Love to Blame Everyone But Themselves for Their Losses

Consider the many times you blamed your broker or the trading floor for your losses. How many times have you blamed the floor for "picking" your stops or the large mutual funds for stopping you out? How often have you blamed your trading adviser or newsletter writers for changing your mind about a trade? Most often we tend to blame everyone but ourselves for losses, but the ultimate responsibility for our trades is our own.

Traders Think Too Much and Take Too Little Action

Thinking is good in many aspects of life, even in trading; however, once you have determined your course of action based on your system or method, you need to *take* action.

Traders Are Inconsistent

At times a trader engages in a behavior or behaviors that are clearly in violation of effective trading rules. Yet, in spite of the fact that rules have been broken, the trade or trades result in a profit. This teaches the trader that consistent following of the rules is not necessary. But because the results of inconsistent rule breaking are random, the trader will never know for certain whether breaking the rules will work or not. The inconsistency of results teaches the trader to react inconsistently.

Traders Can't Accept Too Many Consecutive Losses Before They Begin to Doubt Themselves as Well as Their Trading Systems

The logic and experience of system testing tell us that some of the best-reading systems are subject to considerable drawdowns as well as strings of losing trades. From my experience I'd have to say that taking as many as seven losses (even up to ten losses) in a row is not unusual. Yet this is precisely what causes traders to abandon their systems or to change them midstream. In order to make a system work for you, you have to give it time and plenty of room. Most traders know this intuitively rather than discursively.

Here is how you may embark or stay firmly on the road to consistent profits. First, examine your trading results by looking at your monthly brokerage statements. Attempt to determine why you made the trades you did. This will let you know at once whether your trades were at all systematic or whether they were based on a whim, emotion, tips, rumors, fear or greed. If you're like most traders, then you'll find that a relatively small percentage of your trades were the result of a system and that most of your trades were prompted by other factors, most of which were totally unrelated to any definitive system, method or indicator.

This will alert you to a problem area in your trading. It will let you know, without a doubt, that you are not basing your decisions on a consistent approach. The second step, then, is to fix this problem by looking for a system that has simple, unambiguous rules of application. (See Chapter 9 for a discussion of how to select a trading system.)

MASTERING THE PSYCHOLOGICAL ASPECTS OF COMMODITY TRADING

You can master the psychological end of trading by learning about yourself or by using simple, time-tested, mechanical techniques to overcome the problems. Purists would argue that the latter approach is shallow and not conducive to long-term change. I disagree.

Numerous mechanical techniques can be used to overcome problems of trader discipline. Whether the application of these mechanical methods results in permanent changes is irrelevant. If mechanical methods work, then use them.

What do I mean when I talk about "mechanical methods"? Here are some examples:

1. If too many of your losses are the result of your not using stop losses, don't waste your time trying to figure out why you don't use stops; just have someone enter your stops for you. There are many traders who cannot follow their own systems. To overcome this limitation, simply turn your system over to someone who will implement all the trades for you.
2. How about a method for dealing with overtrading? The answer is simple. Most overtrading comes from either too much contact with the market or attempting to trade too many systems. A mechanical way of dealing with this problem is to eliminate the source or sources of information that stimulate you to make too many trades.
3. Making a verbal contract with your broker can solve other problems. Consider the trader who enters stop losses but who changes them repeatedly as the market approaches the stop. In such cases, the broker and client can agree that once a stop is entered, it will not be changed unless the system so dictates.

Factors Underlying Successful Trading

While there are many things a trader can do wrong in the markets, there are only a few things he or she can do right. We are all well aware of how important are risk management, discipline and a good trading system. Yet, without a doubt, they are all useless in the hands of a trader who is psychologically inept or self-destructive. It is unfortunate that traders still believe in the myth that a better system will make them better traders.

The factors in achieving trading success are primarily psychological or behavioral. My experiences have taught me that three factors comprise perhaps ninety percent of the formula for achieving and maintaining market success: detachment, persistence and a realistic attitude.

Detachment

Many years ago I learned that in order to trade successfully, you have to "not care"—you need to be detached from your work as a trader. At times, being human gets in the way of success by throwing emotional roadblocks in your path. Emotional roadblocks cloud judgment and inhibit success. Just as a surgeon must not become emotionally involved with a patient, a trader must not become emotionally involved with his or her trades, or for that matter, with the idea of success. Keep yourself from caring too much and you'll facilitate success.

Persistence

Clearly, the trader who is a quitter will never succeed, because he or she will not be in the markets when the big moves occur. A truly great trader is willing to come back fighting after a loss or after a string of losses.

Realistic Attitude

Traders must maintain a realistic attitude in order to succeed in the game of high expectations. All too often traders have grossly unrealistic expectations about what they can achieve in the markets. Dreams of striking it rich, of being in on that one trade that makes you fabulously wealthy, are self-destructive and divert your attention from the reality of your goal.

The fact of the matter is that you are far better off trading smaller moves that have a higher degree of accuracy than trading large moves that are not likely to occur and, if they do occur, will take so long to develop that you'll have at least one hundred opportunities to make mistakes.

THE MAJORITY IS USUALLY WRONG— DON'T FORGET IT!

There is a strong relationship between the level of market emotion and short-term market turns. When opinions are very bullish, tops are likely; when opinions are very bearish, bottoms are likely.

Remember these general rules about futures trading and market sentiment. They will serve you well!

1. Most futures traders lose money most of the time.
2. Most futures traders make incorrect decisions at major and minor market turning points.
3. When futures traders are in general agreement that a given market is bullish or bearish, they are usually incorrect.
4. The larger the degree of agreement, the more likely it is that a strongly held opinion will be incorrect.
5. Because most futures traders are buyers rather than sellers, they are most likely to be wrong than they are in strong agreement that a market will move down.
6. It is more important to determine the opinions of average traders as opposed to professional traders.

While these are just a few of the important things to remember if you sincerely want to be a successful futures trader, they are by no means the only prerequisites to success.

I urge you to develop and maintain your own list, derived from your experiences as a futures trader, because your own list will be considerably more meaningful to you.

THE PARADOX OF DISCIPLINE AND EMOTION

The past several decades of technological development have rendered an interesting paradox in the world of commodity investing. With computerized systems and lightning-fast communication and advanced economic forecasting, there should be an overwhelming number of market winners. But in reality, over ninety percent of all investors in commodity futures trading are unsuccessful. The reasons for this lie with the individual trader, for it is the individual who stands in his or her own way when it comes to prospering as a trader. The speculator who takes sophisticated market tools and uses them to create losses rather than gains can only look to his or her own limitations. The average investor who feeds the market with losses can blame only a lack of self-knowledge, self-control and self-discipline.

In spite of overwhelming technological knowledge, the paradox is that most traders still lose money in the futures market. The fact is that knowledge of one's self seems to be more important than the acquisition of so-called facts, news, economic theories or political motivations. The markets of the 1980s and 1990s have continued to violate the market rules of the 1950s and 1960s. It is therefore essential that any speculator hoping to be successful in such a chaotic marketplace have command of his or her emotional self.

The chart patterns studied by technical analysts are little more than a diagram of market psychology. Thus, the various trendlines, reversal patterns, and support and resistance points on a bar chart have no direct relationship to the commodity itself; rather, they reflect the attempts by market traders to cope with forces inside themselves. The rising and falling value of the commodity is a function of what buyers and sellers at any one time and place are willing to pay or receive for it.

Recall the discussion of supply and demand and elasticity of supply and demand. The final act of buying and selling in a marketplace must be performed by people who have examined the situation, considered the variables, studied the charts and arrived at their conclusions. The information available for study is the same for everyone, yet the conclusions can be worlds apart. The explanation for this phenomenon is contained in Francis Bacon's observation: "Man prefers to believe what he prefers to be true."

What a trader prefers to be true is a function of that trader's inner psychological state. Therefore, an understanding of human psychology and human behavior is just as important as an understanding of market fundamentals, trading systems, chart analysis and economic theory, for it is human behavior that causes market behavior.

EMOTIONS, DISCIPLINE AND THE TRADER

What is it about trading that causes us to lose our discipline and to commit many of several hundred errors in our trading? A deceptively simple reply is that we are all human. Because we're human, we are also subject to a virtually endless barrage of emotionally based and emotionally charged inputs, all of which tend to cloud judgment and interfere with reason. The greatest enemy of the trader is his or her own emotions!

The role of emotions in the quest for profitable trading has been the topic of many a book and the source of considerable frustration to traders, since the first trader made the first trade. The simple fact is that the most powerful stimulus for an emotional response in a trader is the very act of trading. Because money represents security, power, prestige, survival and more, it naturally arouses a host of conflicts, wishes, expectations and fears, all of which are emotionally charged. In short, traders are just as scared by the potential for loss as they are excited by the potential for making money.

The fear of losing everything causes traders to become too conservative in their trading. Hence, they tend not to take chances. They tend to use stop losses that are too small. They tend to shy away from trades that seem to be too risky or at all questionable in terms of their potential. They tend to hold on to losing trades, fearing the reality of taking a loss. Traders who are focused on the profit potential of a trade tend to ignore signals to exit or reverse their positions, imbued as they are with the hope of making money. The desire to make money causes traders to take excessive risks, which are often deleterious to their financial health. In addition to the rather obvious ones cited here, there are many subtle and not-so-subtle emotional responses exhibited by traders.

It would seem that the onset of a counterproductive or loss-producing emotional response would be easy to detect. However, we know that this is not the case. Because traders (in fact, all human beings) have a virtually unlimited capacity to avoid dealing with reality, it is difficult—at times, impossible—for us to recognize the onset of a loss-producing emotional response. But we can learn ways of avoiding those responses.

Learning how to avoid loss-producing emotions is a very complex process that traders have spent fortunes and lost fortunes trying to master. They have attended seminars, read books, visited psychologists and psychiatrists, consulted with futures trading professionals, and pondered long and hard about how to overcome these difficulties. The three lists presented here should prove helpful in your quest to keep losing behaviors to a minimum. I hasten to add, though, that the key ingredient to overall success in the markets is personal awareness.

How Emotional Responses Can Lead to Losses

- Reacting emotionally can cloud judgment, leading to bad decisions.
- Fear of taking a loss can lead traders to hold on to positions too long.
- Greed in the form of expecting or wanting larger profits can lead to overtrading.
- Insecurity can lead traders to seek too many opinions, thereby causing confusion and doubt.
- Confusion and doubt can lead to "nervous" trading (which makes it difficult to trade systematically).
- Lack of discipline can cause a good trading system to become a bad trading system.
- Anxiety caused by the fear of loss can cause a trader to exit positions too soon or to enter them too late.
- Hoping that a losing position will turn profitable causes traders to ride losses.
- Hoping that a winning position will become a bigger winner causes traders to hold trades too long.
- Fearing that a profitable trade will become a losing trade causes premature exit and cuts profits short.
- Insecurity caused by the feeling that other traders know more than you do can cause errors.
- Fear of a market moving to the limit against you can cause you to avoid certain markets.

- Concern about keeping losses small can result in using stop losses that are too small.
- Lack of patience, often caused by fear and insecurity, can lead traders to subvert their own trading systems.
- The inability to withstand a series of losing trades and drawdown causes abandonment of one's system.

Behaviors That Tend to Precede Dysfunctional Trader Responses

- Ignoring or overriding signals from your trading system that are contrary to your current position.
- Riding a loss beyond the predetermined stop loss or exit point.
- Failing to do market "homework" due to negative attitude.
- Succumbing to complete dejection and negative attitude following a series of losing trades.
- Deciding to abandon your trading system for a new one that you hope will perform better.
- Changing the rules of your system or method following a few losses.
- Being unwilling to take trading signals from your system following a series of losses.
- Feeling that if you had more information you'd not have lost money.
- Wanting to ride a profitable trade well beyond its price or time target contrary to your system rules.
- Deciding to pyramid a position by adding more contracts than your original position.
- Spreading your position in order to avoid closing out a losing trade.

- Ignoring any information that does not agree with your current positions.
- Feeling that you will always be a loser in the markets, no matter what you do.
- Feeling that there is nothing you can do wrong in the markets (the feeling that you're invincible).
- Subscribing to many different advisory services.
- Having persistent and unfounded feelings that your broker or floor traders are cheating you.

How to Limit Losing Behaviors and Maximize Winning Behaviors

- Keep written records of all your trades, noting the reasons for entry and exit and their outcome.
- Try to remain isolated from the opinions of others; don't use more than three advisory services at once.
- Avoid listening to the popular press such as business television shows, radio market commentaries, etc.
- Develop a set of specific procedures for your trading that will alert you to deviations from your plans.
- Make certain that you don't overextend yourself in terms of margins and positions.
- Don't try to play someone else's game; in other words, develop your own style.
- Make certain that you can accept and be prepared for a string of losses and drawdown.
- Find a trading system or method that fits your style of trading.

- Try to ride profits and cut losses short as opposed to what most traders do (which is the opposite).
- Once you have researched a trading system you feel comfortable with, use it with discipline.
- Avoid making trading decisions that are not based on input from your systems or methods.
- Trade only within the limits of your financial ability and account size.
- Do not pyramid your positions by adding larger positions as the trend continues in your favor.
- Try not to trade when your personal problems are overwhelming.
- Leave your market work at the office; don't take it home with you.
- Try to avoid hope, fear, greed, indecision, wishes, expectations, remorse and lack of confidence.
- Deal only with the facts of your system and not the fantasies of your wishes.

While correcting the emotional problems that can afflict the trader is a process that can take many years, consider taking one of these steps to get started:

1. Read a book such as my *Investor's Quotient,* 2nd ed. (New York: Wiley & Sons, 1994).
2. Take a course or seminar in personal development.
3. Keep a close watch on all of your trading-related behaviors. You can do this by keeping a detailed diary of what you trade, why you trade it and the outcome of the trade. Make

sure you write down all your thoughts and actions. Then analyze the results.

Ultimately, paying close attention to your behaviors and actions will yield the results you want, but it will take time and effort. While the application and understanding of trading methods is relatively simple, their implementation can be difficult if your psychological attitudes toward trading are dysfunctional or excessively emotional. If this is the case, then you need to fix your inner self before you can expect to achieve success as a trader.

WINNERS AND LOSERS

It is not possible for me to overemphasize the fact that great traders are great because they have mastered the discipline of trading as well as the mechanical techniques. I've placed great emphasis on discipline, because it is undoubtedly the weak link in the chain of trading behavior. No consistent success is possible without it.

There are many opinions as to what constitutes discipline. My point of view has been tempered and shaped by over twenty-nine years of trading, writing, and advising that have exposed me to every conceivable type of market and every conceivable type of news event. I have developed an arsenal of time-tested suggestions that I will now share with you. Here they are, not necessarily in order of importance.

FIND YOUR PLACE

One of the most important considerations is for the trader to find his or her place in the vast world of futures trading. There are many things a trader can do, but only a few that can be done at one time. I suggest you find one or more techniques to which you can relate well and with which you feel particularly confident. These are the techniques that you should then use in your trading.

Don't Expect Immediate Results

Many a trader has been sorely disappointed when immediate success was not attainable. Give yourself sufficient time to achieve success. How long will it take, you ask? There is no answer I can give you other than to say, "More than two weeks and less than two years," but this is certainly not a hard-and-fast rule. Some individuals can be successful in several weeks, whereas others are still not capable of achieving consistent success as futures traders even after many years.

Lower Your Expectations

While some books on positive mental attitude will tell you to have great expectations, I caution you against it. Expect to lose at first, but expect that with time you will begin to break even. Expect that with more time you will begin to achieve profitable results.

There are hundreds, if not thousands, of traders who came to the markets with great expectations and a fistful of dollars, but who left the markets beaten, broke and broken. If anything, you ought to expect failure while hoping that through your efforts you can minimize the failures and maximize the successes.

Play Your Own Game

There will always be those who claim to have better systems, better methods, foolproof indicators, outstanding results and fail-safe methods. Before you give any of these serious attention, make sure that what you're doing is not intrinsically better.

While there is nothing wrong with attempting to improve on what you are doing, the act of searching tends to distract you from your goal. Don't be sidetracked from your goal. Persevere and ignore the claims as much as you can.

Admit to Your Losses Quickly

I have stated repeatedly throughout my books, articles and newsletters that the single worst offense a trader can commit is to carry a position beyond its stop loss point. To do so is to violate the essence of futures trading and to expose yourself to all the risks that a futures trader seeks to avoid.

Remember Your Goal as a Trader

I encourage you to have one simple goal every day of your life as a futures trader: Attempt to end each trade with a profit. Place no dollar amount on the profit or it may distract you. To set a goal too high would be unrealistic, and to set a goal too low might be limiting.

Don't Let Good Profits Turn into Losses

Many a good trade has become a bad trade by turning a profit into a loss due to poor risk management. Preservation of capital is essential to consistent success as a futures trader. Develop a follow-up or trailing stop loss procedure.

Don't Force Trades

If you have seen no opportunity for trades but find yourself idly searching through your screens and charts for opportunities, then you are headed for a disaster. Do not attempt to create an opportunity where one does not exist. Be patient. There will be trades tomorrow or the next day. The market always provides opportunities over time, even though none may exist today. Don't ever force yourself to trade if an opportunity is not readily apparent.

Don't Hesitate

Hesitation is one of the worst enemies of the futures trader. The expression "He who hesitates is lost" is truer in the futures markets than anywhere else. Because futures trading occurs in a circumscribed period of time, every moment you lose in entering or exiting a position is a moment that might cost you money. If you choose to hesitate, then do so with premeditation and calculated caution. Do not hesitate out of fear or indecision.

Keep a Diary

Although I have already elaborated on this topic, I emphasize it here once again due to the great importance it can have in helping you learn from your mistakes and, of course, from your successes. A diary should be kept and should be referred to both at the beginning and the end of each trading day. Use it to learn from what you did or didn't do in past trades.

Act According to Your Systems

Some of the techniques I have discussed in my books are so totally mechanical that your presence is not required, nor are live price quotes necessary. Other methods, however, require your presence and close attention. Act accordingly.

When in Doubt, Stay Out

This is a particularly appropriate expression for the futures trader. Not all indicators or signals will be completely clear all the time. Furthermore, there may be other developments such as news reports or short-term fundamentals that make signals unclear or market response uncertain.

In such cases, my best advice is to stay out of the market. There will always be plenty of trades, and there is no need to enter a trade unless its potential outcome is relatively clear and free from the erratic influence of news or other fundamental events.

DO YOUR HOMEWORK

Too many traders become complacent about their market studies, fail to do their homework and then wonder why they lose money. If you intend to succeed, then you must do your homework, no matter how simple or complex it may be. Perhaps you have developed a trading system that requires no homework. This is certainly possible. However, you still need to work on your trading diary and you still need to keep in close touch with trading opportunities that may develop during the next trading day.

MONITOR YOUR PERFORMANCE

Always keep close track of your results on a trade-by-trade and day-by-day basis. Know where you stand at all times, in order to develop effective feedback about the techniques you are using. Unless you know where you stand, you will not have sufficient information about how well your methods are performing, and you will not know when change is necessary. Some traders refuse to monitor their trading results as a form of defense against being distressed by bad results. This is an avoidance technique that can be very costly.

RECOGNIZE THE DANGERS OF PYRAMIDING

Pyramiding is the act of adding increasingly larger units to your position as a market moves in your favor. For example, you may begin by buying one unit and adding two additional units once the trade has moved in your favor. If the trade continues to move in your favor, you may add four new units and then, assuming that it continues in your favor, you might add six or eight units. The essence of pyramiding is that increasingly larger positions are added as the trade moves in your favor. The upside of this methodology is that you will accumulate a very large position consistent with the trend and you will use the capital available in open profits to margin new positions.

The danger of pyramiding is that this is a pyramid clearly built upside down. It is heaviest at the top and rests on only one unit at the bottom. It is therefore subject to violent collapse at the slightest indication of a trend reversal. If you intend to build a pyramid, then do so by establishing your largest position first and following it up with successively smaller numbers of units.

Summary and Conclusions

What do traders really want? You may find that question somewhat amusing or even perplexing. After all, it seems rather obvious that the only thing traders would be interested in is making money. I once thought so as well, but time and experience have taught me otherwise. While it may seem reasonable and logical to assume that the primary goal of traders is to make money, the fact is that there are many other motives that attract traders to the markets.

Chapter 9

DEVELOPING A TRADING STRATEGY

Anyone who desires to become a futures trader will find an overabundance of available help. On any weekend, somewhere in the world an expert is presenting a seminar on a foolproof trading system. Book after book is available on technical analysis, options trading, the Elliot wave, cycles . . . the list goes on. Hundreds of newsletters on the Internet and via the mail provide advice and trading tips. Hotline phone trading advice is available from dozens of market gurus. The newcomer to futures trading finds it easy to get too much help—easy to keep taking in more information and advice. And, with the "coming of age" in the new European and Asian markets, even more information and advisory services are available.

For the individual who is serious about trading in the markets, however, there must be a path through this wilderness of information overload and a way to separate the helpful from the purely extraneous. It should be obvious to anyone who has read this far that making money through futures trading is difficult to the point of being nearly impossible. On the other hand, there are traders who consistently reap tremendous profits from the futures markets.

It has been estimated that approximately ninety percent of all futures traders lose money while only ten percent make money. These figures seem to indicate that the cards are stacked against anyone who tries to play the game. Yet, if there are indeed futures traders who consistently make money by trading, then it would seem that success as a trader might be based on something other than chance.

With that in mind, a prospective trader needs to follow a thoughtful and well-conceived plan while developing a strategy for trading. One such plan is outlined here. If followed, this plan will position a trader to take full advantage of the alternatives that the futures market has to offer.

STEP ONE: EVALUATE THE FACTORS LIMITING YOUR TRADING EFFECTIVENESS

The characteristic that is most damaging to both occasional and full-time futures traders is an unrealistic view of the task and of their own strengths and limitations. The first exercise that every would-be trader must engage in is to list, in a totally honest and unbiased manner, all of the factors that might adversely affect his or her ability to trade effectively. These factors might be listed under several category headings, such as:

1. Limits on my time
2. Financial limitations
3. Equipment limitations
4. Emotional limitations
5. Other limitations

In each of these categories, certain critical questions must be answered, such as:

1. How much time can I give to the market each day (week)?
2. If I can devote time each day, is it during or after market hours?
3. Do I need to buy a computer?
4. Can I afford a computer?

5. Can I afford the exchange fees for real-time quote service?
6. How much can I comfortably allocate to a trading account?
7. Can I take the pressure of intraday trading?
8. Can I ride large losses, or must I settle for small but more frequent losses?
9. Is my family supportive of my undertaking?

Other questions and other categories will occur to each individual who chooses to pursue this exercise. The important thing is to be honest and to let the ideas flow in a brainstorming manner: Simply write down every idea that presents itself without filtering it. Later, evaluate each thought carefully as to its validity.

STEP TWO: LIST YOUR GOALS

Again, the key is to be honest. The list may include financial, personal, social and family goals. They may be long-term or short-term. Financial goals should be listed in terms of dollars or percent return on capital.

After the goals have been listed, they should be reexamined in light of the previous limitations. If any goals are found to be unrealistic, they should be eliminated or modified to match the limitations. It is essential during this step that each goal be practical and achievable. Any deviation from that is a setup for failure.

STEP THREE: ESTABLISH A TRADING APPROACH

At this stage, many decisions must be made. The information to assist you in that decision making is available in this book. Once the decisions have been made, however, a tremendous amount of study and preparation are necessary before effective trading can be accomplished. Some of the decisions to be made are:

1. Will I try to day trade?
2. Will I try to scalp small profits or search for big moves?
3. Will I trade only futures, futures and options, or only options?
4. Will I try to diversify into several markets or limit my trading to one or two?
5. Will I approach market analysis from a fundamental or a technical perspective?
6. Will I develop my own trading system or purchase one of the systems on the market?
7. Do I need a chart service?

Many more questions will occur to the serious trader, and each must be answered carefully and thoughtfully. When a carefully considered answer has been written to each question, then a trading strategy will have taken shape—one that is based on a realistic appraisal of all circumstances that could either inhibit or enhance the trader's effectiveness.

A trader who conscientiously completes each step of this plan is much more likely to be among the successful ten percent than the unsuccessful ninety percent of futures traders, for two reasons. First, a trader who has thoughtfully constructed a trading strategy based on a consideration of personal limitations and the establishment of realistic goals, as well as a careful selection of components and tools, is simply better prepared than most traders. Second, and equally important, that trader has already exhibited the discipline that is absolutely necessary for consistent success. Without discipline, the best plan and strategy will ultimately fail. It is very likely that most of the failures of the ninety percent can be laid at the feet of either poor preparation or poor discipline or both, because they seem to go hand in hand.

DECISIONS, DECISIONS, DECISIONS

In the hope of facilitating a decision for the new trader, or perhaps changing some ideas in an experienced trader, here are some of the things you should consider.

How Much Risk Capital Do You Have?

This is an important first decision, because it will help you decide whether you want to trade futures, options, futures spreads or all of the above. As a rule, if you have less than $5,000, your chances of making money in futures are slim to none.

Will You Use a Technical or Fundamental Method?

Learn the differences between the fundamental approach and the technical approach to trading. Make a decision. Try to be in one camp or the other, but not in both at the same time. Doing both at first will confuse you. For most traders, technical methods are better because they require less work, less attention and fewer decisions.

Will You Trade Short-Term, Day Trade or Position Trade?

Take the time to get in touch with your temperament as a trader. If you have good self-control, discipline, patience and organization, then you may do well as a position trader. But if you're generally impatient, if you can't wait a long time for market moves to occur, or if you thrive on "action," then short-term or day trading might be best for you.

How Much Time Do You Have?

No matter how you look at it, trading does take time. It's a business that requires study, evaluation, preparation, homework, some thought and some degree of organization. You can do your work while the markets are closed, or you can follow the markets all day. You make the choice.

There are pros and cons to each approach, but only you can decide the amount of time you can give to the business. This will be an integral decision for you. It will likely precede all other decisions, with the possible exception of how much starting capital you have.

Do You Need a Computer and Tick-by-Tick Data?

For most traders, the answer to both questions is clearly no. Although those who sell data and computerized systems would have you believe otherwise, there is no guarantee that you'll make money trading futures if you have live quotes, a computer and a computerized trading system.

Do You Need a Chart Service or Newsletters?

In most cases, traders get too much information, and too much information confuses. Be selective. Allow only a small amount of information to affect your decision-making process. Once you have learned the basics, try to go with your own analyses and methods. If you've found a trading adviser, newsletter or hotline that works for you, then trade with it and don't second-guess it.

Do You Have a Broker You Trust and Who Will Work with You?

The relationship between client and broker has not been given enough attention over the years. If you have an antagonistic or otherwise negative relationship with your broker, then your chances of success will be minimized. You should also consider whether a discount broker or a full-service broker is best for you. Generally, full-service brokers tend to be better for new traders or for those who rely on their brokers for implementing trades consistently or according to a certain methodology.

Do You Know the Vocabulary and the Definitions?

Learn the rules of the markets before you risk a single dollar. Learn the vocabulary, the jargon, the meanings and uses of different types of orders. In short, learn before you try to earn.

Do You Know the Rules of the Various Exchanges and Markets?

When you've made the decisions we've discussed here and you've learned what you need to know, you'll be in a much better position to start trading.

ALTERNATIVES TO BEING AN ACTIVE TRADER

Most individuals approaching the futures market will find that the commitment of time and energy necessary to learn about the markets and to maintain a disciplined trading program is simply too great. Unfortunately, many will continue to trade on their own, dabbling, as some call it, and by so doing they will place themselves firmly among the ninety percent of losers.

Others, realizing that such a course of action is much too risky, and not being of a mind to give away their money but still being interested in participating in the futures markets, will look for alternatives to trading on their own. Among the alternatives available to them are commodity funds, managed accounts, directed hotlines and broker discretionary trading. Each has its advantages and disadvantages, but the disciplined individual who approaches the alternatives carefully and with the same degree of scrutiny used in developing a trading strategy will find each of the alternatives to be viable and potentially profitable.

COMMODITY FUNDS

A recent addition to the world of futures trading is the commodity fund, or limited partnership. Based on the concept of a stock mutual fund, investors buy units of a commodity fund, which are then pooled, and the money is traded by a professional trading adviser or, in some cases, a group of advisers. Most funds are closed end—that is, once the initial offering is sold out, no more units are offered publicly. The minimum investment is usually $5,000, or five $1,000 units. Most funds also qualify for Individual Retirement Account (IRA) deposits.

There are those who say that commodity funds mark the coming of age of the futures industry—that funds have opened futures trading to many who would not have considered investing in futures previously. Certainly, the funds are a popular investment vehicle.

The popularity of futures funds is derived from four factors:

1. *Low initial investment.* Many people are willing to risk $5,000 in a fund but are not willing to risk $20,000 to $30,000 in a professionally managed account or in their own trading account.

2. *Reasonable limited risk.* Most funds have a clause in the prospectus that stipulates the fund will cease trading and

return all assets if the total equity in the fund sinks to fifty percent of its original size. This means there is a reasonable likelihood that each investor will lose no more than half of his or her original investment. When compared to the unlimited risk of futures trading, where the original investment can be lost as well as additional money required to meet a margin call, this characteristic of a fund is very attractive.

3. *Professional management.* The trading advisers for a fund are usually veteran traders with proven track records. An investor in a futures fund can be reasonably certain that the person to whom the money is entrusted is a competent trader with proven expertise. On another level, the general partners of the fund are usually knowledgeable about futures trading and money management and will carefully monitor the progress of the trading that goes on in the fund account.
4. *Diversification.* Because a futures fund pools several million dollars in a trading account, the account can be traded on several markets by several advisers, providing the diversification that would be impossible to obtain if the $5,000 investment were traded in a personal account.

As attractive as futures funds seem, however, there are some disadvantages and some pitfalls of which the investor must be wary. The first disadvantage is that the money is tied up in a fund for a minimum time period, often six months from the time of investment. Thereafter, the money can be taken out only when and if the units can be resold. Thus, a futures fund is not a liquid investment vehicle.

Second, although several of the best-performing futures funds do as well as or better than the best mutual funds, it is not uncommon for a futures fund to lose money rather than to make money. Therefore, a fund must be chosen very carefully, with a sharp eye toward the track record of the advisers. Third, funds can be expensive. Many funds charge management fees up front, thereby reducing the amount of the initial investment. Others charge no management fees but do charge advisory incentive fees as a percentage of profits. Moreover, the amount of commissions charged for each trade varies considerably among funds.

A trader who is considering putting money in a futures fund should approach the choice very cautiously. If the fund has been trading for several months, its performance can be tracked through various reporting services.

MANAGED ACCOUNTS

Another popular vehicle for traders who lack the time or expertise to trade their own accounts is a professionally managed account. With this kind of program, the trader establishes a personal trading account with a broker but signs a limited power of attorney that transfers discretionary trading authority to a selected futures trader, who usually is a registered Commodity Trading Advisor (CTA) in the United States or who is registered with the appropriate agency in the various countries. All of the trading decisions are made by the CTA (money manager), but daily trade confirmations, monthly purchases and sale summaries are sent to the person in whose name the account was opened.

One advantage of an individual managed account is the liquidity of the investment. The account holder can take money out, add money, request that trading cease or close the account at any time, with proper notice being given. Another advantage is that the managed account can be monitored closely, allowing the account holder to close the account if he or she does not like the way the money manager is managing it.

Managed accounts do have disadvantages and, as with futures funds, must be approached very cautiously. First, the management fees can be excessive. Some money managers charge only an incentive fee as a percentage of the profits. This can range from 50 percent down to 10 percent. Others charge a management fee, which is often subtracted from the account each month, whether a profit is made or not.

Second, brokerage commissions vary significantly, from the equivalent of discount commissions to full-service commissions. If a money manager trades frequently, the cost of commissions can add up to a significant drain on the account. Third, the money manager who trades the account may have a trading style that conflicts with the personal nature of the account holder. For example, the manager may be a very cautious trader, careful to avoid large losses while being content to take small profits on a high frequency of good trades. The account holder, meanwhile, might like to see his or her account traded in a very aggressive manner, willing to sit through large drawdowns in the interest of catching highly profitable trades. Such a match, obviously, will lead to problems between the money manager and the account holder.

A fourth disadvantage of a managed account is that money managers often require rather large initial investments. Many expect at least $25,000, while some require $50,000 to open an account. A final danger is that the account holder is subject to unlimited risk. A major drawdown can deplete the account and leave the account holder liable for additional losses.

To avoid some of the potential pitfalls of a professionally managed account, the prior performance of a money manager should be evaluated very carefully. Each manager must provide a disclosure document to any person expressing an interest in a managed account. This document describes the trading strategy to be followed, the markets that will be traded, the minimum investment required and the fees to be charged.

Additionally, the disclosure details the money manager's track record for at least the past three years and sometimes longer. This track record must be evaluated carefully, as it will reveal a great deal about the trading style of the manager to see gains of at least one hundred percent per year to justify the risk of futures trading.

Just as important as the percentage of gain, then, is the percentage of loss. How many months of gain are there in relation to the months showing a loss? What is the largest loss in a month or a quarter? Is this a loss that would be tolerable? Is the total profitability for the year based on only one or two very profitable months? Or were there consistent profits month after month?

In evaluating a money manager , therefore, one must look at the trading consistency, the profitability over a reasonable span of time and the size of drawdowns versus the amount of profits. The resulting profile should be consistent with the prospective client's own goals and emotional profile. If the two don't match, then another manager should be chosen.

It should be noted that the rules and regulations governing managed accounts, money managers and reporting requirements differ markedly from one country to the next. Know the rules before you commit any funds.

DIRECTED ADVISORY HOTLINES

A relatively new service offered by some brokers is the directed hotline. With this service, a trader chooses a hotline advisory service he or she likes and then gives the broker the authority to call the hotline and place the trades exactly as recommended. This service works very much like a managed account, but rather than paying a management fee, the client pays a fee for the hotline service.

Many traders who don't have the time to do the necessary market research but still want to be actively involved in trading find that an advisory service, particularly one with a daily hotline recommendation, is an ideal solution. With this kind of service, the trader need only call the hotline number each day to find out which trades are being recommended, then call his or her broker to place the trades.

The advantage of this kind of service is that the trader has ultimate control over his or her account and can choose whether to make a trade and when to cease trading or resume trading. The trader can also select a discount broker, thus saving commission costs. The disadvantage is that many such services can be very expensive, and it may be difficult to find an advisory service that is compatible with the trader's own goals and trading style.

To choose the correct advisory service, a trader must be very careful to thoroughly examine the services being offered. Many hotlines make fantastic claims that, upon closer examination, tend to evaporate. Of critical concern is how specific are the recommendations. Does the hotline recommend what to buy, when to buy and a price to buy at? Or is the recommendation simply a vague statement open to interpretation and leaving all the decision making to the trader?

A second concern when choosing a hotline advisory is whether the timing of the recommendations permits real-time implementation. An advisory service is no good if the trades are signaled too late for implementation.

Another concern is whether the trader has the time and equipment to follow the recommendations. Some hotlines require order entry and update during the day. Others require real-time price information. Both situations may be unrealistic for a trader who works a very busy daytime job.

Finally, a good advisory service should also provide specific price or time objectives, stop loss points and specific follow-up procedures that will leave a trader with alternatives regardless of market conditions. Some services, unfortunately, are excellent at getting a trader into the market but vague and nonspecific about getting him or her out.

When checking the performance record of a hotline, it is important to note certain items:

1. Is the claimed performance based on unrealistic and hypothetical circumstances? Some hotlines, for instance, have been known, in their hypothetical trading, to take extremely large positions, to scale into the market holding losing positions, to purchase or sell extremely large numbers of contracts, or to add more margin to the hypothetical account so as to withstand most losing positions. Such a trading strategy is unrealistic for most small traders, who should not hold more than five to ten positions at any one time.

2. Look closely at the largest single loss, the largest single profit, the average loss, the average profit and the win–lose ratio to determine whether the hotline matches your preferred style. Some services make most of their profits on a few big trades while suffering a large number of small losses. Others make many small gains and few small losses. Still others encounter a few large gains and a few large drawdowns.

3. If the performance record is hypothetical, it is important that the amount deducted for commissions and bad fills be realistic. Generally, this should be in the neighborhood of $100 per trade.

4. Is the track record built on trading markets that are too volatile and risky for a small trader?

5. Does the hypothetical performance require a realistic level of margin? If a trader plans to trade an account of $20,000, the hotline cannot recommend trades that would exceed that margin without adversely affecting the performance of the trader's account.

As a final comment, the trader wishing to use the services of a carefully chosen hotline must be prepared to trade his or her account consistently with the recommendations.

Broker-Assisted and Broker-Discretionary Trading

The most common way many small traders experience the market is probably by trading a small account on the recommendation of a broker. Occasionally, a trader will give discretionary authority to a broker to trade the account without seeking approval on every trade.

If a trader chooses this approach, the same rules apply for checking the track record, because there likely will be no published figures to peruse. The trader must have confidence in the integrity of the broker. With broker-assisted and broker-discretionary trading, there is also a potential conflict of interest, because the broker's reward comes from the number of trades made, not the quality of the individual trades.

Summary and Conclusions

Given the rapid expansion of the international futures markets as well as the ongoing mergers of exchanges, the formation of the new exchanges and the addition of new trading vehicles (i.e., contras), it may be difficult for traders to remain abreast of changes in rules, procedures and acceptable order types. When in doubt (or even if not in doubt) ask your broker if there are any specific rules you need to be concerned about.

Chapter 10

TRADING SYSTEMS IN THE INTERNATIONAL MARKETS

Trading systems and timing indicators are vital tools for technically oriented futures traders. In order to use these methods successfully, they must be tested and validated. Even computers can yield misleading results, and traders should use caution before applying any system.

Merely testing a system and generating highly favorable hypothetical back-tested results does not guarantee the future success of that system. Statistics can easily be manipulated—systems can be (and are) curve-fitted, and results, unless realistic, will not reflect actual performance when the system is implemented. While many systems are developed to show optimum performance, systems must also be tested for the worst. Now that futures trading is truly an international enterprise, the use of trading systems will become more widespread. It is therefore essential that if you intend to use technical methods, indicators and/or systems in your trading, you understand them fully.

HOW TO EFFECTIVELY USE TRADING SYSTEMS IN THE EUROPEAN MARKETS

There is no mystery as to the effective use of trading systems in the foreign markets. As always, the rules of common sense, effective risk management and a diversified trading portfolio apply.

Traders who wish to participate in markets other than their own domestic futures markets are advised to investigate before they attempt to trade them using trading systems or other methods. In many cases, the availability of historical data for the purpose of back testing is limited. As a result, the ability to thoroughly test trading systems in some markets is also limited. In such cases, systems can be tested in related markets or by using cash market data. However, the conclusions derived from such tests may not be sufficiently valid to give traders the sense of security they need prior to committing funds. If testing cannot be done for reasons of limited history and other results are inconclusive, the trader is advised to avoid the given market(s). What's more, those who seek to trade large positions, whether for long-term trading or short-term trading, may find that the size of their positions affects the price at which they are able to buy and/or sell. This, too, will ultimately affect results negatively.

HOW TO DEVELOP A TRADING SYSTEM

Each trader has his or her unique style for developing and testing systems. While my approach may not be the best for you, I think you will benefit from examining my method. Whichever market (s) you plan to trade, I follow several steps.

STEP 1: THE IDEA OR CONCEPT

I begin with an idea or concept about the markets. The idea is usually based on an observation or a direct experience with the market. It is often an outgrowth of something I've read or something that has happened to me in trading. Some of my best systems and indicators have been derived from simple concepts. Here is a real example that will help explain my thought process: For many years traders, myself included, have been fascinated by closing-price patterns. It seems logical that if a market closes lower on eight, nine or even ten days in a row, the next day might bring a recovery. Furthermore, it seems logical that markets also exhibit closing-price patterns of other types, no matter where in the world these markets are traded.

To test the validity of my ideas about closing-price patterns, I consulted the available literature. Perry J. Kaufman,[1] reported results on numerous closing-price pattern analyses. I repeated the Kaufman studies using a historical database that spanned over twenty-five years in most U.S. markets, only to find that the results did not hold up under rigorous and long-term testing. This is not unusual. There is often an inverse relationship between the number of observations in a system test and the accuracy of the system or indicator. The more cases tested, the lower the percentage accuracy.

I found that only several patterns had been correct sixty percent or more of the time since the 1960s. The original Kaufman results were based on a limited historical test and were not, in my opinion, adequately validated. Still, I felt that there must be some validity to the idea that there were closing-price patterns unless, of course, the markets were totally random.

Step 2: The Idea Refined

Since my initial investigation yielded poor results, I decided to refine the technique by examining the closing-price patterns within the constraints of clearly defined uptrends or downtrends. I reasoned that, in an uptrend, the probability of more than several days of successively lower closing prices would be minimal.

Hence, a few days of lower closes should be followed by a higher closing price. I tested my idea and found, again, that there was no statistically valid relationship for futures trading.

---

[1]Kaufman, Perry J., *Trading Systems and Methods, Third Edition*. New York: John Wiley & Sons, 1998.

Nevertheless I was still convinced that my idea had face validity, but how to turn it into a potentially money-making system was still the unanswered question.

Step 3: Change Time Frames

I have found that some ideas may not work profitably in a *one*-day time frame, but that they can work well on an *intra*day basis. I changed the time frame and tested my idea on hourly and half-hourly data. The positive results of my test did not surprise me. Now, with these positive results, I needed to apply the same approach to various other time frames and with different patterns. I decided to test the following:

Buy after three, four, five or six successive higher closes.

Sell and reverse after three, four, five or six successive lower closes.

Test the above on most-active ten-minute, thirty-minute and sixty-minute data.

Step 4: Expand on the Basic Approach

Now that the basic model has proven potentially positive, it's time to refine it by applying stop losses, slippage and commission deductions and by improving time frames.

Step 5: Test It in Real Time

Naturally, the real-time portion of the test is the most important. It's one thing for a system to test well on historical data, but far more important to perform according to expectations in real time. Although it is best to be prepared for the worst-case scenario, you may be pleasantly surprised to find that some systems actually perform better in real time than in hypothetical back-testing.

By using the system in real time, you gain insights that would not ordinarily occur in hypothetical testing. Real-time application of the system will give you hints about refined entry and exit techniques within the basic parameters of your system.

HOW TO TEST A TRADING SYSTEM

Traders test systems for various reasons. Some test a system merely to say they've done so, only to disregard the outcome or to accept mediocre results, rationalizing the negative aspects of their "system." Other traders test systems in order to sell them to the public—their goal is to optimize systems in order to show maximum performance. Then there's the serious futures trader who tests systems to achieve several goals, among them:

- Determining whether a theory or hypothetical construct is valid and/or profitable in historical testing
- Summarizing the overall hypothetical back-tested performance of a system and analyzing its various aspects in order to isolate the strong and the weak
- Determining how different timing indicators interact with one another in order to produce an effective trading system
- Exploring the interaction of risk and reward variables (i.e., stop loss, trailing stop loss, position size, etc.) that would have returned the best overall performance with the smallest drawdown and overall risk

The purpose of testing a trading system is simply to find what will work best for you, based on what appears to have worked best in the past. A thorough test of your trading system should include at least the following information:

NUMBER OF YEARS ANALYZED. It is desirable to test as much data as possible, since many trading systems and indicators do not withstand the test of time. The farther back you test, the less effective most systems will be. Many developers test only ten years of historical data. You must make your own decision regarding the length of your test. In some cases, the test is limited because the data history on many new markets is restricted to no more than several years (or less in some cases).

NUMBER OF TRADES ANALYZED. More important than the number of years analyzed is the number of trades analyzed. You need not have many years of data if you have a large sample of trades. I recommend at least one hundred, provided your system will generate this number of trades in back-testing. Obviously, the more trades you test, the better. *Warning:* There is often a tendency to test fewer trades when you realize that the system is not holding up under back-testing.

Some traders argue that the factors underlying futures market trends twenty-five years ago were distinctly different from those during the past ten years. They feel that testing twenty-five years of data distorts the picture. If they are correct, how would we know when the current market forces change, telling us to change our trading systems? We are much better off finding systems that work in all types of markets. In order to compensate for a lack of futures data in some of the international markets, you can use cash market data if it is available.

MAXIMUM DRAWDOWN. This is one of the most important aspects of a trading system. A very large drawdown is a negative factor, since it eliminates most traders from the game well before the system would have turned in its positive performance. Since most traders are not well capitalized, they cannot withstand a large drawdown. However, drawdown is a function of account size. Obviously, a $15,000 drawdown in a $100,000 account is not unusual; however, the same drawdown in a $35,000 account is serious. You may decide to risk large drawdown in order to achieve outstanding performance, but this is your decision. Note that my figures here are in U.S. dollars. Make the necessary conversions to your currency of choice when considering the international markets.

Evaluate the source of the drawdown by examining the largest losing trade. If the majority of the drawdown occurred on only one trade, you will be better off than if the drawdown was spread out over numerous consecutive losses.

MAXIMUM CONSECUTIVE LOSSES. The impact of this performance variable on the trader is more psychological than anything else. An otherwise excellent trading system may result in losses on many trades in succession. Few traders can maintain their discipline through four or more successive losing trades. Even after the third loss, many traders are ready to abandon their system or find ways to change it. However, at times it is necessary to weather the storm of ten or more successive losses. If you know before you encounter such losses what the worst-case scenario has been, you will be prepared. That's why it's important for your system test to give you this information.

AVERAGE TRADE. This statistic will tell you what the average hypothetical trade has been. The average trade figure is important since it considers all profits, all losses, slippage and commission. You must make certain that when you test your system you deduct slippage and commission from your average trade. Commissions—even discount commissions—add up. Slippage is also an important factor to consider when determining system performance. As a rule of thumb, I recommend deducting between $75 and $100 per trade for slippage and commission. Once you do this, you will often significantly reduce the average trade figure. You must also pay close attention to the largest winning trade and the largest losing trade when evaluating the average trade.

LARGEST SINGLE LOSING TRADE. This important piece of information indicates how much of the maximum drawdown is the result of a single losing trade. This information allows you to see how large the average losing trade has been and to adjust the initial stop loss when you retest the system. If, for example, the average losing trade was $1,055 and the largest single losing trade was $8,466, it's obvious that a good portion of the average losing trade was a function of the largest loser. This, in turn, tells you that if you had a better way of managing the large loser (in hindsight, of course), your overall system performance would have been considerably better. With this information in hand, I strongly recommend close examination of the actual trade that resulted in the single largest loss, especially when this loss is clearly much higher than the average losing trade.

Another question to ask is: *Why was the largest single losing trade so much larger than the stop loss selected?* A single largest losing trade that is several times larger than your selected stop loss, points to a potential problem, perhaps with the system test. You must investigate further in such cases. Remember that a stop loss does not guarantee you will be stopped out of your trade at the given price. Stop-loss orders become market orders when they are hit. As a result, the actual price of exit can, at times, be much worse than the stop-loss price you have entered as your order. Note also that in markets that have daily trading limits, a stop loss might not be executed before the market moves to its daily limit and, as a result, your stop might not be executed until the next day at a much worse price than you had anticipated.

LARGEST SINGLE WINNING TRADE. Perhaps more important than the largest single losing trade is the largest single winning trade. If, for example, your hypothetical profits total $96,780, and $33,810 of this is attributed to only one trade, your average trade figure is distorted. It's often a good idea to remove this one trade from the overall results and recompute them in order to show the performance without this extraordinary winner. You may find that the system you have tested is mediocre, perhaps even a loser, when this trade has been eliminated from the performance summary. If you can wait ten years for the one big trade, then use the system—but I don't advise it. What you're looking for in any system is consistency. In the long run, that is far more important than one or two extremely large winning trades.

Performance summaries will show the largest single winning long and short trades. Frequently, these two trades alone account for a considerable portion of the net profits using that system. While some traders feel that this somehow diminishes the value of the system, I disagree. As long as at least one-half of the overall system performance is due to trades other than the largest single winning long and short trade combined, the system is valid. As far as numbers are concerned, I would not use any system that does not show at least $100 average profit per trade, after deducting reasonable slippage and commission as well as the largest single long and short winners.

More important, because a large portion of the profits in many systems derives from a very small number of trades, it is imperative that you follow the rules on each and every trade as closely as possible. Trading systems are not money machines; they don't grind out one profit after another. They make their money on the bottom line. There are many losers and few winners. The losers are kept in check by using money management stop losses that must, in most cases, be reasonably large. And the winners, only a few of which are very large, make the game worth the candle. The trader who can't stick with a position, or let it ride, is the trader who will be sorely disappointed with the results because the big winners will be cut short.

PERCENTAGE WINNING TRADE. This statistic is not nearly so important as you might think. In actuality few systems result in more than sixty-five percent winning trades; and the more trades in your sample, the smaller this figure will be. Systems that are correct as little as thirty percent of the time can still be good systems; systems that are accurate as much as eighty percent of the time can be bad systems. It's easy to see that even a high degree of accuracy with a large average losing trade and small average winning trade does not make a good system.

OPTIMIZATION AND RETESTING. There has been considerable controversy about trading system optimization. What exactly is wrong with optimizing systems? Can you go too far? Is there a happy medium? Read on.

WHAT IS OPTIMIZATION?

The real issues in system optimization are complex, and they've been exacerbated by the tendency of systems developers to optimize their programs beyond any reasonable degree. To optimize a system is to discover the parameters that provide the best results in hypothetical back-testing. In other words, optimization is a form of discovering what would have produced the best results using numerous if–then scenarios. Before low-cost computer hardware and software, optimization was a long and laborious procedure. To discover the best fit, the systems developer would need to repeatedly backtrack and test several variables. If the system parameters were numerous, the process was virtually impossible. Computers have made this a quick and efficient task.

Such ease of testing and optimizing is both good and bad. On one hand, it allows traders to develop, test and refine (i.e., optimize) systems much more rapidly. On the other hand, it has opened the door to what is called curve fitting. The simple fact is that the powerful system-testing programs now available allow traders as well as systems vendors to repeatedly test a host of timing variables, stop losses and other risk-management devices in order to determine which combinations would have produced the best results. In effect, this procedure fits the best parameters on past history to produce the best hypothetical results. However, the conclusions reached by such methods are often specious and can be deceptive.

The trader who tests and retests to find the best fit will eventually reach his or her goal, but the goal itself may be nothing more than a reflection of the curve-fitted results. Tests tell us what has worked in the past, but may not reveal anything worthwhile about the future. Since the past is not a carbon copy of the future, the optimized parameters may not work. The more parameters in the decision-making model, the less likely they are to work in the future. Overly optimized results lead to false conclusions, which will likely mean losses.

A RATIONAL APPROACH TO DEVELOPING YOUR SYSTEM

Your trading system should have no more than four to six variables. You should search for the best combination of entry and exit variables as well as a reasonable combination of stop-loss and trailing stop-loss amounts. But this is where the optimization should end. The more variables you build into the system, the less likely it is that future performance will achieve your expectations.

MARKET PERSONALITY

Another aspect of system development relates to market personality—a topic that has received little attention from most traders and market analysts. Rather than heavily optimizing a system, I recommend tailoring your system to the personality characteristics of the individual markets, provided that such characteristics exist and that they are sufficiently stable. Given the fact that some of the international markets are relatively new, it is difficult at this time to evaluate their specific "personality traits." However, in the case of markets such as stock-index futures, interest-rate futures, energy futures and grain futures, the markets will likely have similar traits to other world markets that have already established their characteristics.

SYSTEMATIC ENTRY AND UNSYSTEMATIC EXIT

Although some purists will vehemently disagree with me, my words come from the hard knocks of experience. I've found that when it comes to system trading, a good case can be made for systematic market entry based purely on signals generated by the system and for less mechanical exit of positions. That's right, I'm suggesting a hybrid approach to systems trading.

Those who disagree will claim that by not using the system exactly as tested, you will not be trading the system you tested and the results will, therefore, be totally meaningless; your backtesting will be for naught. They'll claim that you might as well trade no system at all. But these are generally the same individuals who will stick doggedly to the system when it is clear that the fundamental situation has changed dramatically. Either unprecedented events are affecting the market or market conditions are not at all similar to those that existed when the system was tested. I believe that such extraordinary cases call for extraordinary measures. I am not suggesting that you make an exit decision based on visceral factors. However, I am suggesting that you may want to exit based on technical indicators that were not part of the original system.

I offer this alternative method of exit because I firmly believe that the experience of a trader counts for something. I am absolutely certain, given my years of market experience, that traders learn much more than their systems, indicators and methods. They learn the internal language of the ticker, the intuitive message of the market that cannot be easily defined in purely mechanical or operational terms. To ignore such valuable knowledge would be a waste of valuable resources. I do not claim that traders become intuitive about the markets through a learning process, but I do not consider the terms "learning" and "intuition" to be mutually exclusive. Take what you have learned from thousands of hours of market experience, what you have learned from your losses and what you've learned from not following your instincts, and use this knowledge—but use it at the right time.

Your intuition won't always be right. You will at times get out too soon, but you'll learn from this experience as well. If you fear losing your position in the market, the answer is simple. When you enter a market, do so with twice the position you usually take. Exit one position strictly by the trading rules, and exit the second system on other indicators if the situation calls for it. See how your results compare.

Perhaps an example will help illustrate my point of view. Let's assume you have entered a long trade in FTSE-100 futures based on an exponential moving average system. As is often the case with good positions, your feelings upon entry are tentative, you're not convinced that this will be a profitable trade, but you are committed to the system and you follow the signal. Soon the market moves in your favor and you're rewarded. The market then begins to move strongly in your favor, and your moving average system is not even close to a possible reversal signal. As you know, moving averages (and most timing signals) are lagging indicators. The higher and faster the market moves, the more the indicators lag. Naturally, you're subject to the trader's perennial fear—what if the market turns sharply lower now, and by the time you exit your trade you've given up too much potential profit? You're somewhat comforted by the fact that your system has a trailing stop loss, yet you fear that by the time your trailing stop loss is triggered, the slippage will be significant and you'll give back too much profit. A trailing stop loss is a procedure by which your stop loss is changed as a market moves in your favor, in order to retain as much profit as possible.

What you're experiencing is not unique. Most (if not all) traders are victims of the same dilemma. What to do? Get out now and cut your profit short, or stay with the system religiously and risk giving back too much profit?

Continuing now with our hypothetical example. Without warning, exciting bullish news develops. The market skyrockets. Your position gains several hundred points within hours after the market opens; it's gained more in several hours than it has in the last three weeks and your open profit has more than doubled within hours after the opening. Now what do you do? You know, given your experience with the markets, that bullish news is often associated with market tops. You know that such dramatic upmoves are inspired by emotion and that this could easily be a *blow-off* top. But you're "locked into" a system. Again the dilemma tugs at your trading conscience, and this time harder than before.

What if you get out too soon? What if this is just the start of another leg on the upside? What if this bullish news is just the beginning of something much more bullish? What if you lose your position and can't get back in? What if you break the rules now and it becomes a habit?

Balancing the logic of following your trading system are the lessons of experience. Is there a happy medium? Can you exit the trade early using another indicator? While dyed-in-the-wool systems followers would object, I recommend you use another timing method to exit the trade if you've decided that a top is imminent.

Another alternative is to exit part of your position. This procedure represents a happy medium between system following and using your market experience to your advantage. Whether this method works for you can only be determined by trying it.

Combining Systems

Another important aspect of system development and testing is the hybridization of systems. For too many years traders have given equal weight to entry and exit signals. In other words, they consider the inverse of a buy signal to be a sell signal. This may not, however, be the most effective approach.

My experience has taught me that buy signals, sell signals and exit signals are not all equal parts of the same methodology. Market tops have distinctly different characteristics than do market bottoms, and downtrends have different characteristics than do sideways or uptrends. Markets top more dramatically than they bottom, and markets drop faster than they rise. A dual moving average crossover buy signal based on a nine-period and eighteen-period moving average will not necessarily work best as a sell signal when used in reverse.

It may very well be that the best combination for buy signals is a nine-day and an eighteen-day moving average crossover, and for sell signals, the best combination may be a seven-day and sixteen-day moving average crossover. It may also be true that when a reversal of the nine-day and eighteen-day moving average parameters occurs, the system may be best off going flat, if a seven-day and sixteen-day sell signal has not already occurred. Remember that my examples are hypothetical; you can easily develop combinations of your own. When you do, use a more sensitive indicator on the sell side, since sell signals and bear markets tend to develop more quickly and decline more quickly than bull markets rise.

KEY TRADING SYSTEMS AND HOW THEY WORK IN INTERNATIONAL MARKETS

The use of a trading system can significantly improve results by adding an objective procedure to your trading. This is no less true in the international markets than it is in the U.S. markets. Professional traders have realized the importance of using an objective approach and have developed numerous mechanical systems for this purpose. As a result, there has been a growing trend toward the use of mechanical-trading systems. Competition in the field of computer manufacturing has resulted in the declining cost of computer systems. Affordable hardware and software have opened the door to intensive computer research on systems and methods. Armed with sufficient historical data and an effective program for developing and back-testing systems, the average trader can develop highly effective trading methods, provided the basic rules of systems development are followed closely. I believe that such an approach is not only viable but also necessary in order to maintain a disciplined approach. I have developed and back-tested a number of systems for the international markets.

These systems are based on systems that were originally developed for use in the U.S. markets. With some small adjustments, they appear to have merit in the European and Asian markets as well. Figures 10.1 through 10.3 illustrate several such systems. They were developed on Omega TradeStation™ software. Note that the results are shown in U.S. dollars with the dollar exchange rate approximated for the market tested. Naturally this will change as exchange rates fluctuate.

FIGURE 10.1

DUAL ORBIT TRADING SYSTEM BACK-TEST RESULTS ON FTSE-100 1984–2000

Performance Summary: All Trades

Total net profit	$39320.00	Open position P/L	$520.00
Gross profit	$68480.00	Gross loss	$-29160.00
Total # of trades	91	Percent profitable	62%
Number winning trades	56	Number losing trades	35
Largest winning trade	$10870.00	Largest losing trade	$-2100.00
Average winning trade	$1222.86	Average losing trade	$-833.14
Ratio avg win/avg loss	1.47	Avg trade (win & loss)	432.09
Max consec. winners	11	Max consec. losers	4
Avg # bars in winners	49	Avg # bars in losers	16
Max intraday drawdown	$-6846.00		
Profit factor	2.35	Max # contracts held	1
Account size required	$6846.00	Return on account	574%

Performance Summary: Long Trades

Total net profit	$44704.00	Open position P/L	$0.00
Gross profit	$52474.00	Gross loss	$-7770.00
Total # of trades	40	Percent profitable	78%
Number winning trades	31	Number losing trades	9
Largest winning trade	$10870.00	Largest losing trade	$-2100.00
Average winning trade	$1692.71	Average losing trade	$-863.33
Ratio avg win/avg loss	1.96	Avg trade (win & loss)	1117.60
Max consec. winners	7	Max consec. losers	2
Avg # bars in winners	71	Avg # bars in losers	17
Max intraday drawdown	$-2920.00		
Profit factor	6.75	Max # contracts held	1
Account size required	$2920.00	Return on account	1531%

Performance Summary: Short Trades

Total net profit	$-5384.00	Open position P/L	$520.00
Gross profit	$16006.00	Gross loss	$-21390.00
Total # of trades	51	Percent profitable	49%
Number winning trades	25	Number losing trades	26
Largest winning trade	$6230.00	Largest losing trade	$-2100.00
Average winning trade	$640.24	Average losing trade	$-822.69
Ratio avg win/avg loss	0.78	Avg trade (win & loss)	-105.57
Max consec. winners	5	Max consec. losers	4
Avg # bars in winners	20	Avg # bars in losers	16
Max intraday drawdown	$-10733.00		
Profit factor	0.75	Max # contracts held	1
Account size required	$10733.00	Return on account	-50%

FIGURE 10.2

2000ST BREAKOUT SYSTEM BACK-TEST RESULTS ON FTSE-100 1984–1999

Performance Summary: All Trades

Total net profit	$38097.20	Open position P/L	$0.00
Gross profit	$84165.59	Gross loss	$-46068.40
Total # of trades	82	Percent profitable	66%
Number winning trades	54	Number losing trades	28
Largest winning trade	$9207.40	Largest losing trade	$-3584.60
Average winning trade	$1558.62	Average losing trade	$-1645.30
Ratio avg win/avg loss	0.95	Avg trade (win & loss)	464.60
Max consec. winners	8	Max consec. losers	4
Avg # bars in winners	38	Avg # bars in losers	27
Max intraday drawdown	$-12647.00		
Profit factor	1.83	Max # contracts held	1
Account size required	$12647.00	Return on account	301%

Performance Summary: Long Trades

Total net profit	$42845.00	Open position P/L	$0.00
Gross profit	$51680.20	Gross loss	$-8835.20
Total # of trades	41	Percent profitable	76%
Number winning trades	31	Number losing trades	10
Largest winning trade	$8649.80	Largest losing trade	$-3486.20
Average winning trade	$1667.10	Average losing trade	$-883.52
Ratio avg win/avg loss	1.89	Avg trade (win & loss)	1045.00
Max consec. winners	9	Max consec. losers	2
Avg # bars in winners	42	Avg # bars in losers	28
Max intraday drawdown	$-3797.80		
Profit factor	5.85	Max # contracts held	1
Account size required	$3797.80	Return on account	1128%

Performance Summary: Short Trades

Total net profit	$-4747.80	Open position P/L	$0.00
Gross profit	$32485.40	Gross loss	$-37233.20
Total # of trades	41	Percent profitable	56%
Number winning trades	23	Number losing trades	18
Largest winning trade	$9207.40	Largest losing trade	$-3584.60
Average winning trade	$1412.41	Average losing trade	$-2068.51
Ratio avg win/avg loss	0.68	Avg trade (win & loss)	-115.80
Max consec. winners	4	Max consec. losers	2
Avg # bars in winners	33	Avg # bars in losers	26
Max intraday drawdown	$-21252.40		
Profit factor	0.87	Max # contracts held	1
Account size required	$21252.40	Return on account	-22%

FIGURE 10.3

ACCUMULATION DISTRIBUTION SYSTEM BACK-TEST RESULTS ON FTSE-100 1984–1999

Performance Summary: All Trades

Total net profit	$59178.01	Open position P/L	$0.00
Gross profit	$105140.81	Gross loss	$-45962.80
Total # of trades	90	Percent profitable	76%
Number winning trades	68	Number losing trades	22
Largest winning trade	$15291.80	Largest losing trade	$-3387.80
Average winning trade	$1546.19	Average losing trade	$-2089.22
Ratio avg win/avg loss	0.74	Avg trade (win & loss)	657.53
Max consec. winners	26	Max consec. losers	3
Avg # bars in winners	32	Avg # bars in losers	26
Max intraday drawdown	$-13204.60		
Profit factor	2.29	Max # contracts held	1
Account size required	$13204.60	Return on account	448%

Performance Summary: Long Trades

Total net profit	$65150.61	Open position P/L	$0.00
Gross profit	$94366.41	Gross loss	$-29215.80
Total # of trades	67	Percent profitable	81%
Number winning trades	54	Number losing trades	13
Largest winning trade	$15291.80	Largest losing trade	$-3387.80
Average winning trade	$1747.53	Average losing trade	$-2247.37
Ratio avg win/avg loss	0.78	Avg trade (win & loss)	972.40
Max consec. winners	21	Max consec. losers	3
Avg # bars in winners	38	Avg # bars in losers	33
Max intraday drawdown	$-9730.00		
Profit factor	3.23	Max # contracts held	1
Account size required	$9730.00	Return on account	670%

Performance Summary: Short Trades

Total net profit	$-5972.60	Open position P/L	$0.00
Gross profit	$10774.40	Gross loss	$-16747.00
Total # of trades	23	Percent profitable	61%
Number winning trades	14	Number losing trades	9
Largest winning trade	$2352.20	Largest losing trade	$-3387.80
Average winning trade	$769.60	Average losing trade	$-1860.78
Ratio avg win/avg loss	0.41	Avg trade (win & loss)	-259.68
Max consec. winners	6	Max consec. losers	4
Avg # bars in winners	8	Avg # bars in losers	15
Max intraday drawdown	$-13820.80		
Profit factor	0.64	Max # contracts held	1
Account size required	$13820.80	Return on account	-43%

JB GAP SYSTEM

This system is based on a simple concept originally popularized by Larry Williams.[2] If a market opens above its previous day's high, you sell short on a stop as the market falls back down below its previous daily high. You exit either on a stop loss, or on the close the same day or on the Nth profitable opening. (Nth refers to the active day of the first profitable opening. The "Nth day" could be the next day, two days later, three days later, etc.) Rather than exit on the first profitable opening, my method exits on the Nth profitable opening. N and X are test variables determined by system optimization. The actual values as determined by back-testing are shown in the text that follows. In addition, my variation on the Williams method takes into consideration gaps that may occur above or below X days back (as opposed to the previous day). Figure 10.4 shows the results of my JB GAP system on the FTSE-100 index. As you can see, the results of this system test are impressive. Accuracy is at seventy-seven percent with an average trade of US$985. The system has a number of different elements:

Long Entry Bars: The number of days for a gap on which to enter a long trade [1]

Short Entry Bars: The number of days for a gap on which to enter a short trade [20]

Short Entry Ticks: The size of penetration on which to go short [2]

Long Entry Ticks: The size of the penetration on which to go long [2]

Minimum Up Gap: The smallest gap up on which to trigger a sell [8]

Minimum Gap Down: The smallest gap down on which to trigger a buy [19]

---

[2]This method is described more clearly in *Short-Term Secrets to Long-Term Trading* by Larry Williams. New York: McGraw-Hill, 1999.

FIGURE 10.4

JB GAP SYSTEM BACK-TEST RESULTS ON FTSE-100 1984–1999

Performance Summary: All Trades

Total net profit	$49359.00	Open position P/L	$-1452.00
Gross profit	$126872.00	Gross loss	$-77513.00
Total # of trades	199	Percent profitable	70%
Number winning trades	140	Number losing trades	59
Largest winning trade	$7273.00	Largest losing trade	$-3287.00
Average winning trade	$906.23	Average losing trade	$-1313.78
Ratio avg win/avg loss	0.69	Avg trade (win & loss)	248.04
Max consec. winners	14	Max consec. losers	3
Avg # bars in winners	18	Avg # bars in losers	19
Max intraday drawdown	$-10751.00		
Profit factor	1.64	Max # contracts held	1
Account size required	$10751.00	Return on account	459%

Performance Summary: Long Trades

Total net profit	$47833.00	Open position P/L	$-1452.00
Gross profit	$99253.00	Gross loss	$-51420.00
Total # of trades	113	Percent profitable	81%
Number winning trades	91	Number losing trades	22
Largest winning trade	$7273.00	Largest losing trade	$-3287.00
Average winning trade	$1090.69	Average losing trade	$-2337.27
Ratio avg win/avg loss	0.47	Avg trade (win & loss)	423.30
Max consec. winners	17	Max consec. losers	3
Avg # bars in winners	25	Avg # bars in losers	32
Max intraday drawdown	$-12255.00		
Profit factor	1.93	Max # contracts held	1
Account size required	$12255.00	Return on account	390%

Performance Summary: Short Trades

Total net profit	$1526.00	Open position P/L	$0.00
Gross profit	$27619.00	Gross loss	$-26093.00
Total # of trades	86	Percent profitable	57%
Number winning trades	49	Number losing trades	37
Largest winning trade	$3281.00	Largest losing trade	$-3057.00
Average winning trade	$563.65	Average losing trade	$-705.22
Ratio avg win/avg loss	0.80	Avg trade (win & loss)	17.74
Max consec. winners	6	Max consec. losers	5
Avg # bars in winners	5	Avg # bars in losers	11
Max intraday drawdown	$-10719.00		
Profit factor	1.06	Max # contracts held	1
Account size required	$10719.00	Return on account	14%

I also optimized the stop (US$2950) and the number of days to exit (29). The parameters are shown in the brackets after each of the variables above. (I deducted $75 for slippage and commission.)

VOLATILITY BREAKOUT SYSTEMS

These systems depend on market breakouts from a trading range, based on the idea that markets generally move sideways. When they break out decisively from their nontrending patterns, they are likely to make large moves. Figure 10.2 shows the results of my back test with FTSE-100, using my volatility system based on the following parameters:

TIME WINDOW: Determine by back-testing a window of time during which prices are monitored for a possible breakout. The window is usually no less than three days and no more than eighteen days. The more volatile a market, the shorter the window should be.

TRADING RANGE: Determine the average trading range for the time window.

PENETRATION LEVEL: Determine a percentage penetration of the average range in the window. Typically a fifty-percent to one hundred fifty-percent penetration above or below the range will be used to trigger a move.

TREND FILTER: Use a momentum trend filter. Take breakouts only if they are in the direction of the trend as determined by the filter.

STOP LOSS AND TRAILING STOP LOSS: These are standard for most systems. For those who are unfamiliar with the development of stop-loss and trailing stop-loss procedures, I recommend the use of an optimization method.

SUMMARY AND CONCLUSIONS

Trading systems and methods are worthwhile and viable on the international markets as long as the rules of system development and testing are followed. This chapter provided a few directions for testing as well as back-testing results from a number of systems. The systems I have provided are merely a very small sample of what can be developed for markets other than those in the United States. In fact, the systems in this chapter were originally developed for the U.S. markets but altered and back-tested on some of the international markets. The TradeStation™ code for these systems appears in Appendix III.

Chapter 11

DAY TRADING THE INTERNATIONAL MARKETS

Effectively day trading in any market mandates a number of prerequisites. They are:

- Sufficient trading volume to allow for ease of position entry and exit.
- Sufficient tick size to allow for profit potential above and beyond commissions and slippage.
- Sufficient intraday volatility—necessary for day-trading opportunities to present themselves.
- Efficient execution of orders to facilitate prompt market entry and exit.
- Availability of viable trading systems and methods to allow for effective day trading.

Unfortunately, there are not too many current markets that meet all of these criteria. Among the markets that do are those located in the United States (various exchanges), the London International Financial Futures Exchange (LIFFE), some of the Japanese markets, some markets at the European Futures Exchange (EUREX) and the ParisBourse SA. Other markets are still relatively new and do not trade sufficient volume to allow for effective day trading. Given the numerous changes in trading volume, I recommend you consult current volume statistics or your broker to determine which markets are the most active.

As an example, consider the differences between the FTSE contract and the S&P 500 futures contract traded in Chicago. Figure 11.1 shows both markets on the same chart. As you can clearly see, the FTSE contract trades between 25,000 and 50,000 contracts daily (although there have been spikes up to 110,000 contracts daily). The S&P trading volume, however, is easily two and a half times as large (with spikes up to 225,000 contracts daily). The Euribor, at the EUREX, trades only about 5,000 contracts on average. On the other hand, the EuroBund, also at the EUREX, trades about 950,000 contracts daily. As you can see, there are significant differences in liquidity, which must be considered by the day trader. This does not mean that the lower volume contracts cannot be day traded; however, it suggests caution due to poor liquidity.

TECHNIQUES FOR DAY TRADING THE INTERNATIONAL MARKETS

There are literally hundreds of techniques available for the purpose of day trading. Details on such methods can be found in three of my books, *The Compleat Day Trader*, *The Compleat Day Trader II* and *Strategies for the Electronic Futures Trader*[1]. Among the more popular techniques are the uses of momentum and/or my thirty-minute breakout method. Both are described in this chapter. Other indicators useful in day trading are described in Chapter 6; some of the systems described in Chapter 10 can also be adapted to day trading.

[1]Bernstein, Jake, *The Compleat Day Trader—Trading Systems, Strategies, Timing Indicators and Analytical Methods* (227 pages). New York: McGraw-Hill, 1995.

Bernstein, Jake, *The Compleat Day Trader II—Covers Advanced Day Trading Techniques, Features Proven Strategies for Precision Trading* (232 pages). New York: McGraw-Hill, 1998.

Bernstein, Jake, *Strategies for the Electronic Futures Trader* (237 pages). New York: McGraw-Hill, 2000.

FIGURE 11.1

FTSE & S&P 500

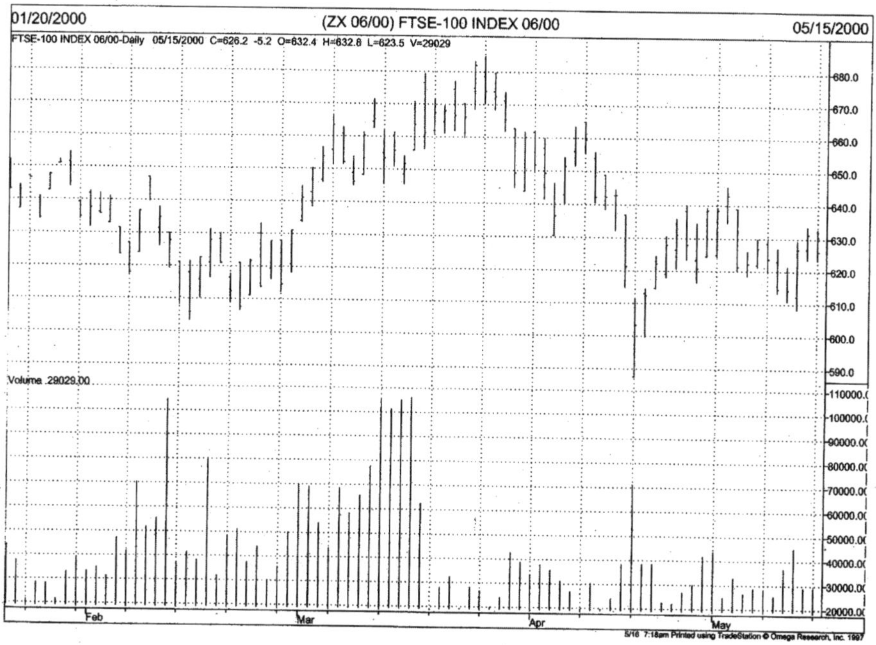

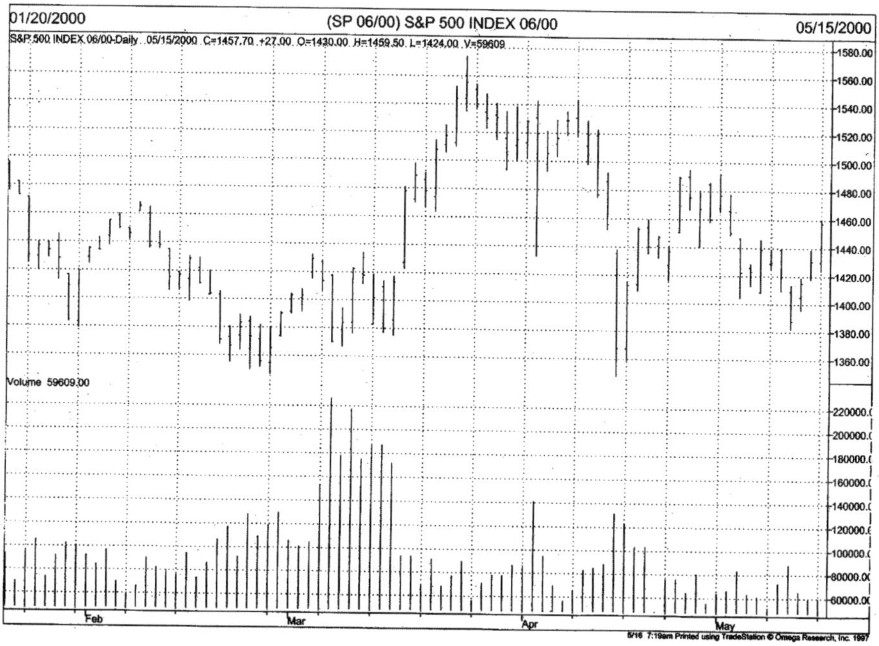

Frequently trading systems that generate their signals using daily price data can be adapted for use with intraday data. This would require changes in the system structure—all of which are relatively simple to accomplish. Note, however, that systems initially designed for day trading do not necessarily transfer successfully to longer-term trading.

MOMENTUM (MOM)

Momentum is a rate-of-change indicator, since it provides you with an idea of trend strength. To calculate the one-day momentum (MOM), simply subtract today's price from yesterday's price. Therefore, if today's price is \$52 and yesterday's price is \$52, today's one-day momentum is +0. To calculate a two-day momentum index, subtract the price two days ago from today's price. For calculating three-, four- and/or five-day momentum, follow the same procedure.

When momentum is moving down very quickly, it is an indication that prices are changing rapidly on the downside; when momentum is rising rapidly, it is an indication that the market is trending higher strongly. Momentum can be used as a trading indicator by applying some simple rules. I must stress at the outset, however, that momentum is not a system, but a trading technique that you will need to work with and refine.

THIRTY-MINUTE BREAKOUT

Of all the day-trading methods I have found or developed during my thirty-plus years in the markets, few can compare to the thirty-minute breakout (30MBO) either in terms of its simplicity or in terms of its ability to grab the "big ones." But do not forget that day trading is a two-way street: It can reward handsomely or sting painfully. While the 30MBO is simple to use, understand and implement, it also requires the trader to do the two things that are most difficult for traders to do. Specifically, it requires traders to buy or sell on a breakout to new high ground for the day or to new low ground for the day, and thereafter to maintain their position until the end of the day, unless stopped out.

The 30MBO rules are as follows:

1. Do not enter any trades for the first thirty minutes of trading in the markets for which the 30MBO is being used.
2. Make note of the high and low prices for the first thirty minutes of trading.
3. *After* the first thirty minutes, buy if the ending price of the thirty-minute interval is greater than the high of the first thirty-minute price bar by a predetermined number of ticks.
4. *After* the first thirty minutes, sell short if the ending price of the thirty-minute interval is less than the low of the first thirty-minute price bar by a predetermined number of ticks.
5. Understand that your stop loss can be either a predetermined signal (i.e., fail-safe or "dead" stop) or the opposite signal (i.e., a sell signal after an initial buy signal, or vice versa).
6. Use a trailing stop loss to follow up an open position, since it has reached a given profit objective.
7. Liquidate your current position in the event of a stop loss on a reversing signal and establish an opposite one.
8. Exit your trade at the end of the day either several minutes before the close of trading or MOC (market on close).
9. Trade only in active markets.
10. Take your profit if a long trade moves limit up in your favor; if a short trade moves limit down in your favor, then take your profit (assuming that the market you are trading has a daily trading limit).

Figure 11.2 shows an example of the 30MBO in FTSE. No system, method or indicator can be effective at all times. The 30MBO in its present state of refinement is not different from other methods; it is not a panacea or the Holy Grail. It is merely

FIGURE 11.2

THIRTY-MINUTE BREAKOUT FTSE

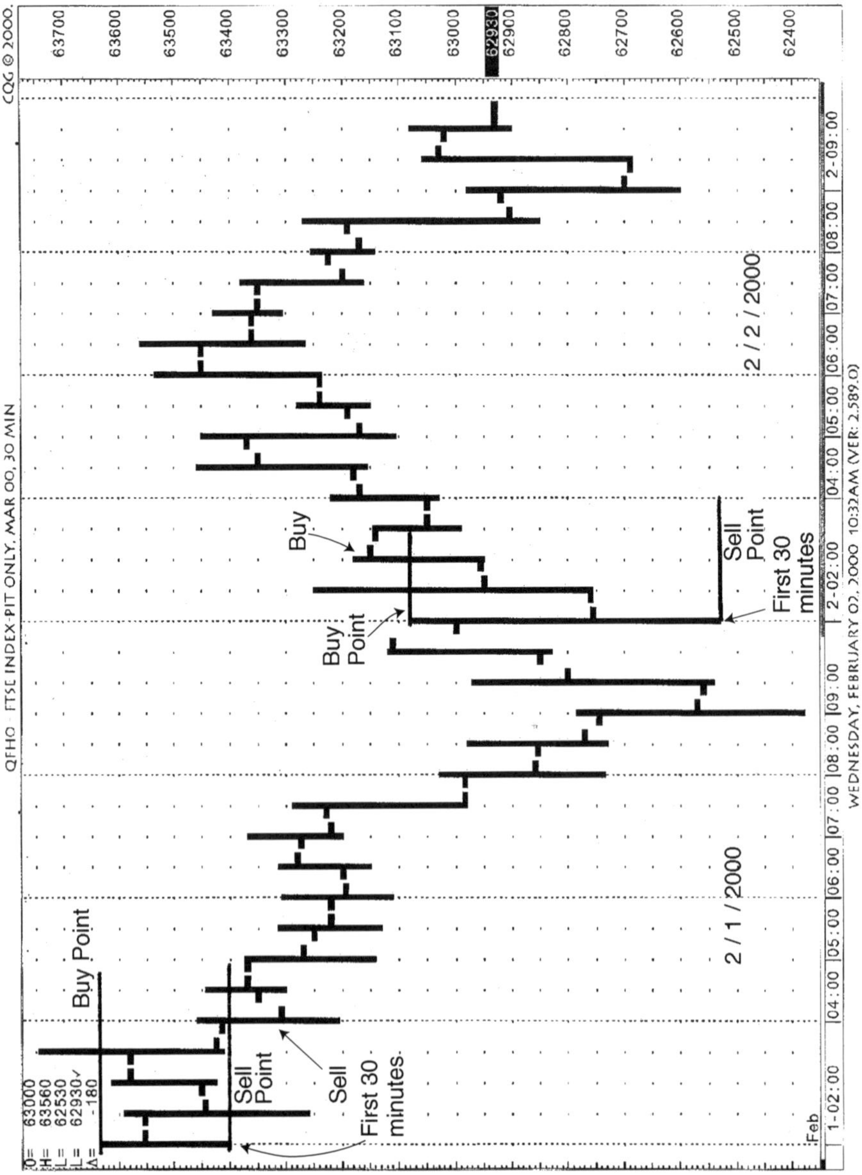

a way of interpreting and dealing with the reality of the markets. Systems take losses when they're wrong. The further inescapable reality is that systems can and will occasionally be wrong on a successive number of trades.

INTERNATIONAL MARKETS SUITABLE FOR DAY TRADING

Since many of the world markets are still in their formative stages, trading volume tends to be small when compared with that of markets in the United States. With U.S. Treasury bonds trading about 600,000 contracts daily and S&P futures at about 104,000 contracts daily, other markets look small by comparison. A look at trading volumes at the LIFFE, EUREX and ParisBourse SA recently (January 2000) yielded the following trading volume figures in number of contracts traded daily:

Italian Government Bond	190	(unsuitable for day trading)
FTSE	30,000	
Japanese Bond	3,000	(unsuitable for day trading)
Short Sterling	160,000	
Gilt	25,000	
CAC-40	130,000	
EuroBund	800,000	
DAX	56,000	

Due to these limitations, there are relatively few markets that are viable day-trading vehicles. However, the fact that these markets do allow for day trading should allow traders to broaden their perspectives. Here is a list of markets, in order of preference, that I feel are currently viable (excluding U.S. markets) for off-the-floor day trading:

FTSE-100 Stock Index (LIFFE)
Short Sterling (LIFFE)
Euribor (EUREX)
Gilt (LIFFE)
DAX Index (LIFFE & EUREX)
CAC-40 (ParisBourse SA)

As trading volume on the international exchanges increases, more markets will become viable for day trading. The growing turmoil in world economies and currency relationships virtually guarantees an active day-trading market for many years to come. I consider trading volume of at least 15,000 contracts daily (on the average) to be a reasonable benchmark when selecting markets to be day traded.

WHY DAY TRADE THE INTERNATIONAL MARKETS?

Although traders in the United States are fortunate to have some of the best day-trading markets in the world at their disposal, the time is not far off when other markets will challenge the U.S. leadership in market activity. The LIFFE exchange in London is now the world's third most-active exchange with an impressive volume of trading. Many of the markets traded at the LIFFE are viable for day trading by U.S. traders. (This will even improve if their trading hours are changed.)

Summary and Conclusions

In addition to the active markets traded in the United States, a number of markets in other countries are suitable for day trading. My experience with the active international markets leads me to believe that the systems, methods and timing indicators I am currently using will continue to perform well in these markets. In this chapter, I have reviewed two timing indicators and day-trading methods as well as discussed which markets are currently appropriate for day trading. As always, the individual trader must determine which markets offer the greatest profit potential with the lowest risk and the greatest liquidity.

Chapter 12

MAKING THE INTERNATIONAL FUTURES MARKETS WORK FOR YOU

What you have read in this book is intended to serve as an introduction to the international futures markets. I have attempted to achieve several goals in the preceding chapters:

- To introduce the basic concepts underlying futures trading and the futures markets;
- To explain the economic functions of futures trading;
- To explain the roles of speculators, hedgers, commercial interests and brokers in the futures markets;
- To provide a general understanding of fundamental and technical analysis and to give examples of each; and
- To highlight the various aspects of the futures industry as well as different opportunities available to you as an independent trader, broker or market analyst.

HOW TO IMPROVE YOUR ODDS OF SUCCESS AS A TRADER

In order to achieve a thorough understanding of this challenging but rewarding field, I suggest you follow these steps:

1. *Learn more.* Throughout this book I have stressed the value and, indeed, the necessity of education. If you plan to seri-

ously pursue a job in the area of futures trading or if you plan to trade for your own account, you must learn as much as you can. There are literally hundreds of books for beginners and advanced students and many classroom courses you can take.

2. *Get your feet wet.* Once you've taken the time to learn more from books or course work, get involved in futures trading. Open a small account and trade for yourself or work with a broker. Don't risk a great deal, particularly if you can't afford it. Consider the money you put into your account as part of your tuition. If you lose it, you've helped further your education; if you win, you've learned something as well as having something to show for it other than just the learning itself.

3. *Ask questions.* Be sure to ask questions. If you know other traders, use them as resources to learn more. If you open a trading account, ask your broker questions. You'll learn more by asking questions than you will from any book. Best of all, the answers usually won't cost you anything!

4. *Visit a broker's office.* You can learn a great deal by watching brokers do their work. If you have the opportunity to watch your broker work, do so. You'll get to see exactly how orders are entered, time stamped, and reported back to the broker and customers. This will further your understanding of the different types of orders, when they are used and how to use them.

5. *Visit one of the futures exchanges.* Every futures exchange provides public tours. Take some time to visit the exchanges. The firsthand experience of witnessing the markets in real-time operation will add to your appreciation of how the futures markets work the role of traders, runners and exchange officials; computerized price reporting; govern-

ment regulation; and more. Even after all of my years as a futures trader, I still enjoy an occasional visit to the exchange. If you know someone who can get you onto the trading floor, this is an even more exciting educational thing to do.

6. *Familiarize* yourself with the different exchanges and contracts they trade.

7. *Use the Internet to visit the web sites of the various exchanges.* This will help you learn their rules, policies and markets.

8. *Read some of the trade publications.* While such regular reading as the *Wall Street Journal* will keep you informed on current events, it is also helpful to regularly read trade publications such as *The Financial Times.* It may not be a good idea to take anything you read in these publications too seriously, but it is a good idea to keep informed on industry trends and events.

9. *Do your own research.* If you have some market ideas of your own, don't be afraid to test them. Home computer systems, historical futures data and analytical software are so reasonably priced nowadays that systems testing is not so expensive a proposition as it was in the past. If you have ideas about trading systems that merit further investigation and development and if you have the funds to pursue this direction, then I encourage you to do so.

These are just a few suggestions that may help you to develop your skills or find employment in the futures industry. How you use this information and what you eventually decide to do is, of course, a matter of individual preference. I do, however, encourage you to consider being involved in futures trading in one way or another.

THE FACTS OF MARKET LIFE

I would like to share with you nineteen facts of market life, compiled from my many years of experience as a trader. I believe they will be of great benefit to you. I urge you to read them, analyze them, study them and think about them.

1. The More You Trade, the Less You Make

The simple fact is that more frequent trading is not necessarily synonymous with more profitable trading. The cost of commissions and the cost of poor order execution on entry and exit all add up. In the long run, they can prove very costly. The idea is not to trade more but to trade better. Know that a good trading system is one that "knows" when to keep you out of the market, not necessarily one that keeps you in the market all the time or one that causes you to trade too often.

2. More Decisions = Less Profit

Because most decisions a trader makes are wrong, the more decisions a trader has to make, the more losing decisions there will be. The moral is this: Traders must use simple methods and systems that do not require too many decisions. Furthermore, each decision for a trader can arouse mental conflicts. Mental conflicts increase the probability of making an emotionally based decision as opposed to a logical decision.

3. More Complicated = Less Effective

This cogent point is clearly related to the first two points. In my many years as a trader, I've traded or tested the vast majority of systems that exist. In addition to finding most of them mediocre, I've found that the simple systems seem to work best as well as most consistently. So keep it simple. There are literally hundreds, if not thousands, of trading systems available, often for obscenely large amounts of money. In choosing a system, bear in mind that the complexity of a system is in no way correlated with the value of a system.

4. More Calls to Broker = Less Profit

When you call your broker you often open yourself up to emotional responses that will not serve you well. Call your broker only when you need to place an order, pick up a fill, or ask a valid question. Unless you depend on your broker for recommendations, I suggest you avoid your broker's input, particularly if you trade your own system.

5. Think More, Make Less Money

Too much analysis and thought, once a system has given its signals, is the enemy of successful trading. All too often traders think themselves into losing positions and out of winning positions.

6. Analyze More, Make Less, Lose More

Analysis is fine, but too much analysis can cost you lost opportunities. Find a simple system and use it without too much, if any, second-guessing or analysis. The result will be very much to your liking.

7. More Information In = Less Money Out

With the plethora of books, newsletters, services, systems, computer bulletin boards and trading courses on today's market (not to mention all of the "free" opinions offered in the media), the odds of being overloaded with information are very high. The danger in being overloaded with information is that you will get confused and you will get too many recommendations. You will begin to doubt your own opinions and ideas.

8. More Emotion = Less Profit

Emotion will make you get in too soon, out too late, in too late and out too soon. It will cause you to lose sleep over positions and it will cause you to add to positions when you should subtract from them. Yet emotion is the most difficult thing for a trader to control.

9. Care More, Make Less

The more you care, the less you'll make; the less you care, the more you'll make. Care about what? About being right, about making money, about losing, about making a lot, about being wrong. If you care, then you lose your objectivity, and that will lead to losses.

10. Smaller Stop Losses = Less Profits

Most trading systems don't work if the stop losses you use are too small. All markets contain a certain amount of random behavior, expressed as whipsaws, that occurs during the day. Whipsaws stop traders out of otherwise good positions as losses when, in fact, a wider stop loss might have resulted in a profit. Do not use stop losses that are too small. You will guarantee yourself a loss if your stop losses aren't large enough to allow for random market fluctuations.

11. Try Not to Ask "Why" Things Happen

Every market has a significant random element that affects outcomes, and sometimes a cause and effect cannot be discerned. In futures trading, don't always attempt to know why something happens. Knowing why will not necessarily help you, and it may in fact hinder you.

12. What Most Traders Do Doesn't Work

What most traders do in the market doesn't make money. Furthermore, most technical trading systems do not work over the long run. Over the short term they may show some good profits, but over an extended period of time they're losers. Therefore, don't be swayed by what most traders do. Play your own game and choose your own indicators.

13. Commission Costs Make a Big Difference

Don't get fooled into paying excessively high commissions and don't pay a percentage or option premium as commission. Keep commissions reasonable!

14. Patterns Are the Best Indicators

The more work I do with patterns, the more I realize that patterns are exceptionally valid as indicators and trading methods. As more research is done, I think it will become more evident that patterns are the best indicators available.

15. Live Data and Real-Time Quotes Aren't Necessary

Traders erroneously believe that closer contact with the markets in the form of live, tick-by-tick quotes will make them more money. In fact, the reverse is often true. Traders who are undisciplined are unable to cope with the large influx of information. They begin attending to every tick, watching every market, working with a host of indicators. The end result is that they lose money, not only on the cost of the data, but in their trading as well.

16. Most Traders Can't Accept More Than Three Consecutive Losses Before Losing Their Discipline

It is the nature of all trading systems to lose money at times. Drawdown of equity is a universal problem with trading systems. In addition to dollar drawdown, the number of consecutive losing trades can play on a trader's mind and undermine a trader's discipline. The more consecutive losses a system takes, the less a trader will be inclined to remain disciplined with that system. This lack of discipline can only lead to losses.

17. The Experts' Forecasts Are Unimportant

Forecasts have nothing to do with precise timing, and timing is what will make you money in the futures markets. Forecasts won't do anything for you.

18. How You Place and Use Orders Is Important

Most traders are unfamiliar with the different types of orders they can use. Using the right order at the right time is very important. Frequently it can mean the difference between a profit and a loss. The use of a stop limit order as opposed to a simple stop order, for example, can save you hundreds if not thousands of dollars in the long run, provided you know when to use it. If you aren't familiar with the kinds of orders that are appropriate in specific situations, make it your goal to learn about them.

19. The Vast Majority of Traders Lack Discipline

Discipline in doing your market work and in sticking to a trading system is a very important skill to acquire if you want to succeed as a trader. The underlying reason for most losses is not system related but discipline related. Although an effective trading system can be a great help on the road to success, even the most profitable system will become a losing system if implemented by a trader who lacks discipline.

Summary and Conclusions

These nineteen points are some of the most important facts of commodity life in the international markets. Understand them, learn them and use them to come closer to achieving success as a trader. I am certain that you have developed some rules of your own. Add them to the facts I've given you and embark on your road to profits.

Chapter 13

SUMMARIZING THE INTERNATIONAL TRADING EXPERIENCE

The 1990s witnessed explosive growth in international commodities trading. Futures exchanges have been started throughout the world. The disintegration of the Soviet Union and the fall of communism have contributed to the development and initiation of futures exchanges in the individual Soviet states. Furthermore, futures exchanges can now be found in the smallest and most remote countries of the world.

Yet, in spite of the significant growth of such exchanges, the mere presence of these institutions does not *ipso facto* guarantee the viability or liquidity of trading vehicles. As time passes, new exchanges will develop not only their own specific trading vehicles, but also their own methods and procedures of operations, their own scope of coverage and their own membership. This, in turn, will add significantly to the liquidity of contracts traded.

Whereas international futures trading offers great promise to the speculator as well as the bona fide hedger and commercial user, there is still considerable risk involved, particularly if such trading is conducted in markets that are either illiquid or otherwise inappropriate. In order to avoid the attendant problems that can confront the trader who wishes to use the international markets, it is clear that a number of prerequisite steps must be taken.

My extensive research in preparation of this book has crystallized the following conclusions, caveats and considerations with regard to the international trading experience.

- Although there are many markets that one can trade, there are relatively few that offer sufficient liquidity and trading volume at this time. It is strongly suggested that those interested in conducting trades in a given market closely monitor daily trading volume and open interest in order to determine if transactions are viable.
- Given the distinct differences from one market to the next, both in terms of contracts specifications and trading regulations, it is imperative that the trader or speculator be totally familiar with the methods of operation and other specific details on each of the exchanges where he or she wishes to trade.
- Such important details as margin requirements, first notice day, delivery, accepted order types and other unique characteristics of different exchanges must also be considered if problems are to be avoided.
- Notwithstanding the above considerations, there are also specific legal requirements and individual brokerage house requirements that must be complied with or fulfilled. It is imperative that the speculator or trader who wishes to operate in these markets be totally familiar with, and in compliance with, these regulations and requirements.
- Although trading practices and procedures are fairly standard throughout the world, there are a number of significant differences and variations on the theme, particularly in Japan, which must be considered if you are to trade successfully in these locations.
- For the trader who has never participated in markets other than in his or her own country, I recommend, in fact, urge you to trade only in markets where liquidity is high. In order to have the information you need, you can either contact the given exchanges, their web sites or your broker. A thorough

study may prevent some costly losses due to ignorance or uncertainty.

- Use of various price orders can vary from market to market. Orders that are accepted on U.S. exchanges may not necessarily be accepted for orders in Europe, Asia or Japan. Consequently, it is important to determine which types of orders are acceptable and how they are used.
- Some foreign exchanges have restrictions on the use of their markets by individuals who are not citizens of the particular country. Naturally, you'll need to avoid such markets unless there are exceptions or other ways to circumvent the restrictions legally.

Summary and Conclusions

The international futures markets offer considerable profit potential to traders and investors. But with profit potential also comes the risk of loss. Fortunately, education and awareness of the rules and regulations that govern the operations of these markets will mitigate the potential for loss while increasing the probability of profits. The rapid growth of futures trading in virtually every country of the world will continue. Although exchanges and markets will merge and consolidate, the new era of futures trading will likely continue to expand.

For those who have the discipline, persistence, trading capital and knowledge, the opportunity to achieve great success in international futures will be significant. Those who prefer day trading will find that there are not too many markets as of yet that offer significant intraday volume to accommodate such trading. But these markets will also grow and expand over time. We stand at the threshold of a brave new world of futures trading. The global economy is a reality. The realization of this reality may also prove to be the vehicle to great success in international futures trading.

Appendix I

WORLD FUTURES MARKETS

Following is a list of world commodity exchanges and markets. While every effort has been made to ensure the accuracy of this information, please note that because the world markets change very frequently we cannot guarantee complete accuracy of the information. Up-to-the-minute information can be obtained from your broker or from the listed exchanges, many of which have Internet addresses.

African & Middle Eastern Exchanges

ISRAEL

Tel Aviv Stock Exchange Ltd., The (TASE)
Tel: (972) (3) 567-7411
Fax: (972) (3) 510-5379
Address: 54 Ahad Ha'am St., Tel Aviv, 65202, Israel
Established: 1953
E-mail address: webmaster@tase.co.il
Web site: http://www.tase.co.il

TURKEY

Istanbul Stock Exchange (ISE)
Tel: (90) (212) 298-21 00
Fax: (90) (212) 298-25 00
Address: Istinye 80860 Istanbul, Turkey
Established: 1985
E-mail address: info@ise.org
Web site: http://www.ise.org

SOUTH AFRICA

South African Futures Exchange (SAFEX)
Tel: (27-11) 728 5960
Fax: (27-11) 728-5970

Address: 105 Central Street, Houghton Estate 2198,
P.O. Box 4406, Johannesburg 2000, Republic of South Africa
Established: 1988
E-mail address: root@safex.co.za
Web site: http://www.safex.co.za

ASIAN EXCHANGES

CHINA

Beijing Commodity Exchange (BCE)
Tel: (86) (010) 6492-8347
Fax: (86) (010) 6499-3365
Address: 306 Chenyun Building, No. 8 Beichen East Road,
Chaoyang District, Beijing, China 100101
Established: 1992
E-mail address: sunli@intra.cnfm.co.cn
Web site: http://www.cnfm.co.cn

China-Commodity Futures Exchange, Inc. of Hainan (CCFE)
Tel: (86) (898) 670-0107
Fax: (86) (898) 670-0099
Address: Huaneng Building, 36 Datong Road, Haikou,
Hainan Province, China
Established: 1993
E-mail address: mayuechao@ccfe.org
Web site: http://www.ccfe.org

China Zhengzhou Commodity Exchange (CZCE)
Tel: (86) (371) 561-3236
Fax: (86) (371) 554-5424
Address: 69 Weilai Road, Zhengzhou, China 450003
Established: 1993
E-mail address: hyzhang@czce.com.cn
Web site: http://www.czce.com.cn

Guangdong United Futures Exchange (GUFE)
Tel: (86) (20) 8755-2109
Fax: (86) (20) 8755-1654
Address: JingXing Hotel, 91 LinHe West Road, Guangzhou, China
Established: 1994

Shanghai Cereals and Oils Exchange (SCOE)
Tel: (86) (21) 5831-1111
Fax: (86) (21) 5831-9308
Address: 199 Shangheng Road, Pudong New District, Shanghai, China
E-mail address: liangzhu@public.sta.net.cn

Shanghai Metals Exchange (SHME)
Tel: (86) (21) 6257-0000
Fax: (86) (21) 6244-7543
Address: 2550 Zhongshan North Road, Shanghai, China 200063
Established: 1992
E-mail address: info@shme.com.cn
Web site: http://www.shme.com

Shenzhen Mercantile Exchange (SZME)
Tel: (86) (755) 3343-502
Fax: (86) (755) 3343-502
Address: 1/F Bock B, Zhongjian Overseas Decoration, Hua Fu Road, Shenzhen, China
Established: 1992

HONG KONG

Hong Kong Futures Exchange Limited (HKFE)
Tel: (852) 2842-9333
Fax: (852) 2509-0555

Address: 6/F Asia Pacific Finance Tower, Citibank Plaza, 3 Garden Road, Central, Hong Kong
Established: 1976
E-mail address: prm@hfke.com
Web site: http://www.hkfe.com

Chinese Gold and Silver Exchange Society
Tel: (852) 544-1945
Fax: (852) 854-0869
Address: Gold and Silver Commercial Building, 12018 Mercer Street, Hong Kong

INDIA

OTC Exchange of India (OTCEI)
Tel: (91) (22) 21-88-164
Fax: (91) (22) 21-88-012
Address: 92 Maker Towers F, Cuffe Parade, Bombay, India
E-mail address: otc.otcindia@gems.vsnl.net.in

EUROPEAN EXCHANGES

EUROPEAN ECONOMIC UNION

European Futures Exchange (EUREX)

EUREX Frankfurt
Address: GmbH Borsenstrasse 7-11, D-60313, Frankfurt, Germany
Tel: (49) (0) 69-21 01-1700
Fax: (49) (0) 69-21 01-3941

EUREX Main Germany Zurich
Address: Selnaustrasse 30, CG-8021 Zurich, Switzerland
Tel: (41) (0) 1-229 2942
Fax: (41) (0) 1-229 2466

EUREX London
Address: 50 Cannon Street, GB-London EC4N 6JJ, UK
Tel: (44) 171-778-9331
Fax: (44) 171-778-9321

EUREX Chicago
Address: 190 South LaSalle Street, Chicago, IL 60603, USA
Tel: (312) 782-2223
Fax: (312) 782-2225
Established: 1998

Established through the merger of DTB (Deutsche Terminborse) and the Swiss Options and Financial Exchange (SOFFEX)

E-mail address: info@eurexchange.com

Web site: http://www.eurexchange.com

AUSTRIA

Wiener Borse AG (WBAG)
Tel: (43) (1) 531 65-0
Fax: (43) (1) 531 65-140
Address: Wiener Borse AG Strauchgasse 1-3 Postbox 192, A-1014, Austria
Established: 1991

Formerly the Vienna Stock Exchange and the Austrian Futures and Options Exchange (OTOB)

E-mail address: info@wbag.at
Web site: http://www.wbag.at

BELGIUM

Belgium Futures and Options Exchange (BELFOX)
Tel: (32) (2) 512-8040
Fax: (32) (2) 513-8342
Address: Palais de la Bourse, Rue Henri Maus—Henri Mausstraat, 2, B-1000 Brussels, Belgium

Established: 1991
E-mail address: marketing@belfox.be
Web site: http://www.belfox.be

BULGARIA

Sofia Commodity Exchange (SCE)
Tel: (35) (92) 954-93-68
Fax: (35) (92) 80-10-42
Address: 1 Bulgaria Sq., National Palace of Culture, Administrative Building, Ground Floor, Tryditsa Municipality, Sofia, Bulgaria
Established: 1991
E-mail address: sce@online.bg
Web site: http://www.online.bg/sce

DENMARK

FUTOP Market—Copenhagen Stock Exchange and the FUTOP Clearing Centre
Tel: (45) (33) 93-3366
Fax: (45) (33) 8613
Address: Nikolaj Plads 6, Box 1040, Copenhagen DK-1007, Denmark
Established: 1988
E-mail address: xcse@xcse.dk
Web site: http://www.xcse.dk

FINLAND

Finnish Options Exchange Ltd. (FOEX)
Suomen Optioporssi Oyj
Tel: (358) (9) 439-1030
Fax: (358) (9) 439-10340
Address: Westendintie 1 A, 02160 Espoo, Finland
Established: 1986
E-mail address: info@foex.fi
Web site: http://www.fi/foexinfo.htm

HEX Ltd., Helsinki Securities and Derivatives Exchange, Clearinghouse

Tel: (358) (9) 616-671
Fax: (358) (9) 6166-7366
Address: Fabianinkatu 14, PL 361, FIN-00131, Helsinki, Finland
Established: 1999

Due to the merger of the Finnish Option Market (FOM, and the Helsinki Stock Exchange (HSE)

E-mail address: paivi.kumpulainen@hex.fi
Web site: http://www.hex.fi

FRANCE

ParisBourse SA
Paris Office
Tel: (33) (0) 1-40-27-10-00
Fax: (33) (0) 1-49-27-14-33
Address: 39, rue Cambon, Paris Cedex 01, France
Chicago Office
Tel: (312) 338-2770
Fax: (312) 338-2777
Address: 30 South Wacker Drive, Suite 1520, Chicago, IL 60606, USA
Established: 1999

Four French market operations—SBF, MATIF SA, MONEP SA and Societé du Nouveau Marché—merged to form a single entity. Although MATIF SA no longer exists as a market operator, the MATIF as a market for interest-rate and commodity derivatives is still performing along the MONEP, another of the derivatives markets of the ParisBourse SA.

E-mail address: dominique.lande@www.bourse-de-paris.fr
Web site: http://www.bourse-de-paris.fr

GERMANY

WTB Warenterminborse Hannover
Tel: (49) 5111 30159-0

Fax: (49) 5111 30159-30
Address: Prinzenstrasse 17, D-30159, Hannover, Germany
Established: 1998
E-mail address: info@wtb-hannover.de
Web site: http://wtb-hannover.de

GREECE

Athens Stock Exchange (ASE)
Tel: (30) (1) 32-11-301
Fax: (30) (1) 32-13-938
Address: 10 Sophocleous str., Athena 105-59, Greece
Established: 1995
E-mail address: webmaster@asg.gr
Web site: http://ase.gr

Athens Derivatives Exchange S. A. (ADEX)
a wholly owned subsidiary of the Athens Stock Exchange
Web site: http://adex.ase.gr

HUNGARY

Budapest Commodity Exchange (BCE)
Tel: (36) (1) 465-6971
Fax: (36) (1) 465-6981
Address: H-1134 Robert Karoly Krt. 61-65, P.O. Box 495, 1343 Budapest, Hungary
Established: 1989
Initially trading as the Produce Exchange Ltd., it changed its name in 1990.
E-mail address: bce@bce-bat.com
Web site: http://www.bce-bat.com

Budapest Stock Exchange (BSE)
Tel: (36) (1) 429-6700
Fax: (36) (1) 429-6800
Address: H-1052 Budapest, Deak Ferenc u. 5., Hungary
Established: 1990
It began trading futures in 1995.

E-mail address: business@tozsdeforum.hu
Web site: http://www.fornax.hu/fmon

IRELAND

Irish Futures and Options Exchange (IFOX)
Tel: (353) (1) 676-7413
Fax: (353) (1) 661-4645
Address: Segrave House, Earlsfort Terrace, Dublin 2, Ireland
Established: 1988

ITALY

Italian Stock Exchange (ISE)
Its subsidiaries: the **Italian Derivatives Market (IDEM)** *and the* **Italian Financial Futures Market (MIF)**

Consiglio de Borsa Italiana
Tel: (39) (02) 724-261
Fax: (39) (02) 720-0433
Address: Piazza degli Affari 6, 20123, Milan, Italy
Established: 1994
E-mail address: info@borsaitalia.it
Web site: http://www.borsaitalia.it

THE NETHERLANDS

Amsterdam Exchanges (AEX—Opitebeurs)
Tel: (31) (20) 550-4444
Fax: (31) (20) 550-4912
Address: Rokin 65, 1012 KK Amsterdam, The Netherlands
Established: 1999

NORWAY

Oslo Stock Exchange (OSLO)
Oslo Bors
Tel: (47) (22) 34-1700
Fax: (47) (22) 41-6590
Address: Tollbugt 2, P.O. Box 460, Sentrum, N-0105, Oslo, Norway

Established: 1990
E-mail address: info@ose.no
Web site: http://www.ose.no

PORTUGAL

Portuguese Futures and Options Exchange (BDP)
Bolsa de Derivados do Porto
Tel: (351) 2 618 58 58
Fax: (351) 2 618 58 97
Address: Avenida da Boavista, 3433, 4100 Porto, Oporto, Portugal
Established: 1996
E-mail address: bdp@bdp.pt
Web site: http://www.bdp.pt

ROMANIA

Romanian Commodities Exchange (BRM)
Bursa Romana de Marfuri
Tel: (40) (1) 224-45-60
Fax: (40) (1) 224-28-78
Address: Piata Presei Libere nr.1 Bucuresti, Romania
Established: 1992
E-mail address: brm@starnets.ro
Web site: http://www.brm.ro

Sibiu Monetary-Financial and Commodities Exchange (SMFCE)
Bursa Monetar-Financiara si de Marfuri Sibiu
Tel: (40) (69) 211-153
Fax: (40) (69) 211-798
Address: 69, Piata 1 Decembrie 1918, 2400 Sibiu, Romania
Established: 1994
E-mail address: office@bmfms.ro
Web site: http://www.bmfms.ro

Transylvania Commodity Exchange (TCE)
Tel: (40) (64) 414-481
Fax: (40) (64) 414-484

Address: 3400 Cluj-Napoca, 4 N. Titulescu, Transilvania, Romania
Established: 1994
E-mail address: bursa@bursa.codec.ro
Web site: http://www.twc.ro/bt

RUSSIAN FEDERATION

Moscow Commodity Exchange (ME)
Tel: (7) (095) 187 83 07
Fax: (7) (095) 187 9982
Address: Pavilion No. 4, Russian Exhibition Centre, Moscow
Established: 1994

Moscow Interbank Currency Exchange (MICEX)
Tel: (7) (095) 705-9627
Fax: (7) (095) 705-9622
Address: 21/1, Sadovaya-Spasskay, Moscow
Established: 1991
E-mail address: inmices@micex.com
Web site: http://www.micex.com

Russian Exchange, The (RE)
Tel: (7) (095) 262 06 53
Fax: (7) (095) 262 06 53
Address: Myasnitskaya ul 26 Moscow
Established: 1990

This exchange was organized by the Russian Commodities and Raw Materials Exchange in 1990—the first trading floor in Russia since the 1917 Revolution.

E-mail address: assa@vc.rtsb.msk.ru
Web site: http://www.re.ru

St. Petersburg Futures Exchange (SPBFE)
Tel: (7) (812) 327-90-18
Fax: (7) (812) 294-86-59
Address: Ligovski pr. 274, St. Petersburg 196006 Russia
E-mail address: seva@spbfe.futures.ru
Web site: http://www.futures.ru

Siberian Stock Exchange (SibEx)
Tel: (383) (2) 21-06-90
Fax: (383) (2) 21-06-90
Address: Box 233, 630076, Novosibirsk, Frunze st. 5
Established: 1991
E-mail address: sibex@sse.nsk.su
Web site: http://www.sse.nsk.su

SLOVENIA

Commodity Exchange of Ljubljana (CEL)
Tel: (386) (0) 61 18 55 100
Fax: (386) (0) 61 18 55 101
Address: Smartinska 152, 1530, Ljubljana, Slovenia
Established: 1994
E-mail address: infos@bb-lj.si
Web site: www.eunet.si/commercial/bbl/bbl-ein

SPAIN

Citrus Fruit and Commodity Futures Market of Valencia (FC&M)
Futuros de Citricos y Mercanderias de Valencia
Tel: (34) (5) 387-801 88
Fax: (34) (6) 394-36 30
Address: 2, 4 Libreros 46002, Valencia, Spain
Established: 1995
E-mail address: fcm@fcym.com
Web site: http://www.fcym.com

Spanish Financial Futures Market (MEFF RF)
MEFF Renta Fija
Tel: (34) (3) 412-11 28
Fax: (34) (3) 268-47 69
Address: Via Laietana, 58 (6a planta), 08003, Barcelona, Spain
Established: 1990
E-mail address: meffrv@meff.es
Web site: http://www.meff.es

Spanish Equity Derivatives Exchange (MEFF RV)
MEFF Renta Variable
Tel: (91) 585-08 00
Fax: (91) 571-95 42
Address: Torre Picasso, Planta 26, 28020 Madrid, Spain
E-mail address: meffrv@meffrv.es
Web site: http://www.meff.es

Mercado do Opciones y Futuros
Tel: (34) (3) 412-1128
Fax: (34) (3) 268-4769
Address: Via Laietana, 58, 08003 Barcelona, Spain

SWEDEN

OM Stockholm Exchange (OM)
Tel: (46) (8) 613-8800
Fax: (46) (8) 10-8110
Address: Stockholms Fondbors, Kallargrand 2, S-105, Stockholm, Sweden
Established: 1999
Formed through the merger of the Stockholm Stock Exchange and OM Stockholm.
E-mail address: info@xsse.se
Web site: http://www.xsse.se *or* http://www.omgroup.com/transaction

UNITED KINGDOM

International Petroleum Exchange of London (IPE)
Tel: (44) (171) 481-0643
Fax: (44) (171) 481-8485
Address: International House, 1 St. Katharine's Way, London E1 9 UN, UK

IPE U.S. Office
Tel: (212) 425-6969
Fax: (212) 425-2282
Address: One Exchange Plaza, 55 Broadway, Suite 2602, New York, NY 10006

Established: 1980
E-mail address: info@ipe.uk.com
Web site: http://www.ipe/uk.com or www.energylive.com

London Commodity Exchange (LCE)
Tel: (44) (171) 481-2080
Fax: (44) (171) 702-9923/4
Address: 1 Commodity Quay, St. Katharine Docks, London, UK
Established: 1987
E-mail address: webmaster@liffe.com
Web site: http://www.liffe.com

London International Financial Futures Exchange (LIFFE)
Tel: (44) (171) 623-0444
Fax: (44) (171) 588-3624
Address: Cannon Bridge, London EC4R 3XX, UK
Established: 1982
E-mail address: webmaster@liffe.com
Web site: http://www.liffe.com

London Metal Exchange (LME)
Tel: (44) (0171) 264-5555
Fax: (44) (0171) 680-0505
Address: 56 Leadenhall Street, EC3A 2DX, London, UK
Established: 1877
E-mail address: info@lme.co.uk
Web site: http://www.lme.co.uk

SOUTH AMERICAN EXCHANGES

ARGENTINA

Buenos Aires Grain Exchange (BAGE)
Bolsa de Cereales de Buenos Aires SA
Tel: (541) 311-9541/312-2000
Fax: (541) 311-9540
Address: Corrientes 127- (1043) Buenos Aires, Republicia Argentina

Established: 1854
E-mail address: bolcer@datamarkets.com.ar
Web site: http://www.bolcereales.com

Buenos Aires Futures Market (MATBA)
Mercado a Termino de Buenos Aires SA
Tel: (54) (1) 311-47-16
Fax: (54) (1) 312-47-16
Address: Bouchard 454 5th, (1106), Buenos Aires, Argentina
Established: 1907
E-mail address: info-matba@matba.com.ar
Web site: http://www.matba.com.ar

Buenos Aires Stock Exchange (BCBA)
Bolsa de Comercio de Buenos Aires
Tel: (54) (1) 313-3334
Fax: (54) (1) 312-9332
Address: Sarmiento 299, Buenos Aires, Argentina
Established: 1854
E-mail address: cau@sba.com.ar
Web site: http://www.merval.sba.com.ar

Rosario Board of Trade
Bolsa de Comerico de Rosario
Tel: (54) (11) 4316-7000
Fax: (54) (11) 4316-7000
Address: Sarmiento 299, Buenos Aires, Argentina
Established: 1854
E-mail address: dg@bcba.sba.com.ar
Web site: http://www/bcba.sba.com.ar/bolsa

Rosario Futures Exchange (ROFEX)
Mercado a Termino de Rosario
Tel: (54) (41) 425-9610
Fax: (54) (41) 421-5097
Address: Cordoba 1402 2000 Rosario, Santa Fe, Argentina

Established: 1909
E-mail address: info@rofex.com.ar
Web site: http://www.rofex.com.ar

BRAZIL

Commodity & Futures Exchange, The (BM&F)
Bolsa de Mercadorias y Futuros
Tel: (55) (11) 3119-2000
Fax: (55) (11) 232-7565
Address: Praca Antonio Prado, 48 São Paulo, SP, Brazil 01010-901
Established: 1991

This exchange was established through the merger of the Mercantile & Futures Exchange (BM&F), which was established in 1985 and the São Paolo Commodities Exchange (BMSP), founded in 1917 as the first Brazilian exchange for forward trading. In 1997, BM&F was strengthened when the Brazilian Futures Exchange (BBF) merged with the exchange.

E-mail address: bmf@bmf.com.br
Web site: http://www.bmf.com.br

Rio de Janeiro Stock Exchange
Tel: (55) (21) 271-1001
Fax: (55) (21) 221-2151
Address: Praca XV de Novembro, 20, 20010-001, Rio de Janeiro, Brazil
Established: 1845
E-mail address: info@bvrj.com.br
Web site: http://www.bvrj.com.br

CHILE

Santiago Stock Exchange (SSE)
Bolsa de Comercio de Santiago
Tel: (56) (2) 698-2001
Fax: (56) (2) 672-8046

Address: La Bolsa 64, Casilla 123-D, Santiago, Chile
Established: 1991
E-mail address: ahucke@comercio.bolsantiago.cl
Web site: http://www.bolsantiago.cl

VENEZUELA

Caracas Stock Exchange (BVC)
Bolsa de Valores de Caracas, C.A.
Tel: (58) (2) 905-55-11
Fax: (58) (2) 952-26-40
Address: Ediflcio Atrium, Calle Sorocaima entre avenidas Venezuela y Tamanaco, Urbanizacion El Rosal, Apartado de Correos 6274-A, Caracas 1060-A, Venezuela
Established: 1947
E-mail address: bvc@caracasstock.com
Web site: http://www.caracasstock.com

North American Exchanges

BERMUDA

Bermuda Commodities Exchange (BCOE)
Tel: (44) 296-6100
Fax: (44) 296-6101
Address: 29 Richmond Road, Pembroke, Bermuda HM08
Established: 1996
E-mail address: info@bcoe.bm
Web site: http://www.bcoe.bm

CANADA

Montreal Exchange (ME)
Bourse de Montreal
Tel: (514) 871-2424
Fax: (514) 871-3531
Address: Tour de la Bourse, P.O. Box 61, 800 Victoria Square, Montreal, Quebec H4Z 1A9 Canada

Established: 1874
E-mail address: info@me.org
Web site: http://www.me.org

Toronto Futures Exchange (TFE)
Tel: (416) 947-4487
Fax (416) 947-4272
Address: Two First Canadian Place, The Exchange Tower, Toronto, Ontario M5X 1J2 Canada
Established: 1983
E-mail address: info@tfe.com
Web site: http://www.tfe.com

Toronto Stock Exchange (TSE)
Tel: (416) 947-4487
Fax (416) 947-4272
Address: Derivative Markets, Two First Canadian Place, The Exchange Tower, Toronto, Ontario M5X 1J2 Canada
Established: 1983
E-mail address: info@tse.com
Web site: http://www.tse.com

Winnipeg Commodity Exchange (WCE)
Tel: (204) 925-5000
Fax (204) 943-5448
Address: 500 Commodity Exchange Tower, 360 Main St., Winnipeg, Manitoba R3C 3Z4 Canada
Established: 1887
E-mail address: wce@wce.mb.ca
Web site: http://www.wce.mb.ca

UNITED STATES OF AMERICA

Chicago Board Options Exchange (CBOE)
Tel: (312) 786-5600 or (800) 678-4667
Fax: (312) 786-7409
Address: 400 S. LaSalle St., Chicago, IL 60605, USA

Established: 1973
E-mail address: investorservices@cboe.com
Web site: http://www.cboe.com

Chicago Board of Trade (CBOT)
Tel: (312) 435-3500
Fax: (312) 341-3306
Address: 141 W. Jackson Blvd., Chicago, IL 60604, USA
Established: 1848
E-mail address: comments@cbot.com
Web site: http://www.CBOT.com

Chicago Mercantile Exchange (CME)
Tel: (312) 930-1000
Fax: (312) 936-3439
Address: 30 S. Wacker Dr., Chicago, IL 60606, USA
Established: 1919
The Chicago Produce Exchange, founded in 1874, gave birth to Butter and Egg Board in 1898. This was incorporated as CME in 1919.)
E-mail address: info@cme.com
Web site: http://www.cme.com

Kansas City Board of Trade (KCBOT)
Tel: (816) 753-7500 or (800) 821-5228
Fax: (816) 753-3944
Address: 4800 Main St., Suite 303, Kansas City, KS 64112, USA
Established: 1856
E-mail address: kCBOT@kCBOT.com
Web site: http://www.kCBOT.com

MidAmerica Commodity Exchange (MidAm)
(affiliated with the CBOT since 1987)
Tel: (312) 341-3000
Fax: (312) 341-3027
Address: 141 W. Jackson Blvd., Chicago, IL 60604, USA
Established: 1880

E-mail address: comments@cbot.com
Web site: http://www.midam.com

Minneapolis Grain Exchange (MGE)
Tel: (612) 321-7101
Fax: (612) 339-1155
Address: 400 S. Fourth St., Minneapolis, MN 55415, USA
Established: 1881
E-mail address: mgex@ix.netcom.com
Web site: http://www.mgex.com

New York Board of Trade (NYBOT)
Tel: (212) 742-6000
Fax: (212) 742-5026
Address: Four World Trade Center, New York, NY 10048, USA
Established: 1998

In 1998, the Coffee, Sugar & Cocoa Exchange, Inc., which originated in 1882; the New York Cotton Exchange, which began in 1870; the New York Futures Exchange (FINEX) and Citrus Associates of the NYCE merged into the NYBOT.

E-mail address: info@nybot.com
Web site: http://www.nybot.com

New York Mercantile Exchange (NYMEX/COMEX)
Tel: (212) 229-3000
Fax: (212) 301-4670
Address: One North End Avenue, World Financial Center, New York, NY 10282, USA
Established: 1998

NYMEX in its original form was established in 1872 as Butter and Cheese Exchange of New York.

E-mail address: exchangeinfo@nymex.com
Web site: http://www.nymex.com

Pacific Rim Exchanges

AUSTRALIA

Sydney Futures Exchange Limited (SFE)

Tel: (61) (2) 9256-0555

Fax: (61) (2) 9256-0666

Address: 30-32 Grosvenor Street, Sydney, NSW 2000, Sydney, Australia

Established: 1960

Initially called the Sydney Greasy Wool Futures Exchange.

E-mail address: sfe@hutch.com.au

Web site: http://www.sfe.com.au

INDONESIA

Indonesian Commodity Exchange Board
Badan Pelaksana Bursa Komoditi

Tel: (62) (21) 344 1921

Fax: (62) (21) 3480 4426

Address: Gegung Bursa, Jalan Medan Merdeka Selatan 14, 4th Floor, Jakarta Pusat, Indonesia

Established: 1995

JAPAN

Chubu Commodity Exchange (C-COM)

Tel: (81) (52) 951-2171

Fax: (81) (52) 961-6407

Address: 3-2-15, Nishiki Kaka-ku, Nagoya 460 Japan

Established: 1996

Created from the merger of the Nagoya Grain & Sugar Exchange, Nagoya Textile Exchange, and Toyohasi Dried Cocoon Exchange.

Kanmon Commodity Exchange (KCE)
Kanmon Shohin Torihikijo
Tel: (81) (832) 31-1313
Fax: (81) (832) 23-1947
Address: 1-5 Nabe-cho, Shimonoseki, Yamaguchi 750-8650, Japan
Established: 1953
Originally established as Kanmon Grain Exchange in 1805 and restructured in 1953.
E-mail address: webmaster@kce.or.jp
Web site: http://www.kce.or.jp

Kansai Commodities Exchange (KANEX)
Tel: (81) (6) 531-7935
Fax: (81) (6) 541-6832
Address: 1-10-14 Awaza, Nishi-ku, Osaka 550, Japan
Established: 1997
Established in 1997 through the merger of the Kansai Agricultural Commodities Exchange (originally established in 1993 through the merger of three historic exchanges: the Osaka Grain Exchange, the Kobe Grain Exchange and the Osaka Sugar Exchange) and the Kobe Raw Silk Exchange.
E-mail address: kex-1@kanex.or.jp
Web site: http://kanex.or.jp

Maebashi Dried Cocoon Exchange (MDCE)
Maebashi Kanken Torihikijo
Tel: (81) (272) 52-1401
Fax: (81) (272) 51-8270
Address: 1-49-1 Furuichi-machi 1-chrome, Maebashi 371, Japan
Established: 1952

Osaka Mercantile Exchange (OME)
Tel: (06) 244-2191
Fax: (06) 244-2194
Address: 2-5-28 Kyutaromachi, Chuo-ku, Osaka 541-0056, Japan
Established: 1997

Formed through the merger of the Kobe Rubber Exchange and the Osaka Textile Exchange.

E-mail address: ome-web@osamex.com

Web site: http://www.osamex.com

Osaka Securities Exchange (OSE)
Osaka Shoken Torihikijo

Tel: (81-6) 229-8643

Fax: (81-6) 231-2639

Address: 8-16, Kitahama 1-chome, Chuo-ku, Osaka 541-0041, Japan

Established: 1949

Its predecessor was the Osaka Stock Exchange, which began trading in 1878.

E-mail address: osakaexc@po.iijnet.or.jp

Web site: http://www.ose.or.jp

Tokyo Commodity Exchange (TOCOM)
Tokyo Kogyoin Torihikijo

Tel: (81) (3) 3661-9191

Fax: (81) (3) 3661-7568

Address: 14th Floor, S. Wing, Riverside Yomiuri Bldg., 36-2 Nhionbashi-Hakozakicho, Chuo-ku, Tokyo 103, Japan

Established: 1984

Established through the consolidation of the Tokyo Gold Exchange, which began in 1983; the Tokyo Rubber Exchange, which was instituted in 1952; and the Tokyo Textile Exchange, which began trading in 1951.

E-mail address: int-aff@tocom.or.jp

Web site: http://www.tocom.or.jp

Tokyo Grain Exchange (TGE)
Tokyo Kokumotsu Shohin Torihikijo

Tel: (81) (3) 3668-9321

Fax: (81) (6) 3661-4564

Address: 12-5 Nihonbashi Kakigara-cho, 1-chome, Chuo-ku, Tokyo 103, Japan

Established: 1952

TGE began trading in the building that housed the Tokyo Rice Exchange, which closed before World War II and had hoped to resume rice futures trading at a later date. It merged with the Tokyo Sugar Exchange in 1993 to become the largest agricultural commodity futures market in Japan. In 1995, it also merged with the Hokkaido Grain Exchange—originally established as Otaru Rice, Herring and Fertilizer Exchange in 1893 and reopened in 1951 as Agricultural and Fishery Products Exchange.

E-mail address: webmas@tge.or.jp

Web site: http://www.tge.or.jp

Tokyo International Financial Futures Exchange (TIFFE)

Tel: (81) (3) 5223-2400

Fax: (81) (6) 5223-2450

Address: 1-3-1 Marunouchi, Chiyoda-ky, Tokyo 100, Japan

Established: 1989

E-mail address: tiffe@tkb.att.ne.jp

Web site: http://www.tiffe.or.jp/e

Tokyo Stock Exchange (TSE)

Tokyo Shoken Toribikijo

Tel: (81) (3) 3666-0141

Fax: (81) (3) 3663-0625

Address: 2-1 Nihombashi-Kabuto-cho, Chuo-ku, Tokyo 103-8220 Japan

Established: 1949

E-mail address: info@www.tse.or.jp

Web site: http://www.tse.or.jp

Yokohama Raw Silk Exchange (YRSE)

Yokohama Kiito Toribikjo

Tel: (81) (45) 641-1341

Fax: (81) (45) 641-1346

Address: Silk Center, 1 Yamashita-cho, Naka-ku, Yokohma 231, Japan

Established: 1993

KOREA (SOUTH)

Korea Futures Exchange (KOFEX)
Tel: (82) (2) 3774-9000
Fax: (82) (2) 786-0263
Address: 33 Yoido-dong, Youngdeungpo-gu, Seoul, South Korea 150-010
Established: 1999
E-mail address: world@www.kse.or.kr
Web site: http://:www.kofex.com/html

Korea Stock Exchange (KSE)
Tel: (02) (3) 774-9065
Address: 33 Yoido-dong, Youngdeungpo-gu, Seoul, South Korea 150-010
Established: 1956
It began trading stock-index futures in 1996.
E-mail address: world@www.kse.or.kr
Web site: http://www.kse.or.kr

MALAYSIA

Commodity and Monetary Exchange of Malaysia (COMMEX)
Tel: (6) (3) 293-6822
Fax: (6) (3) 0274-2215
Address: 4th Floor, Citypoint, Dayabumi Complex, Jalan Sultan Hishamuddin, P.O. Box 11260, 50740 Kuala Lumpur, Malaysia
Established: 1998
Formed in December 1998 by the merger of the Kuala Lumpur Commodity Exchange (KLCE) and the Malaysia Monetary Exchange (MME).
E-mail address: klce@jaring.my or mme@po.jaring.my
Web site: http://www.commex.com.my

Kuala Lumpur Options & Financial Futures Exchange (KLOFFE)
Tel: (60) (3) 253-8199
Fax: (60) (3) 253-5911
Address: 10th Floor, Wisma Chase Perdana, Off Jalan Semantan, Damansara Heights, 50490 Kuala Lumpur, Malaysia

Established: 1993
E-mail address: kloffe@kloffe.com.my
Web site: http://www.kloffe.com.my

NEW ZEALAND

New Zealand Futures & Options Exchange Ltd. (NZFOE)
a wholly owned subsidiary of the Sydney Futures Exchange
Tel: (64) (9) 309-8308
Fax: (64) (9) 309-8817
Address: 12th Floor Stock Exchange Centre, 191 Queen Street, Auckland, New Zealand
Established: 1985
E-mail Address: infoe@nzfoe.co.nz
Web Site: http://www.nzfoe.co.nz

PHILIPPINES

Manila International Futures Exchange (MIFE)
Tel: (63) (2) 818-5496
Fax: (63) (2) 818-5529
Address: 7th Floor, Producers Bank Center, Paseo de Roxos, Makati, Metro Manila 1200, Philippines
Established: 1986

SINGAPORE

Singapore Commodity Exchange Limited (SICOM)
Tel: (0617) (65) 338-5600
Fax: (0617) (65) 338-9116
Address: 111 North Bridge Road #23-04/05, Peninsula Plaza, Singapore 179098
Established: 1994
Originated as the Singapore Chamber of Commerce Rubber Association in the 1920s, then became the Rubber Association of Singapore in 1992 and renamed the Singapore Commodity Exchange in 1994.
E-mail address: sicom@pacific.net.sg
Web site: http://www.sicom.com

Singapore International Monetary Exchange Ltd. (SIMEX)
Tel: (65) 535-7382
Fax: (65) 535-7282
Address: 1 Raffles Place, No. 07-00, OUB Centre,
Singapore 048616

SIMEX America Ltd.
Tel: (212) 481-8080
Fax: (212) 481-7373
Address: 10 E. 40th St., Suite 4205, New York, NY 10016, USA
Established: 1984
E-mail address: simex@pacific.net.sg
Web site: http://www.simex.com.sg

APPENDIX II

CONTRACT SPECIFICATION LISTINGS

The following is a list of world commodity contracts. While every effort has been made to assure the accuracy of this information, please note that the world markets and their products change frequently, so we cannot guarantee complete accuracy of the information. Also note that some exchanges listed in Appendix I will not have any specific contracts shown here due to the fact that their product line is currently being determined and/or not readily available. Up-to-the-minute information can be obtained from your broker or from the listed exchanges.

CURRENCIES

Australian Dollar

Chicago Mercantile Exchange (CME)

Bolivar/U.S. Dollar Exchange Rate

Caracas Stock Exchange (BVC)

British Pound

Budapest Commodity Exchange (BCE)
Chicago Mercantile Exchange (CME)
MidAmerica Commodity Exchange (MidAm)
New York Board of Trade (NYBOT)
New York Mercantile Exchange (NYMEX/COMEX)
Singapore International Monetary Exchange Ltd. (SIMEX)

British Pound/German Mark Exchange Rate

New York Board of Trade (NYBOT)

Canadian Dollar

Chicago Mercantile Exchange (CME)

Czech Koruna

Budapest Commodity Exchange (BCE)
Singapore International Monetary Exchange Ltd. (SIMEX)

Euro (ECU)

Budapest Commodity Exchange (BCE)
Chicago Mercantile Exchange (CME)
Commodity Exchange of Ljubljana (CEL)
London International Financial Futures Exchange (LIFFE)
MidAmerica Commodity Exchange (MidAm)
New York Board of Trade (NYBOT)
New York Mercantile Exchange (NYMEX/COMEX)

French Franc

Chicago Mercantile Exchange (CME)

German Mark/French Franc Exchange Rate

New York Board of Trade (NYBOT)

German Mark/Italian Lira Exchange Rate

New York Board of Trade (NYBOT)

German Mark/Japanese Yen Exchange Rate

New York Board of Trade (NYBOT)

German Mark/Swiss Franc Exchange Rate

New York Board of Trade (NYBOT)

Italian Lira

Budapest Commodity Exchange (BCE)
Commodity Exchange of Ljubljana (CEL)

Japanese Yen

Budapest Commodity Exchange (BCE)
Chicago Mercantile Exchange (CME)
Commodity Exchange of Ljubljana (CEL)
London International Financial Futures Exchange (LIFFE)
New York Board of Trade (NYBOT)
New York Mercantile Exchange (NYMEX/COMEX)
Singapore International Monetary Exchange Ltd. (SIMEX)
Tokyo International Financial Exchange (TIFFE)

Jumbo U.S. Dollar/Guilder Exchange Rate

European Options Exchange (EOE)

Korean Won

Korea Futures Exchange (KOFEX)

Mexican Peso

Chicago Mercantile Exchange (CME)

MICEX

St. Petersburg Futures Exchange (SPBFE)

MICEX/U.S. Dollar

The Russian Exchange (RE)

New Zealand Dollar

New Zealand Futures & Options Exchange Ltd. (NZFOE)

Rolling Forex

Hong Kong Futures Exchange Limited (HKFE)

Romanian Dollar/German Mark Exchange Rate

Sibiu Monetary-Financial and Commodities Exchange (SMFCE)
Transilvania Commodity Exchange (TCE)

Romanian Dollar/Euro Exchange Rate

Sibiu Monetary-Financial and Commodities Exchange (SMFCE)
Transilvania Commodity Exchange (TCE)

Romanian Dollar/U.S. Dollar Exchange Rate

Sibiu Monetary-Financial and Commodities Exchange (SMFCE)
Transilvania Commodity Exchange (TCE)

Spanish Peseta/German Mark Exchange Rate

Spanish Financial Futures Market (MEFF RF)

Spanish Peseta/U.S. Dollar Exchange Rate

Spanish Financial Futures Market (MEFF RF)

SPCEX

St. Petersburg Futures Exchange (SPBFE)

Sterling

London International Financial Futures Exchange (LIFFE)

Swiss Franc

Budapest Commodity Exchange (BCE)
Chicago Mercantile Exchange (CME)
London International Financial Futures Exchange (LIFFE)
New York Board of Trade (NYBOT)
New York Mercantile Exchange (NYMEX/COMEX)

U.S. Dollar

Budapest Commodity Exchange (BCE)
The Commodity & Futures Exchange (BM&F)
Commodity Exchange of Ljubljana (CEL)
Korea Futures Exchange (KOFEX)
Tokyo International Financial Futures Exchange (TIFFE)

U.S. Dollar/Belgium Franc Exchange Rate

Belgium Futures and Options Exchange (BELFOX)

U.S. Dollar/British Pound Exchange Rate

Manila International Futures Exchange (MIFE)

U.S. Dollar/Brazilian Real Exchange Rate

The Commodity & Futures Exchange (BM&F)

U.S. Dollar/Euro (ECU) Exchange Rate

Amsterdam Exchanges (AEX—Optiebeurs)
Sibiu Monetary-Financial and Commodities Exchange (SMFCE)

U.S. Dollar/German Mark Exchange Rate

Commodity Exchange of Ljubljana (CEL)
European Futures Exchange (EUREX)
Manila International Futures Exchange (MIFE)

U.S. Dollar/Guilder Exchange Rate

Amsterdam Exchanges (AEX—Optiebeurs)
European Options Exchange (EOE)

U.S. Dollar/Japanese Yen Exchange Rate

Manila International Futures Exchange (MIFE)

U.S. Dollar/Korean Wan Exchange Rate

Korea Futures Exchange (KOFEX)

U.S. Dollar/Peso Exchange Rate

Manila International Futures Exchange (MIFE)
Santiago Stock Exchange (SSE)

U.S. Dollar/Rouble Exchange Rate

The Russian Exchange (RE)
Siberian Stock Exchange (SibEx)

U.S. Dollar/Swiss Franc Exchange Rate

Manila International Futures Exchange (MIFE)

ENERGY

Coal

New York Mercantile Exchange (NYMEX/COMEX)

Crude Oil

(including Brent, Light, Sweet and Middle East Sour)

International Petroleum Exchange of London (IPE)

New York Mercantile Exchange (NYMEX/COMEX)

New Zealand Futures & Options Exchange Ltd. (NZFOE)

Singapore International Monetary Exchange Ltd. (SIMEX)

Sydney Futures Exchange Limited (SFE)

Electricity

(including California/Oregon Border, Cinergy, Entergy, NSW Base Load Electricity, NSW Peal Period Electricity, NZ, Palo Verde, PJM, VIC Base Load Electricity and VIC Peak Period Electricity)

New York Mercantile Exchange (NYMEX/COMEX)

Sydney Futures Exchange Limited (SFE)

Fuel Oil

(including High Sulfur)

International Petroleum Exchange of London (IPE)

Singapore International Monetary Exchange Ltd. (SIMEX)

Gas Oil

International Petroleum Exchange of London (IPE)

Singapore International Monetary Exchange Ltd. (SIMEX)

Gasoline
(including New York Harbor Unleaded and Unleaded)

Guangdong United Futures Exchange (GUFE)
International Petroleum Exchange of London (IPE)
New York Mercantile Exchange (NYMEX/COMEX)
Singapore International Monetary Exchange Ltd. (SIMEX)
Sydney Futures Exchange Limited (SFE)

Heating Oil

New York Mercantile Exchange (NYMEX/COMEX)
Sydney Futures Exchange Limited (SFE)

Natural Gas
(including Henry Hub and Western)

Kansas City Board of Trade (KCBOT)
New York Mercantile Exchange (NYMEX/COMEX)
New Zealand Futures & Options Exchange Ltd. (NZFOE)
Sydney Futures Exchange Limited (SFE)

Propane Gas

New York Mercantile Exchange (NYMEX/COMEX)
Sydney Futures Exchange Limited (SFE)

Foods

Black Pepper

OTC Exchange of India (OTCEI)

Cocoa
(including #8)

China-Commodity Futures Exchange, Inc. of Hainan (CCFE)
Commodity and Monetary Exchange of Malaysia (COMMEX)

London Commodity Exchange (LCE)
London International Financial Futures Exchange (LIFFE)
New York Board of Trade (NYBOT)

Coffee
(including Arabica, Conillion and Robusta)
The Commodity & Futures Exchange (BM&F)
China-Commodity Futures Exchange, Inc. of Hainan (CCFE)
Indonesian Commodity Exchange Board
London Commodity Exchange (LCE)
London International Financial Futures Exchange (LIFFE)
Manila International Futures Exchange (MIFE)
New York Board of Trade (NYBOT)
ParisBourse SA
Singapore Commodity Exchange Limited (SICOM)
Tokyo Grain Exchange (TGE)

Copra
Manila International Futures Exchange (MIFE)

Frozen Concentrated Orange Juice
New York Board of Trade (NYBOT)

Oranges
(including Naval and Valencia)
Citrus Fruit and Commodity Futures Market of Valencia (FC&M)

Orange Juice
New York Board of Trade (NYBOT)

Potato Starch
Chubu Commodity Exchange (C-COM)
Kanmon Commodity Exchange (KCE)

Potatoes

Amsterdam Exchanges (AEX—Optiebeurs)
London International Financial Futures Exchange (LIFFE)
London Commodity Exchange (LCE)
New York Board of Trade (NYBOT)
OTC Exchange of India (OTCEI)
ParisBourse SA
WTB Warenterminborse Hannover

Sugar

(including #11, #14, Crystal, Domestic, Icumsa, Raw, Refined White and World)

Chubu Commodity Exchange (C-COM)
The Commodity & Futures Exchange (BM&F)
Kanmon Commodity Exchange (KCE)
Kansai Commodities Exchange (KANEX)
Kasai Agricultural Commodities Exchange (KACEX)
London Commodity Exchange (LCE)
London International Financial Futures Exchange (LIFFE)
Manila International Futures Exchange (MIFE)
New York Board of Trade (NYBOT)
ParisBourse SA
Tokyo Grain Exchange (TGE)

Turmeric

OTC Exchange of India (OTCEI)

Equity Options

Anglo American

South African Futures Exchange (SAFEX)

BIFFEX (Dry Freight Futures)

London International Financial Futures Exchange (LIFFE)

B-Gold Index

Belgium Futures and Options Exchange (BELFOX)

BTC

Commodity Exchange of Ljubljana (CEL)

BXF (Futures of BEL-20 Index of the Brussels Stock Exchange)

Belgium Futures and Options Exchange (BELFOX)

Eurotop

London International Financial Futures Exchange (LIFFE)

FTSE-100 and 250

London International Financial Futures Exchange (LIFFE)

HKFE Taiwan Index Futures

Hong Kong Futures Exchange Limited (HKFE)

Hang Seng China-Affiliated Corporations Index Options (Red-Chip Futures)

Hong Kong Futures Exchange Limited (HKFE)

Hang Seng Index Futures
(including 100 Futures)

Hong Kong Futures Exchange Limited (HKFE)

KID

Commodity Exchange of Ljubljana (CEL)

LEPO on Swiss Equities

European Futures Exchange (EUREX)

KRKA

Commodity Exchange of Ljubljana (CEL)

Norwegian Equity Futures

Oslo Stock Exchange (OBX)

Norwegian Government Bond, Ten-year

Oslo Stock Exchange (OBX)

TOPIX

Tokyo Stock Exchange (TSE)

Financial Futures and Options

FIM Government Bond

HEX Ltd., Helsinki Securities and Derivatives Exchange, Clearinghouse

Financial Index

South African Futures Exchange (SAFEX)

Industrial Index

South African Futures Exchange (SAFEX)

Long Bond
(including R150, R153, R157 and R162)

South African Futures Exchange (SAFEX)

Mining Index

South African Futures Exchange (SAFEX)

OBX Index

Oslo Stock Exchange (OBX)

Rand/U.S. Dollar

South African Futures Exchange (SAFEX)

Short-Term Interest Rate

South African Futures Exchange (SAFEX)

GRAINS AND OILSEEDS

Azuki (Red Beans)

China Zhengzhou Commodity Exchange (CZCE)
Chubu Commodity Exchange (C-COM)
Kanmon Commodity Exchange (KCE)
Kansai Commodities Exchange (KANEX)
Kasai Agricultural Commodities Exchange (KACEX)
Manila International Futures Exchange (MIFE)
Tokyo Grain Exchange (TGE)

Barley

(including Forage, Malting and Western)

Budapest Commodity Exchange (BCE)
China-Commodity Futures Exchange, Inc. of Hainan (CCFE)
Commodity Exchange of Ljubljana (CEL)
London International Financial Futures Exchange (LIFFE)
Minneapolis Grain Exchange (MGE)
Shenyang Commodity Exchange
Sofia Commodity Exchange (SCE)
Winnipeg Commodity Exchange (WCE)

Beans

Beijing Commodity Exchange (BCE)
China-Commodity Futures Exchange, Inc. of Hainan (CCFE)
Chubu Commodity Exchange (C-COM)
Dalian Commodity Exchange
Kanmon Commodity Exchange (KCE)
Kasai Agricultural Commodities Exchange (KACEX)
Shanghai Cereals and Oils Exchange (SCOE)
Suzhou Commodity Exchange

Black Sunflower

Sofia Commodity Exchange (SCE)

Bread Wheat

Buenos Aires Futures Market (MATBA)

Canola

Winnipeg Commodity Exchange (WCE)

Castorseeds

OTC Exchange of India (OTCEI)

Corn

Beijing Commodity Exchange (BCE)
Budapest Commodity Exchange (BCE)
Buenos Aires Futures Market (MATBA)
Buenos Aires Grain Exchange (BAGE)
Chicago Board of Trade (CBOT)
The Commodity & Futures Exchange (BM&F)
Dalian Commodity Exchange
Guangdong United Futures Exchange (GUFE)
Kanmon Commodity Exchange (KCE)
MidAmerica Commodity Exchange (MidAm)
New York Mercantile Exchange (NYMEX/COMEX)
ParisBourse SA
Rosario Futures Exchange (ROFEX)
Shanghai Cereals and Oils Exchange (SCOE)
Sofia Commodity Exchange (SCE)
Tokyo Grain Exchange (TGE)

Crude Palm Oil
(including Kernel Oil)

China-Commodity Futures Exchange, Inc. of Hainan (CCFE)
Commodity and Monetary Exchange of Malaysia (COMMEX)

Field Peas

Winnipeg Commodity Exchange (WCE)

Flaxseed

Winnipeg Commodity Exchange (WCE)

Green Bean (Mung Bean)

Beijing Commodity Exchange (BCE)
China Zhengzhou Commodity Exchange (CZCE)

Maize

Commodity Exchange of Ljubljana (CEL)
South African Futures Exchange (SAFEX)

Oats

Chicago Board of Trade (CBOT)
MidAmerica Commodity Exchange (MidAm)
Winnipeg Commodity Exchange (WCE)

Peanut Kernel

Beijing Commodity Exchange (BCE)
China Zhengzhou Commodity Exchange (CZCE)
Shenyang Commodity Exchange

Rapeseed (Canola)

Budapest Commodity Exchange (BCE)
ParisBourse SA
Winnipeg Commodity Exchange (WCE)

Red Corn

Buenos Aires Futures Market (MATBA)

Rice

Beijing Commodity Exchange (BCE)
Chicago Board of Trade (CBOT)

Dalian Commodity Exchange
Guangdong United Futures Exchange (GUFE)
Shanghai Cereals and Oils Exchange (SCOE)

Rye

Winnipeg Commodity Exchange (WCE)

Sorghum

Shenyang Commodity Exchange

Soybeans

Beijing Commodity Exchange (BCE)
Buenos Aires Futures Market (MATBA)
Buenos Aires Grain Exchange (BAGE)
Chicago Board of Trade (CBOT)
Chubu Commodity Exchange (C-COM)
The Commodity & Futures Exchange (BM&F)
Dalian Commodity Exchange
Guangdong United Futures Exchange (GUFE)
Kanmon Commodity Exchange (KCE)
Kansai Commodities Exchange (KANEX)
Kasai Agricultural Commodities Exchange (KACEX)
Manila International Futures Exchange (MIFE)
MidAmerica Commodity Exchange (MidAm)
New York Mercantile Exchange (NYMEX/COMEX)
Shanghai Cereals and Oils Exchange (SCOE)
Tokyo Grain Exchange (TGE)

Soybean Meal

Beijing Commodity Exchange (BCE)
Budapest Commodity Exchange (BCE)
Chicago Board of Trade (CBOT)
Dalian Commodity Exchange
Guangdong United Futures Exchange (GUFE)

MidAmerica Commodity Exchange (MidAm)
New York Mercantile Exchange (NYMEX/COMEX)

Soybean Oil

Beijing Commodity Exchange (BCE)
Chicago Board of Trade (CBOT)
Dalian Commodity Exchange
Kanmon Commodity Exchange (KCE)
MidAmerica Commodity Exchange (MidAm)
New York Mercantile Exchange (NYMEX/COMEX)

Sweet Potato Starch

Chubu Commodity Exchange (C-COM)

Sunflower Seed

Budapest Commodity Exchange (BCE)
Buenos Aires Futures Market (MATBA)
Buenos Aires Grain Exchange (BAGE)

Wheat
(including Bread, Durum, Feed, Milling and White)

Amsterdam Exchanges (AEX—Optiebeurs)
Beijing Commodity Exchange (BCE)
Budapest Commodity Exchange (BCE)
Buenos Aires Futures Market (MATBA)
Buenos Aires Grain Exchange (BAGE)
Chicago Board of Trade (CBOT)
China Zhengzhou Commodity Exchange (CZCE)
Chubu Commodity Exchange (C-COM)
Dalian Commodity Exchange
Kansas City Board of Trade (KCBOT)
London International Financial Futures Exchange (LIFFE)
MidAmerica Commodity Exchange (MidAm)
Minneapolis Grain Exchange (MGE)

New York Mercantile Exchange (NYMEX/COMEX)
ParisBourse SA
Rosario Futures Exchange (ROFEX)
Shanghai Cereals and Oils Exchange (SCOE)
Sofia Commodity Exchange (SCE)
South African Futures Exchange (SAFEX)
Sydney Futures Exchange Limited (SFE)
Winnipeg Commodity Exchange (WCE)

White Beans

Sofia Commodity Exchange (SCE)

Indexes

All Ordinaries Index

Sydney Futures Exchange Limited (SFE)

Bankers Acc, Ninety-Day

Sydney Futures Exchange Limited (SFE)

BEL 20 Index

Belgium Futures and Options Exchange (BELFOX)

BHKP Index (Bleached Hardwood Kraft Pulp)

Finnish Options Exchange Ltd. (FOEX)

BIFFEX

London Commodity Exchange (LCE)

Brady Bonds Index

Chicago Mercantile Exchange (CME)

Brazilian Real Index

Chicago Mercantile Exchange (CME)

Business Activity Index

The Russian Exchange (RE)

CAC-40 Index

ParisBourse SA

CECE-Index (CEX)

Wiener Borse AG (WBAG)

CRB Price Index

New York Board of Trade (NYBOT)

New York Futures Exchange (NYFE)

CTX—Czech Traded Index

Wiener Borse AG (WBAG)

DAX Index (German Stock Index)
(including Xetra Electronically traded DAX)

European Futures Exchange (EUREX)

Dollar Index

New York Board of Trade (NYBOT)

Dow Jones
(including Euro STOXX 50, STOXX 50, STOXX Bank, STOXX Energy, STOXX L&M Insurance, STOXX L&M Media, STOXX L&M Pharmacy, STOXX L&M Technology and STOXX Telecom)

European Futures Exchange (EUREX)

ParisBourse SA

Dutch Top 5 Index

Amsterdam Exchanges (AEX—Optiebeurs)

European Options Exchange (EOE)

Euro Bund

European Futures Exchange (EUREX)

Euro (ECU) Bond

ParisBourse SA

EOE Index

OM London (OMLX)

Eurotop 100 Index

Amsterdam Exchanges (AEX—Optiebeurs)
European Options Exchange (EOE)
New York Mercantile Exchange (NYMEX/COMEX)
OM London (OMLX)

EuroMark
(including One-Month and Three-Month)

European Futures Exchange (EUREX)

FIB-30 Index

Italian Derivatives Market (IDEM)

FOX Index Futures

HEX Ltd., Helsinki Securities and Derivatives Exchange, Clearinghouse

FTSE/ASE-20

Athens Derivatives Exchange S.A. (ADEX)

FTSE Eurotop Index
(including 100, 250 and 300)

Amsterdam Exchanges (AEX—Optiebeurs)
London International Financial Futures Exchange (LIFFE)
New York Mercantile Exchange (NYMEX/COMEX)

GEMx Index

OM London (OMLX)

Gold Index

Belgium Futures and Options Exchange (BELFOX)
The Commodity & Futures Exchange (BM&F)
South African Futures Exchange (SAFEX)

Goldman Sachs Commodity Index

Chicago Mercantile Exchange (CME)

Greek Government Bond, Ten-Year

Athens Derivatives Exchange S.A. (ADEX)

The Guy Carpenter Catastrophe Index (GCCI)

Bermuda Commodities Exchange (BCOE)

Hang Seng Index
(including Hang Seng 100 Index, Hang Seng China-Affiliated Corporations Index—Red Chip and Hang Seng Properties Sub-Index)

Hong Kong Futures Exchange Limited (HKFE)

HKFE Taiwan Index

Hong Kong Futures Exchange Limited (HKFE)

HTX—Hungarian Traded Index

Wiener Borse AG (WBAG)

Ibovespa Futures

The Commodity & Futures Exchange (BM&F)

Jumbo Pfanbrief-Future

European Futures Exchange (EUREX)

Large Milk Index

New York Board of Trade (NYBOT)

Major Market Index

Chicago Mercantile Exchange (CME)

European Options Exchange (EOE)

MDAX Index

European Futures Exchange (EUREX)

MSCI Hong Kong Index

Singapore International Monetary Exchange Ltd. (SIMEX)

NASDAQ
(including Composite and 100 Index)

Chicago Mercantile Exchange (CME)

MidAmerica Commodity Exchange (MidAm)

Nikkei Index
(including 225, 300 and Stock Average)

Osaka Securities Exchange (OSE)

Singapore International Monetary Exchange Ltd. (SIMEX)

Notionnel Bond

ParisBourse SA

NYSE 40 Index

New Zealand Futures & Options Exchange Ltd. (NZFOE)

OX Index

European Options Exchange (EOE)

OM London (OMLX)

Oslo Stock Exchange (OBX)

PIX Index
Finnish Options Exchange Ltd. (FOEX)

PTX—Polish Traded Index
Wiener Borse AG (WBAG)

Paper Index
(including A4 B-copy, Ctd WF and LWC Indexes)
Finnish Options Exchange Ltd. (FOEX)

Potato Index
South African Futures Exchange (SAFEX)

Pulp Index
(including NBSK Index)
Finnish Options Exchange Ltd. (FOEX)

RDX—Russian Index
(including Depository Receipts and Russian Traded Indexes)
Wiener Borse AG (WBAG)

RJSC UES Index
The Russian Exchange (RE)

RTS (Russian Trading System) Index
The Russian Exchange (RE)

Rosafe Soybean Index
Rosario Futures Exchange (ROFEX)

Rubber Cash Settled Index
Singapore Commodity Exchange Limited (SICOM)

S&P 500
(including BARRA Growth, BARRA Value, MidCap 400 and Indexes)

Chicago Mercantile Exchange (CME)

Schatz

European Futures Exchange (EUREX)

SMI Index

European Futures Exchange (EUREX)

SPCEX

St. Petersburg Futures Exchange (SPBFE)

Swedish OMX Index

OM Stockholm Exchange (OM)

Swiss Bond, Ten-Year

European Futures Exchange (EUREX)

Swiss Market Index

European Futures Exchange (EUREX)

Toronto 35

Toronto Futures Exchange (TFE)

TSE 300 Spot

Toronto Futures Exchange (TFE)

Value Line
(including Value Line—Mini, VLA5 Value Line/A and VLC5 Value Line/G)

Kansas City Board of Trade (KCBOT)

VOLAX Index

European Futures Exchange (EUREX)

Interest Rates

Accepted Bank Bill, Ninety-Day

Sydney Futures Exchange Limited (SFE)

All Ordinaries Index

Sydney Futures Exchange Limited (SFE)

ATHIBOR, Three-Month

Athens Derivatives Exchange S.A. (ADEX)

AUS Bond, Ten-Year

Sydney Futures Exchange Limited (SFE)

Bank Accepted Bills, Ninety-Day

New Zealand Futures & Options Exchange Ltd. (NZFOE)
Sydney Futures Exchange Limited (SFE)

BAX—Canadian Bankers' Acceptance, Three-Month

Montreal Exchange (ME)

BCP

Portuguese Futures & Options Exchange (BDP)

BGB—Belgian Government Bond

Belgium Futures and Options Exchange (BELFOX)

BIBOR, Three-Month

Belgium Futures and Options Exchange (BELFOX)

BOBL—German Government Bond *(Bundes obligationen)*
(including medium and long term)

European Futures Exchange (EUREX)
London International Financial Futures Exchange (LIFFE)

Bonos—Spanish Government Bond
(including Three-Year, Five-Year and Ten-Year and E-5, E-10 and E-30)

London International Financial Futures Exchange (LIFFE)
Spanish Financial Futures Market (MEFF RF)

Brady Bond Index

Chicago Board Options Exchange (CBOE)

BTP—Italian Government Bond
(including Five-Year and Ten-Year and BTP 10 Medium Term and BTP 30 Long Term)

Italian Stock Exchange (ISE)
London International Financial Futures Exchange (LIFFE)
Mercato Italian Futures (MIF)

BUBOR
(including One-Month and Three-Month)

Budapest Commodity Exchange, Ltd. (BCE)
Spanish Financial Futures Market (MEFF RF)

CAC-40 Index
(including Odd-Lot, Short Term and Long Term)

ParisBourse SA

CD Interest Rate, Three-Month

Korea Futures Exchange (KOFEX)

CIBOR, Three-Month

FUTOP Market—Copenhagen Stock Exchange and the FUTOP Clearing Centre

CIMBOR

Portuguese Futures & Options Exchange (BDP)

COMI

European Futures Exchange (EUREX)

CONF

European Futures Exchange (EUREX)

CT2 and CT5 Mortgage Bond

OM Stockholm Exchange (OM)

DIBOR, Three-Month

Irish Futures and Options Exchange (IFOX)

Danish Government Bond
(including Medium Term and Long Term)

FUTOP Market—Copenhagen Stock Exchange and the FUTOP Clearing Centre

Dutch Government Bond

Amsterdam Exchanges (AEX—Optiebeurs)

European Options Exchange (EOE)

EBond, Thirty-Year

ParisBourse SA

EDP

Portuguese Futures & Options Exchange (BDP)

ENote, Two-Year

ParisBourse SA

Euribor
(including One-Month and Three-Month)

European Futures Exchange (EUREX)
Italian Stock Exchange (ISE)
London International Financial Futures Exchange (LIFFE)
ParisBourse SA
Spanish Financial Futures Market (MEFF RF)

Euro All Sovereigns

ParisBourse SA

EuroBund
(including Long and Short Term)

European Futures Exchange (EUREX)
London International Financial Futures Exchange (LIFFE)

Euro Five-Year Bond

ParisBourse SA

EuroDollar
(including Three-Month)

Chicago Mercantile Exchange (CME)
London International Financial Futures Exchange (LIFFE)
New York Mercantile Exchange (NYMEX/COMEX)
Singapore International Monetary Exchange Ltd. (SIMEX)
Tokyo International Financial Futures Exchange (TIFFE)

Euro (ECU)
(including Three-Month)

London International Financial Futures Exchange (LIFFE)

EuroLibor

London International Financial Futures Exchange (LIFFE)

EuroLira
(including Three-Month)
London International Financial Futures Exchange (LIFFE)

EuroMark
(including One-Month and Three-Month)
Chicago Mercantile Exchange (CME)
London International Financial Futures Exchange (LIFFE)
Singapore International Monetary Exchange Ltd. (SIMEX)

Euro Notional Bond
ParisBourse SA

EuroSwiss
(including Three-Month)
London International Financial Futures Exchange (LIFFE)

EuroYen
(including Three-Month)
Chicago Mercantile Exchange (CME)
London International Financial Futures Exchange (LIFFE)
Singapore International Monetary Exchange Ltd. (SIMEX)
Tokyo International Financial Futures Exchange (TIFFE)

Fed Funds Rate
Chicago Mercantile Exchange (CME)

Federal Funds, Thirty-Day
Chicago Board Options Exchange (CBOE)

Flexible T-Notes
(including Two-Year, Five-Year and Ten-Year)
Chicago Board Options Exchange (CBOE)

Flexible U.S. T-Bonds
Chicago Board Options Exchange (CBOE)

French Government Bond, Medium Term

ParisBourse SA

French Treasury Bond

ParisBourse SA

General Market Price Index

The Commodity & Futures Exchange (BM&F)

Gilt
(including Five-Year and Long)

London International Financial Futures Exchange (LIFFE)

GKO (Russian Treasury Bills)

The Russian Exchange (RE)

Government of Canada Bond
(including CGF Five-Year and CGB Ten-Year)

Montreal Exchange (ME)

GSZ (Federal Savings Loan Bonds)

The Russian Exchange (RE)

HELIBOR FRA Interest Rate

HEX Ltd., Helsinki Securities and Derivatives Exchange, Clearinghouse

HELIBOR, Three-Month

Hong Kong Futures Exchange Limited (HKFE)

HIBOR Futures, One-Month

Hong Kong Futures Exchange Limited (HKFE)

Interbank Deposits
(including One-Day and Thirty-Day)

The Commodity & Futures Exchange (BM&F)

IFOX Interest Rate Swaps

Irish Futures and Options Exchange (IFOX)

IMM Forward Rate

OM Stockholm Exchange (OM)

Individual Share

Sydney Futures Exchange Limited (SFE)

Interbank Deposit
(including One-Day and Thirty-Day)

The Commodity & Futures Exchange (BM&F)

Irish Gilt
(including Five-Year and Twenty-Year)

Irish Futures and Options Exchange (IFOX)

JGB—Japanese Government Bond
(including Five-Year, Ten-Year and Twenty-Year)

London International Financial Futures Exchange (LIFFE)
Singapore International Monetary Exchange Ltd. (SIMEX)
Tokyo Stock Exchange (TSE)

KLIBOR
(including Three-Month)

Commodity and Monetary Exchange of Malaysia (COMMEX)

KO—Four-Year Bond

ParisBourse SA

LIBOR

Chicago Mercantile Exchange (CME)
Singapore International Monetary Exchange Ltd. (SIMEX)

LISBOR, Three-Month

Portuguese Futures & Options Exchange (BDP)

Malaysian Government Securities, Five-Year

Commodity and Monetary Exchange of Malaysia (COMMEX)

MIBOR
(including Three-Month, Ten-Year, E-90, 90 Plus and E-360)

Spanish Financial Futures Market (MEFF RF)

Mortgage Credit Bond, Long Term

FUTOP Market—Copenhagen Stock Exchange and the FUTOP Clearing Centre

Municipal Bond Index

Chicago Board Options Exchange (CBOE)

Norwegian Government Bond
(including Five-Year and Ten-Year)

Oslo Stock Exchange (OBX)

Notionnel Bond (GLOBEX)

ParisBourse SA

Notional Government Bond
(including Three-Year, Five-Year and Ten-Year)

Mercato Italian Futures (MIF)
Spanish Financial Futures Market (MEFF RF)

Notional Guilder Bond

Amsterdam Exchanges (AEX—Optiebeurs)

Notional Mortgage Bond
(including Two-Year and Five-Year)

OM Stockholm Exchange (OM)

Notional Swedish Bond
(including Five-Year and Ten-Year)

OM Stockholm Exchange (OM)

Notional TBills

OM Stockholm Exchange (OM)

OMR Swap Ten-Year

OM Stockholm Exchange (OM)

OT 10 Government Bond

Portuguese Futures & Options Exchange (BDP)

PIBOR, Three-Month

ParisBourse SA

PT

Portuguese Futures & Options Exchange (BDP)

SB5 Mortgage Bond

OM Stockholm Exchange (OM)

Shekel/Dollar Exchange Rate

Tel Aviv Stock Exchange, Ltd. (TASE)

Short Sterling
(including Three-Month)

London International Financial Futures Exchange (LIFFE)

Short-Term Interest-Rate Futures

Commodity Exchange of Ljubljana (CEL)

STIBOR, Three-Month

OM Stockholm Exchange (OM)

SXF—S&P Canada 60 Index

Montreal Exchange (ME)

Swedish Government Bond, Two-Year

OM Stockholm Exchange (OM)

Swiss Bond, Ten-Year

European Futures Exchange (EUREX)

Treasury Bills

Chicago Mercantile Exchange (CME)

Treasury Bonds

(including Three-Year and Ten-Year)

New York Mercantile Exchange (NYMEX/COMEX)
New Zealand Futures & Options Exchange Ltd. (NZFOE)
Sydney Futures Exchange Limited (SFE)

Treasury Yield Curve Spread

Chicago Board Options Exchange (CBOE)

U.S. Dollar

New Zealand Futures & Options Exchange Ltd. (NZFOE)
Tokyo International Financial Futures Exchange (TIFFE)
Tokyo Stock Exchange (TSE)

U.S. Treasury Bond

Chicago Board Options Exchange (CBOE)
Tokyo Stock Exchange (TSE)

U.S. Treasury Notes

(including Two-Year, Five-Year and Ten-Year)

Chicago Board Options Exchange (CBOE)
MidAmerica Commodity Exchange (MidAm)
New York Board of Trade (NYBOT)

Meat and Dairy Products

Butter

Chicago Mercantile Exchange (CME)

Cheddar Cheese

New York Board of Trade (NYBOT)

Chilled Carcass Beef

South African Futures Exchange (SAFEX)

Feeder Cattle

Chicago Mercantile Exchange (CME)
The Commodity & Futures Exchange (BM&F)

Fluid Milk

Chicago Mercantile Exchange (CME)
New York Board of Trade (NYBOT)

Lean Hogs

Chicago Mercantile Exchange (CME)
New York Mercantile Exchange (NYMEX/COMEX)

Live Cattle

Chicago Mercantile Exchange (CME)
The Commodity & Futures Exchange (BM&F)
MidAmerica Commodity Exchange (MidAm)
Sydney Futures Exchange Limited (SFE)

Live Hogs
(including #1 and #2)

Amsterdam Exchanges (AEX—Optiebeurs)
Budapest Commodity Exchange (BCE)
Chicago Mercantile Exchange (CME)
MidAmerica Commodity Exchange (MidAm)
WTB Warenterminborse Hannover

Milk

New York Board of Trade (NYBOT)
Chicago Mercantile Exchange (CME)

National Average Beef Index

South African Futures Exchange (SAFEX)

Non-Fat Dry Milk

New York Board of Trade (NYBOT)

Piglets

Amsterdam Exchanges (AEX—Optiebeurs)

Pork Bellies

Chicago Mercantile Exchange (CME)

Shrimp

Minneapolis Grain Exchange (MGE)

Metals

Aluminum

(including Alloy, High Grade and Primary)

Beijing Commodity Exchange (BCE)
Guangdong United Futures Exchange (GUFE)
London Metal Exchange (LME)
New York Mercantile Exchange (NYMEX/COMEX)
Shanghai Metals Exchange (SHME)
Shenyang Commodity Exchange
Tokyo Commodity Exchange (TOCOM)

Copper

Beijing Commodity Exchange (BCE)
Guangdong United Futures Exchange (GUFE)
London Metal Exchange (LME)
New York Mercantile Exchange (NYMEX/COMEX)
New Zealand Futures & Options Exchange Ltd. (NZFOE)
Rosario Board of Trade
Shanghai Metals Exchange (SHME)

Gold

Amsterdam Exchanges (AEX—Optiebeurs)
Belgium Futures and Options Exchange (BELFOX)
The Commodity & Futures Exchange (BM&F)
Commodity and Monetary Exchange of Malaysia (COMMEX)
Chicago Board of Trade (CBOT)
European Options Exchange (EOE)
Hong Kong Futures Exchange Limited (HKFE)
Korea Futures Exchange (KOFEX)
MidAmerica Commodity Exchange (MidAm)
New York Mercantile Exchange (NYMEX/COMEX)
New Zealand Futures & Options Exchange Ltd. (NZFOE)
Rosario Board of Trade
The Russian Exchange (RE)
Singapore International Monetary Exchange Ltd. (SIMEX)
South African Futures Exchange (SAFEX)
Tokyo Commodity Exchange (TOCOM)

Lead

London Metal Exchange (LME)
Rosario Board of Trade
Shanghai Metals Exchange (SHME)

Nickel

London Metal Exchange (LME)
Rosario Board of Trade
Shanghai Metals Exchange (SHME)

Palladium

New York Mercantile Exchange (NYMEX/COMEX)
Tokyo Commodity Exchange (TOCOM)

Platinum

MidAmerica Commodity Exchange (MidAm)
New York Mercantile Exchange (NYMEX/COMEX)
Tokyo Commodity Exchange (TOCOM)

Silver

Amsterdam Exchanges (AEX—Optiebeurs)
Chicago Board of Trade (CBOT)
European Options Exchange (EOE)
MidAmerica Commodity Exchange (MidAm)
New York Mercantile Exchange (NYMEX/COMEX)
New Zealand Futures & Options Exchange Ltd. (NZFOE)
Rosario Board of Trade
Tokyo Commodity Exchange (TOCOM)
Toronto Futures Exchange (TFE)

Tin

Commodity and Monetary Exchange of Malaysia (COMMEX)
London Metal Exchange (LME)
Shanghai Metals Exchange (SHME)

Zinc (including Special High Grade)

London Metal Exchange (LME)
Rosario Board of Trade
Shanghai Metals Exchange (SHME)

Stock-Index Futures

All Ordinaries Share-Price Index

Sydney Futures Exchange Limited (SFE)

All Share Index

South African Futures Exchange (SAFEX)

Amsterdam Exchanges Index

Amsterdam Exchanges (AEX—Optiebeurs)

BET Index

Sibiu Monetary-Financial and Commodities Exchange (SMFCE)

Bovespa Stock Index

The Commodity & Futures Exchange (BM&F)

CAC-40 Index

ParisBourse SA

Cheung Kong Limited

Hong Kong Futures Exchange Limited (HKFE)

China Resources Enterprise Limited

Hong Kong Futures Exchange Limited (HKFE)

China Telecom Limited

Hong Kong Futures Exchange Limited (HKFE)

CITIC Pacific Limited

Hong Kong Futures Exchange Limited (HKFE)

CLP Holdings Limited

Hong Kong Futures Exchange Limited (HKFE)

DAX MIDCAP Stock Index

European Futures Exchange (EUREX)

DAX Xetra (Electronically Traded DAX)

European Futures Exchange (EUREX)

Dow Jones Euro STOXX 50

ParisBourse SA

Dow Jones STOXX 50

ParisBourse SA

EOE Stock Index

Amsterdam Exchanges (AEX—Optiebeurs)

European Options Exchange (EOE)

Euro IBEX-35 Index

Spanish Equity Derivatives Exchange (MEFF RV)

FTSE-100 Stock Index

Chicago Mercantile Exchange (CME)

London International Financial Futures Exchange (LIFFE)

Gazprom RJSC

The Russian Exchange (RE)

Government Stock
(both Three-Year and Ten-Year)

New Zealand Futures & Options Exchange Ltd. (NZFOE)

Hang Seng Bank Limited

Hong Kong Futures Exchange Limited (HKFE)

Henderson Land Development Company

Hong Kong Futures Exchange Limited (HKFE)

Hong Kong Electric Holdings Limited

Hong Kong Futures Exchange Limited (HKFE)

Hong Kong Telecommunications Limited

Hong Kong Futures Exchange Limited (HKFE)

Hopewell Holdings Limited

Hong Kong Futures Exchange Limited (HKFE)

HSBC Holdings

Hong Kong Futures Exchange Limited (HKFE)

Hutchison Whampoa Limited

Hong Kong Futures Exchange Limited (HKFE)

IBEX 35 Stock Index

Spanish Equity Derivatives Exchange (MEFF RV)

IBEX 35 Plus Stock Index

Spanish Equity Derivatives Exchange (MEFF RV)

IBC Stock Index Futures Contract

Caracas Stock Exchange (BVC)

IPSA Index

Santiago Stock Exchange (SSE)

ISE

Istanbul Stock Exchange (ISE)

ISENN (Brazilian) Stock Index

Rio de Janeiro Stock Exchange

KFX Share Index

FUTOP Market—Copenhagen Stock Exchange and the FUTOP Clearing Centre

KLSE CI—Kuala Lumpur Stock Exchange Composite Index

Kuala Lumpur Options & Financial Futures Exchange (KLOFFE)

KOSPI (including 50, 100 and 200)

Korea Stock Exchange (KSE)

LEAPS (Long-Term Equity Anticipation Securities)

Toronto Stock Exchange (TSE)

LUKOIL

The Russian Exchange (RE)

Malaysia/Thailand Stock Index

Singapore International Monetary Exchange Ltd. (SIMEX)

MIB 30

Italian Stock Exchange (ISE)

MIDEX

Italian Stock Exchange (ISE)

Mexican IPC Stock Index

Chicago Mercantile Exchange (CME)

MSCI Hong Kong Stock Index

Singapore International Monetary Exchange Ltd. (SIMEX)

MSCI Taiwan Stock Index
(including Ox3e I)

Singapore International Monetary Exchange Ltd. (SIMEX)

Nikkei 225 Stock Average Index

Chicago Mercantile Exchange (CME)

NYSE Indexes
(including Composite, Small Composite and Utility Composite)

New York Board of Trade (NYBOT)

NZSE-10 Share Index

New Zealand Futures & Options Exchange Ltd. (NZFOE)

OBX-Index
Oslo Stock Exchange (OBX)

PSE Technology Index
New York Board of Trade (NYBOT)

RTS Stock Index
St. Petersburg Futures Exchange (SPBFE)

Russell 2000 Stock Price Index
Chicago Mercantile Exchange (CME)

STOXX
HEX Ltd., Helsinki Securities and Derivatives Exchange, Clearinghouse

S&P Index
(including 100 and 500)
Chicago Board Options Exchange (CBOE)
Chicago Mercantile Exchange (CME)

Selective Stock Price Index IPSA
Santiago Stock Exchange (SSE)

Sherbank
The Russian Exchange (RE)

Shanghai Industrial Holdings Limited
Hong Kong Futures Exchange Limited (HKFE)

Singapore Stock Index
Singapore International Monetary Exchange Ltd. (SIMEX)

Stock Futures
Hong Kong Futures Exchange Limited (HKFE)

Swiss Market Index
European Futures Exchange (EUREX)

TA-100 Index
Tel Aviv Stock Exchange, Ltd. (TASE)

TA-25 Index
Tel Aviv Stock Exchange, Ltd. (TASE)

TAC3m Interest Rate Future Contract
Caracas Stock Exchange (BVC)

TIPS Index
(including 35 and 100)
Toronto Stock Exchange (TSE)

Toronto 35 Index Futures
Toronto Stock Exchange (TSE)

Toronto 100 Stock Index
Toronto Futures Exchange (TFE)

TSE Index Futures
Toronto Stock Exchange (TSE)

Turnover (NIS, 000)
Tel Aviv Stock Exchange, Ltd. (TASE)

U.S. Dollar Interbank Exchange Rate
Santiago Stock Exchange (SSE)

Textiles

Cotton
The Commodity & Futures Exchange (BM&F)

New York Board of Trade (NYBOT)
OTC Exchange of India (OTCEI)

Cotton Yarn

Chubu Commodity Exchange (C-COM)
Osaka Mercantile Exchange (OME)
Tokyo Commodity Exchange (TOCOM)

Dried Cocoon

Chubu Commodity Exchange (C-COM)
Maebashi Dried Cocoon Exchange (MDCE)
Manila International Futures Exchange (MIFE)
Toyahashi Dried Cocoon Exchange (TDCE)

Hussein

OTC Exchange of India (OTCEI)

Jute Goods (Sacking)

OTC Exchange of India (OTCEI)

Linen

Rosario Futures Exchange (ROFEX)

Raw Jute

OTC Exchange of India (OTCEI)

Raw Silk

Kansai Commodities Exchange (KANEX)
Kobe Raw Silk Exchange (KRSE)
Yokohama Raw Silk Exchange (YRSE)

Staple Fiber Yarn (Staple Fiber Yarn–Dull)

Chubu Commodity Exchange (C-COM)
Osaka Mercantile Exchange (OME)

Wool
(including Broad, Fine, Greasy and New Zealand)

New Zealand Futures & Options Exchange Ltd. (NZFOE)
Sydney Futures Exchange Limited (SFE)

Woolen Yarn

Chubu Commodity Exchange (C-COM)
Osaka Mercantile Exchange (OME)
Tokyo Commodity Exchange (TOCOM)

Other Industrials

International 1 Ribbed Smoked Sheet—RRSS 1

Singapore Commodity Exchange Limited (SICOM)

International 3 Ribbed Smoked Sheet—RSSS 3

Singapore Commodity Exchange Limited (SICOM)

Rubber

Beijing Commodity Exchange (BCE)
China-Commodity Futures Exchange, Inc. of Hainan (CCFE)
Commodity and Monetary Exchange of Malaysia (COMMEX)
Indonesian Commodity Exchange Board
Osaka Mercantile Exchange (OME)
Singapore Commodity Exchange Limited (SICOM)
Tokyo Commodity Exchange (TOCOM)

Rubber—RSS3

Osaka Mercantile Exchange (OME)

Technically Specified Rubber 20—TSR

Singapore Commodity Exchange Limited (SICOM)

OTHER PRODUCTS

Anhydrous Ammonia

Chicago Board of Trade (CBOT)

Diammonium Phosphate

Chicago Board of Trade (CBOT)

Gur

OTC Exchange of India (OTCEI)

Lumber

Chicago Mercantile Exchange (CME)

Plywood

Beijing Commodity Exchange (BCE)
Chicago Mercantile Exchange (CME)
China-Commodity Futures Exchange, Inc. of Hainan (CCFE)
Shenyang Commodity Exchange
Suzhou Commodity Exchange

Polypropylene

Beijing Commodity Exchange (BCE)

Polyvinyl Chloride

Beijing Commodity Exchange (BCE)
Suzhou Commodity Exchange

Sodium Carbonate

Beijing Commodity Exchange (BCE)

Wood

Shenyang Commodity Exchange

Appendix III

SYSTEM DETAILS AND COMPUTER CODE

The following system codes, originally developed for use in the U.S. markets using Omega TradeStation™, are presented with the understanding that they will need to be altered and developed for use in other futures markets.

The system codes are written in EasyLanguage™ and can only be used with Omega Research™ such as SuperCharts™, TradeStation™ and ProSuite 2000I™. Nevertheless, with a little programming skill they can be adapted for use with other trading software programs. Furthermore, although they have been specifically developed for the U.S. markets, they appear to have validity in many of the European and Asian markets.

Note that these systems require daily price data to have an opening, high, low and closing price. If trading activity is insufficient and, therefore, does not generate this data, the systems included in this appendix will not function well. Finally, these systems can also be adapted to intraday data where volume is sufficient.

```
{
Type  :  System
Name :  mbh.Range BreakOut
Notes :  Jake Bernstein, 2000ST System © 2000 Jake Bernstein


Inputs:  ATR.Bars        (03)  Length of Average TrueRange
         ATR.Mult      (0.62)  Multiplier for ATR (Volatility Factor)
         MOM.Bars        (28)  Length of Momentum Indicator
         MOM.Back        (10)  Length of Momentum LookBack Period
         HLC.Mode        (00)  Toggle [High / Low / Close] of last bar
                               0=Close (Default) ; Non-Zero=High/Low


Inputs:  ATR.Bars        (03),  { Length of Average TrueRange }
         ATR.Mult      (0.62),  { Multiplier for ATR (Volatility Factor) }
         MOM.Bars        (28),  { Length of Momentum Indicator }
         MOM.Back        (10),  { Length of Momentum LookBack Period }
         HLC.Mode        (00) ; { Toggle [High / Low / Close] of last bar }
                                {   0=Close (Default) ; Non-Zero=High/Low  }

Inputs:  MinFloor      (1000),      Percent       (0.90) ;
IncludeSystem:     "jb.Trailing Stop %", MinFloor, Percent ;

 *}

Vars   :  App.Name ("mbh.Range BreakOut") ;

Vars   :  ATR.val          (00),
          MOM.val          (00),      MOM.Trnd      (00) ;
Vars   :  le.Price   (+999999),       se.Price (-999999) ;


if      BarNumber <= 01 then begin
  Print ("System: '", App.Name, "' (",
        ATR.Bars:1:0, ", ",                    ATR.Mult:1:4, ", ",
        MOM.Bars:1:0, ", ",                    MOM.Back:1:0, ", ",
        HLC.Mode:1:0, ", ",
```

```
            MinFloor:1:2, ", ",                Percent :1:4, ", ",
            ProfOpen:1:0, ") ;") ;
end ;

le.Price  =  +999999 ;
se.Price  =  -999999 ;
ATR.Val   =  Average (TrueRange, ATR.Bars) * ATR.mult ;

MOM.Val    = Momentum (Close,   MOM.Bars) ;
MOM.Trnd   = +00 ;
if @BarNumber >= MOM.Back then begin
 if MOM.Val  > MOM.Val [MOM.Back] then MOM.Trnd = +01 ;
 if MOM.Val <  MOM.Val [MOM.Back] then MOM.Trnd = -01 ;
end ; { Sufficient bars have passed to initialize all values }

if MOM.Trnd > +00 then begin
 if HLC.Mode <> 00 then le.Price = High + ATR.Val
              else le.Price = Close + ATR.val ;
{*
 Plot1 (le.Price, "le.Price") ; { Blue or Green }
 *}
 if MarketPosition <> +01
   then Buy ("le.2000ST") at le.Price stop ;
end ; { Buy Mode }

if MOM.Trnd <  +00 then begin
 if HLC.Mode <> 00 then se.Price = Low   -  ATR.Val
                   else se.Price = Close -  ATR.val ;
{*
 Plot2 (se.Price, "se.Price") ;  { Red }
 *}
 if MarketPosition <> -01
   then Sell ("se.2000ST") at se.Price stop ;
end ; { Sell Mode }

{
```

page 2

```
{
Type   : System (Top Level)
Name   : jb.DBO System
Notes  : Jake Bernstein, System w/ Day Of Week filter

Input  :
Alert  :
Calls  :
Uses   :

}


Inputs : Day.Num        (1)  ;   { if zero then take all trades }

Inputs : le.Ticks       (5),     { number of ticks for long entry stop }
         se.Ticks       (5) ;    { number of ticks for short entry stop }

Vars   : App.Name ("jb.DBO System") ;
Vars   : le.Points (MinMove  * le.Ticks Points),
         se.Points (MinMove  * se.Ticks Points) ;
Vars   : le.Price (+999999),      se.Price (-999999),
         Dummy          (0)  ;

if DataCompression  = 2 then begin { must be daily data }
  le.Price = +999999 ;
  se.Price = -999999 ;

  if Day.Num = 0 or
    Day.Num = DayOfWeek (Date)
  then begin
   if Open              <  Close {and
     Open Next Bar <= High  and
     Open Next Bar >=  Low }
    then le.Price = High + le.Points ;

   if Open              > Close {and
     Open Next Bar <= High  and
     Open Next Bar >=  Low }
```

```
    then se.Price =  Low - se.Points ;
  end ;
end ;

if DataCompression <  2 then begin { intraday data }
  le.Price = +999999 ;
  se.Price = -999999 ;

  Dummy = MRO (Date > Date[1], MinList (MaxBarsBack - 1, Day.Num), 1) ;
  if Day.Num = 0 or
    Day.Num = Dummy + 1
  then begin
   if Open              <  Close {and
     Open Next Bar <= High  and
     Open Next Bar >=  Low }
    then le.Price = High + le.Points ;

   if Open              > Close {and
     Open Next Bar <= High  and
     Open Next Bar >=  Low }
    then se.Price =  Low - se.Points ;
  end ;
end ;

if  le.Price <  +999990 then Buy  ("le.DBO") at le.Price stop ;
if  se.Price  > -999990 then Sell ("se.DBO") at se.Price stop ;

{*
if Exit.MCO and Time = Sess1EndTime
then begin
  if MarketPosition  = +1 then ExitLong  ("lx.MOC") on the close ;
  if MarketPosition  = -1 then ExitShort ("sx.MOC") on the close ;
end ;
 *}
```

```
{
Type   : System
Name   : jb.DualOrbit
Notes  : Jake Bernstein © Copyright 2000 MBH Commodity Advisors, Inc.


Inputs : en.Mode   (+0) ;
Inputs : hi.Len     (10),      hi.Cross     (01),
         lo.Len     (10),      lo.Cross     (01),
         rn.Len     (06) ;

Inputs : MinFloor (1000),     Percent  (0.10) ;

Vars   : App.Name        ("jb.DualOrbit Var. #C") ;
Vars   : hi.Val          (0),        lo.Val       (0),      rn.Val     (0),
         hi.XOver        (0),        lo.XOver     (0),
         Cond01  (FALSE),
         Cond02  (FALSE) ;

IncludeSystem: "jb.Trailing Stop %", MinFloor, Percent ;


hi.Val   = @Momentum (High, hi.Len) ;
lo.Val   = @Momentum ( Low, lo.Len) ;
rn.Val   = @Momentum ((High-Low), rn.Len) ;
hi.XOver = vrt.CrossOver (hi.Val, rn.Val,  0) ;
lo.XOver = vrt.CrossOver (lo.Val, rn.Val,  0) ;

if hi.Cross >= 0 and lo.Cross >= 0 then begin
  Cond01 = (MRO (lo.XOver  = +1, lo.Cross + 1, 1)     =   lo.Cross) and
           (MRO (lo.XOver <>  0, lo.Cross,      1)     =          -1) ;
  Cond02 = (MRO (hi.XOver  = +1, lo.Cross + 1, 1)     =    o.Cross) and
           (MRO (hi.XOver <>  0, lo.Cross,      1)     =          -1) ;

  if (lo.Val   > rn.Val) and (hi.Val   > rn.Val) and
   (Cond01 or Cond02)
  then begin
   if (en.Mode  >     -1)
   then Buy  ("le.DlOrb") at Market ;
```

```
   ExitShort   ("sx.DlOrb") at Market ;
  end ;
end ;

if hi.Cross >= 0 and lo.Cross >= 0 then begin
  Cond01 = (MRO (hi.XOver  = -1, hi.Cross + 1,  1)  = hi.Cross) and
               (MRO (hi.XOver <>  0, hi.Cross,        1)  =        -1) ;
  Cond02 = (MRO (lo.XOver  = -1, hi.Cross + 1,  1)  = hi.Cross) and
               (MRO (lo.XOver <>  0, hi.Cross,        1)  =        -1) ;

  if (hi.Val  <  rn.Val) and (lo.Val  <  rn.Val) and
     (Cond01 or Cond02)
  then begin
    if (en.Mode <       +1)
      then Sell ("se.DlOrb") at Market ;
    ExitLong    ("lx.DlOrb") at Market ;
  end ;
end ;

if CheckCommentary then begin
  CommentaryCl (MarKetPosition:3:0, ", ", BarsSinceEntry:4:0, ", ",
              EntryDate:7:0, ", ", EntryTime:5:0, ", ", EntryPrice, ", $",
              PositionProfit:1:2, NewLine) ;
  CommentaryCL ("  hi.Val= ", hi.Val, ", hi.xOver= ", hi.xOver:5:0,
             ",  lo.Val= ", lo.Val, ", lo.xOver= ", lo.xOver:5:0,
             ",  rn.Val= ", rn.Val) ;
end ;
```

page 2

Printed using TradeStation PowerEditor by Omega Research Version 4.02.19—Dec 02 1996

```
{
Type   : System (Top Level)
Name   : jb.Gap System
Notes  : Jake Bernstein, Bar Opening Gap System

Input:
Alert:
Calls:
Uses :

}

Inputs:  le.Bars      (2),    { number of days back to check for low }
         se.Bars      (2),    { number of days back to check for high }
         le.Ticks     (2),    { number of ticks for long entry stop }
         se.Ticks     (2),    { number of ticks for short entry stop }
         le.MnGap     (2),    { minimum number of gap ticks for lEntry }
         se.MnGap     (2) ;   { minimum number of gap ticks for sEntry }
{*
Vars  : Start        (FALSE) ;
*}
Vars  : le.Price    (+999999),        se.Price (-999999) ;

Inputs: Cnt.FPOX   (1) ;
IncludeSystem: "skt.1st Prof Open",        Cnt.FPOX ;

Inputs: Cnt.FPCX   (1) ;
IncludeSystem: "skt.1st Prof Close",       Cnt.FPCX ;

Inputs: Exit.MOC (FALSE) ;
IncludeSystem: "skt.Market On Close",      Exit.MOC ;

{*
Inputs: MinFloor (1000),                 Percent  (0.20) ;
IncludeSystem: "vrt.Trailing Stop %", MinFloor, Percent ;
 *}

Vars   :  App.Name ("jb.Gap System") ;
Vars   :  le.Points (MinMove * le.Ticks Points),
          se.Points (MinMove * se.Ticks Points),
          le.GapPts (MinMove * le.MnGap Points),
          se.GapPts (MinMove * se.MnGap Points) ;
```

Printed using TradeStation PowerEditor by Omega Research Version 4.02.19—Dec 02 1996

```
if CurrentBar <= 1 then begin
  Print ("") ;
  Print ("System: '", App.Name, "'") ;
  Print ("------------------------------") ;
  Print ("") ;
  Print ("    Date  Next Open  HI or LO  Gap Size     Entry") ;
  Print ("------------------------------------------------------") ;
end ;

if Date  > Date[1] then begin
{*
  Start   =   TRUE ;
 *}
  le.Price = +999999 ;
  se.Price = -999999 ;
end ;

if MarketPosition = +1 then begin
  if BarsSinceEntry = 0 then begin
    le.Price = +999999 ;
  end ;
end ;

if MarketPosition = -1 then begin
  if BarsSinceEntry = 0 then begin
    se.Price = -999999 ;
  end ;
end ;

if Open Next Bar <   Lowest ( Low, le.Bars) - le.GapPts
then begin
  le.Price = Lowest ( Low, le.Bars) + le.Points ;
{*
  Print ("le: ", Date:6:0,
          Open Next Bar,
           Lowest ( Low, le.Bars) - le.GapPts,
           Lowest ( Low, le.Bars) - Open Next Bar, le.Price) ;
 *}
end ;
```

page 2

```
if Open Next Bar  > Highest (High, se.Bars) + se.GapPts
then begin
  se.Price = Highest (High, se.Bars) - se.Points ;
{*
  Print ("se: ", Date:6:0,
          Open Next Bar,
          Highest (High, se.Bars) - se.GapPts,
          Open Next Bar - Highest (High, se.Bars), se.Price) ;
 *}
end ;

if le.Price <  +999990 then Buy  ("le.Gap") at le.Price stop ;
if se.Price  > -999990 then Sell ("se.Gap") at se.Price stop ;

{* Cannot use Tomorrow's price and close order in same system
if MarketPosition  = +1 then begin
  ExitLong  ("lx.MOC") on the close ;
end ;

if MarketPosition  = -1 then begin
  ExitShort ("sx.MOC") on the close ;
end ;
 *}
```

page 3

Printed using TradeStation PowerEditor by Omega Research Version 4.02.19—Dec 02 1996

Moving Average Crossover System

```
Input: Length1(9),Length2(18);

IF CurrentBar > 1 and Average(Close,Length1) crosses over
Average(Close,Length2) Then Buy on Close;

IF CurrentBar > 1 and Average(Close,Length1) crosses below
Average(Close,Length2) Then Sell on Close;
```

Printed using TradeStation PowerEditor by Omega Research Version 4.02.19—Dec 02 1996

```
{
Type   : System (Top Level)
Name : jb.ADD System
Notes : Jake Bernstein, Accumulation Distribution
© 2000 Jake Bernstein

}

Inputs : le.nBars          (1),     se.nBars        (1),
         Length            (28),    Rng.Mode        (2) ;

Inputs : MinFloor       (1000),       Percent  (0.20) ;
IncludeSystem: "vrt.Trailing Stop %", MinFloor, Percent ;

{*

Inputs: Exit.MOC (FALSE) ;
 *}
Vars  : App.Name ("jb.ADD System") ;
Vars  : AD.val       (0),       AD.xavg    (0),
        le.bars      (-1),      se.bars    (-1) ;


AD.val    =          jb.Acc_Dist (Rng.Mode) ;
AD.xavg  = Average (jb.Acc_Dist (Rng.Mode), Length) ;

le.Bars  = -1 ;
se.Bars = -1 ;

le.Bars  = MRO (AD.val <= AD.xavg, le.nBars  + 1, 1) ;
se.Bars = MRO (AD.val >= AD.xavg, se.nBars + 1, 1) ;

if le.Bars   = le.nBars and MarketPosition <> -1
  then Sell("se.ADD") at market ;
if se.Bars  = se.nBars and MarketPosition <> +1
  then Buy("le.ADD") at market ;

{*
if Exit.MOC and Time = Sess1EndTime
```

```
then begin
 if MarketPosition  =  -1 then ExitShort  ("sx.MOC") on the close ;
 if MarketPosition  = +1 then ExitLong ("lx.MOC") on the close ;
end ;
 *}
```

INDEX